FOR
GOODNESS
SAKE

FOR GOODNESS SAKE

Religious Schools and Education for
Democratic Citizenry

WALTER FEINBERG

Routledge
Taylor & Francis Group
New York   London

Routledge is an imprint of the
Taylor & Francis Group, an informa business

Published in 2006 by
Routledge
Taylor & Francis Group
270 Madison Avenue
New York, NY 10016

Published in Great Britain by
Routledge
Taylor & Francis Group
2 Park Square
Milton Park, Abingdon
Oxon OX14 4RN

Printed in the United States of America on acid-free paper
10 9 8 7 6 5 4 3 2 1

International Standard Book Number-10: 0-415-95378-2 (Hardcover) 0-415-95379-0 (Softcover)
International Standard Book Number-13: 978-0-415-95378-8 (Hardcover) 978-0-415-95379-5 (Softcover)
Library of Congress Card Number 2005028002

Library of Congress Cataloging-in-Publication Data

Feinberg, Walter, 1937-
   For goodness sake : religious schools and education of democratic citizenry / Walter Feinberg.
      p. cm.
   Includes bibliographical references and index.
   ISBN 0-415-95378-2 (hb : alk. paper) -- ISBN 0-415-95379-0 (pb : alk. paper)
   1. Church and education. 2. Moral education. 3. Religious education. 4. Democracy. I. Title.

LC375.F44 2006
371.07--dc22   2005028002

Taylor & Francis Group
is the Academic Division of Informa plc.

Visit the Taylor & Francis Web site at
http://www.taylorandfrancis.com

and the Routledge Web site at
http://www.routledge-ny.com

To my grandchildren, Alicia, Keith, and Austin, in their quests
and
To my wife, Eleanor, for all her
love and support

Contents

**Part III   The Reconstruction of Religious Education:
                 A Pragmatic Framework**

Acknowledgments

The Spencer Foundation's tradition of encouraging work in the humanities and social sciences as it relates to the understanding and improvement of education is a unique national resource, and I am grateful to the foundation for its support of this project. In addition, I owe a significant debt of gratitude to the many dedicated administrators and teachers, and to their students, in faith-based schools who welcomed me into their classrooms and who spent many hours helping me to understand the nature of their work.

During the research on the book, I had the help of some exceptional and dedicated graduate assistants. Jason Odeshoo and Nathan Raybeck's knowledge of contemporary theology and biblical scholarship was invaluable in helping me launch this project. As a former student in a Catholic high school, Rashid Robinson provided considerable insight into the informal student culture and kept me informed about some of the racial issues that arise in some of these schools. Jill Wightman, Michelle Wibbelsm, and Steve Maas, all doctoral students in the Anthropology Department of the University of Illinois, provided guidance on organizing and coding the observations and interviews. Jill and Steve also helped with the fieldwork. In addition, my advisees, Scott Johnston and Jeffrey Thibert, read earlier drafts of the manuscript and made important suggestions.

Colleagues both at the University of Illinois and around the world were most supportive throughout this project. This support includes the detailed and insightful comments of Robert McKim and Michael Merry on different chapters; the critical response provided by Eric Bredo and Dwight Boyd to the entire manuscript; the detailed criticism of those who attended the two-day conference on an early draft of the manuscript held at Cambridge University and arranged by Terry McLaughlin; the important feedback provided by the members of the Philosophy of Education Society of Great Britain, to whom I delivered a keynote address at its 2004 annual meeting; the instructive comments and comparative information provided by Klas Roth and his colleagues at the Stockholm Institute of Education, where I gave a series of lectures relating to the book; the discussions I had with Phillip Barnes at his home in Northern Ireland, which provided much of the early inspiration for this study; my lunches with my colleague, Daniel Walsh, which helped to orient me to the different sides of Catholic educational practice; and my conversations with Jeff McMahan and his thoughtful and probing comments that were very useful in helping me maintain a critical perspective. I also want to extend my appreciation to the faculty and students of the Department of Educational Policy Studies for providing a stimulating and supportive intellectual environment. In addition, I owe considerable appreciation to my daughter, Deborah, for her help in understanding aspects of Jewish thought and tradition.

Introduction

One of the most significant features of educational discourse in the United States is the extent to which religious groups of all kinds are forcefully asserting that religion should play a central role in the moral education of children in public schools. And one of the most poignant silences of this same time is to be found in the reticence of the public to deliberate about the moral qualities of religious schools—as if only those within a religious community had any serious interest in the moral education of children in religious schools.[1] This book seeks to change that and to open up a dialogue about the appropriate aims of religious education and about the teaching of religion in liberal, democratic societies. Its main thesis is that the public has a strong interest in the work of religious schools and that this interest extends beyond the academic performance of their students into the shared moral understandings required to sustain and reproduce liberal, pluralistic democracies. It concludes by offering a conceptualization of the aims of religious education that is consistent with both the educational requirements of liberal, pluralistic societies and the concern of many religious parents and educators to be able to provide a strong religious education for their children.

The book is a response to a confluence of different events following from 9/11, when religious fanaticism was blamed for the terrorist act; to the U.S. Supreme Court decision to allow tax dollars to be used to support religious school tuition; to the increasing popularity of religious schools; to the success of Catholic schools in working with poor and minority children.[2] Its point is simple. In light of these events, we need to reconceptualize the role of religious education in the construction of a democratic citizenry.

This book contributes to that reconceptualization by

1. Exploring the values that religious schooling represents.
2. Analyzing those values in relation to the educational requirements of liberal democracy.
3. Drawing on the work of some religious educators as they address the dual mission of advancing both faith and democracy.
4. Addressing the public's responsibility for the moral education of children in religious schools.

A reconception of the role of religious education is also needed at this time because in light of recent Supreme Court decisions that allow public funds to flow to religious schools, a long-standing consensus has broken down and there is a need for the relationship between religion content and public interests to be reexamined. The original consensus was defined by a decision by the U.S. Supreme Court in 1925 in *Pierce v. Society of Sisters*.[3] In that decision the Court ruled that parents have a right to send their children to private schools but did not require that the state provide the means for them to do so. In other words, while *Pierce* gave parents the right to educate their children as they wish, within broad limits, it also placed the financial burden for religious education on the parents themselves, hence tilting the financial field in favor of nonreligious public schools. By allowing vouchers to be paid to support tuition in religious schools, the recent *Zelman* decision of 2002[4] alters that tilt[5] but in doing so implicitly makes it clear that religious education is everyone's business.

Two responses are likely as a result of the *Zelman* decision. First, some groups will organize to extend vouchers to all states, challenging those whose constitutions prohibit aid to religious schools, while other groups will demand greater accountability from religious schools, especially those receiving public funds. Hence we can no longer assume that religious education will continue to be just a small part of most children's education, something they do one day a week while attending secular public schools the rest of the time.

The time has come for a national discussion about the aims of religious education in liberal, pluralistic democracies and the interest that the public has in the aims of religious schools. This conversation must, of course, include the voices of religious educators and parents, as they express the values of religious schools as they see them, but the conversation needs also to address the interest that the secular public has in the workings of religious schools. Here it helps to understand the secular interest as not opposed to religion—we are all secularists when looking at another person's religion—but as the interest that everyone has in advancing a fair and just society and in providing space for both religious and nonreligious interpretations of the good society.

This book is written from a secular point of view. In other words, it contextualizes religious schools within the general aims of liberal democracy. However, the fullest expression of this standpoint requires an acknowledgment of the deeply felt human needs that all religions work to serve. Thus the book begins with an attempt to understand the uniquely human values that religions serve, values that arise out of a species awareness of our own vulnerability and that define a religious education in terms of ultimate faith and fundamental commitment. To look inside religious schools is, hopefully, to understand how these values guide the school program and the diverse ways in which they are expressed in different and exclusive religious formulations. It is also to understand the extent to which different expressions of them are compatible with the aims of both liberalism and pluralism.

Breaking the Silence

The silence regarding the practices of religious schools contrasts dramatically with the interest expressed in the role of religion within the public school. Here the discussion is robust and serious, joined by believers and nonbelievers alike. Should prayer be allowed in the public schools? Should students in public schools be taught about religion? Should creationist theory be placed on a par with evolution in the classroom? These questions have been vigorously debated in educational and legal forums, and whatever one's opinion may be about the different questions that are addressed, the intensity of the debate communicates an important truth—the education of children in a democratic society is everybody's business. However, the situation is vastly different when it comes to discussions of religious schools. Here there is little public discussion about the desirability of a given form of religious education. The partition that is open and inviting from one side suddenly seems like a solid, towering wall from the other, as if once children are sent off to a religious school, the public no longer has an interest in their development. But, as I will show, this is far from the case.

Religious education is a matter of faith in more than the familiar sense of the term. To fail to broaden the debate about the appropriate aims of religious education in liberal, democratic societies beyond the confines of a single faith community is to assume that the attitudes, skills, and dispositions required to reproduce liberal, democratic society can be placed on automatic and grow themselves. This assumption is false. The skills required for liberal democracy are multifaceted, the dispositions deep, and the attitudes complex. Having taken centuries of political struggle, philosophical debate, and popular upheaval to shape, they are still subject to revision. They are satisfied not just when people vote. They are expressed in the way citizens treat one another at home, at work, and on the street. They are embodied in a willingness to share power, to examine evidence, and to take up the standpoint of the other—believers and nonbelievers alike—to evaluate policy from the standpoint of general fairness. They are reflected in people's willingness to take responsibility and to hold themselves and their representatives accountable. They are also represented in attitudes toward people of different races, religions, genders, and sexual orientations. There may be a one hundred percent turn out for elections, but if these other requirements are not present, neither is democracy. True, a robust liberal democracy can tolerate some free riders, people who hold to their own point of view so absolutely that any nod to the fortunes of liberal plural-ism is given begrudgingly. However, democracy cannot survive many free riders. It depends on a general citizenry who is committed to advancing its principles as robustly as any one citizen is to advancing any one particular set of beliefs and commitments.

Regardless of the silence surrounding religious schools, and regardless of the resistance or the height of the wall and the reluctance to enter the space in which religious business is carried out, everyone has a stake in what goes on inside religious schools because everyone has a stake in maintaining and advancing an informed and democratic citizenry. While there are good reasons to constrain state intervention in religious schools in certain respects, there is no good reason to restrain dialogue, to stand outside of the religious school classroom, and to refrain from engaging in a discussion about the proper aims of a religious education in the context of a liberal, democratic society. The object in opening such a discussion, in peering across the wall from the other side, is not to alter the religious character of faith-based schools but to fasten them as well to the aims of liberalism and pluralism. This book shows how this can be done.

Others, such as Warren Nord, Nel Noddings, and Robert Nash,[6] have addressed the teaching of religion in a public school context. I share Warren Nord's belief that study of religion should be an integral part of a general and liberal education, but I am making a different point here. Nord is interested in representing a religious viewpoint in the secularized curriculum for the sake of "balance" and to expose students to a religious alternative to what he sees as oversecularized disciplines. I am concerned with the practices of religious schools and with the extent to which they may develop the critical reflective skills and the attitude of respect for differences that democracy requires. This includes both respect for other systems of belief, religious and nonreligious, and respect for evidence that guides belief.

Stanley Fish offers an insightful analysis of the increasing importance of religion among college students, suggesting that universities need to do more than take "religion as an object of study [but should also] . . . take religion seriously." And he proposes that "to take religion seriously would be to regard it not as a phenomenon to be analyzed at arm's length, but as a candidate for truth."[7] Fish does not say how this might be done or what standards we might use in evaluating competing religious claims to truth, but he is quite right to suggest that religion constitutes a new imperative for education and that it must be taken seriously in its own right. Just how to do that in the context of competing religious truth claims and without sacrificing the commitment of liberal democracy to critical thinking and autonomy is a major concern of this book. In the concluding chapters I suggest ways in which educators can gain the perspective that is needed to help students think about religious truth claims.

Why the Concern for Religious Schools?

There is no doubt that religion has left us with a wealth of moral understanding that helps to make human beings human. From the idea of charity, to the treatment of strangers, to the humane care of animals, religions have been in the business of constructing moral communities for a long time. Nevertheless, modern, liberal democracies have their own sets of requirements, from the need for autonomy and critical reflection demanded by liberalism to the requirement for tolerance, mutual recognition, and respect for differences demanded by pluralism.

Thus, regardless of the merits[8] or deficits of individual religious schools, a focus on religious education is in order precisely because, unlike public schools, these schools are not answerable to a public formed through a democratic process, and because, perhaps out of disinterest, their curriculum is largely veiled from public scrutiny and shielded from public debate. It is also in order because there are certain features of some religions that *appear to be* in tension with the requirements of democratic deliberation. These include claims to absolute truth and hierarchy as opposed to consensus building, an emphasis on exclusivity as opposed to openness, and the need to control belief instead of to test it against scientific standards. In addition, global economic factors are forcing many people to immigrate to the West, many of whom have not been a part of the religious consensus forged in much of Europe and the United States.

As religious groups assert their educational authority in the public square, every modern nation has had to come to terms with the implications of this for liberal, pluralist democracy, and they have done so in different ways. The French government now insists that children leave ostentatious religious symbols behind when they enter public schools. The Netherlands supports multiple types of religious schools, but they all must follow strict state regulations. England, after much anguish and debate, has decided that it *can* fund Islamic as well as Christian and Jewish schools, among others; while some provinces in Canada will support only public and Catholic schools. And, as mentioned earlier, the U.S. Supreme Court has decided that individual states may, if they choose, support, through vouchers, separate religious schools. And even in those countries where the government sets minimum academic requirements, the everyday practices of teachers are often beyond the range of public view.

Yet, at least in the United States, much of this is taking place without a significant discussion of the aims of religious education in the modern context. Given the direction of political events, the increase in anti-Muslim and anti-Jewish sentiment in much of the Western world, and the fact that many religious schools take strong stances on public issues such as women's rights, homosexual marriage, birth control, and abortion, this silence is disturbing. Given the importance of these issues, the absence of dissenting voices in a school can be dangerous. Yet there is also danger in overregulation—in a state that feels it has the right to micromanage religious education.

The tendency among scholars in addressing religious education has been to examine only those dimensions of religious schools that can be mapped onto public schools, and most importantly academic achievement, and to relegate the rest to the private realm. Yet this is the easiest part of the task. The more difficult task is to speak to the obligation to shape citizens whose identity extends beyond that of a single congregation and to the society as a whole. This task does not have an end point but is a part of the continuing construction of democracy.

Orienting This Study: The Double Paradox of Religious Education

Some people take the historical role of religion in the construction of moral communities as proof that a religious education is an essential foundation for moral education and that an education in the absence of religion must be self-serving and, hence, in this view, utilitarian and amoral. Secularists, including those secularists who are also religious but who believe that religious matters are best kept separate from political matters, reject this claim because they know that there are many ways to think about moral issues; some overlap with religious ideas of morality, while others are independent or even in conflict with them.[9] From the secular point of view, there are many reasonable ways to deliberate about moral issues that do not require religion. Secularists are also skeptical about the claims made for religious education because they take seriously situations where religious people have behaved badly. Pedophilic priests, zealous ministers, uncompromising rabbis, and fanatical ayatollahs offer strong empirical evidence to counter the claim that religion necessarily provides *the* road to moral wisdom. Given the available evidence, anecdotal though some of it may be, the claim that one needs a religious education to be a moral person is surely suspect, and in any event, the suggestion that morality must follow religion is obviously false, a fact that is implicitly acknowledged by the important role that forgiveness plays in most religions.[10] To be more precise, secularists may well object to the arrogance and the hypocrisy involved in making this claim and interpret it as saying, "Only those like me can be moral." Or, to put the paradox in terms that a religious person could recognize: when religious leaders assert the moral superiority of their way of life, are they committing "the sin of pride"? Indeed, from the secular standpoint, this looks like a performative contradiction where the very making of the claim contradicts the claim that is being made.

To take this road though would handicap the study and would result in silencing the voice of religious educators, some of whom take a more modest view of the connection between religion and morality, even before they had an opportunity to speak. Once we do this, then we give ourselves the license that Fish warns against and reduce religion and religious education to something else—a psychological or sociological phenomena—and we will have difficulty understanding the moral instruction that takes place in religious schools as anything different than that which takes place in nonreligious public schools.

One way for skeptical secularists to guard against that is to look at the "mote in our own eye" and to see the contradiction in our own response. To dismiss the claim of superiority made by believers as hypocrisy seems to be affirming that "real" religion, in fact, would provide a higher moral standard and that *truly* religious people would not be self-serving and hypocritical. To accept this conclusion would be to allow that religious education, in the *true* sense of the term, is the best possible kind of moral education. Granted, we could nitpick these paradoxes until they were dissolved, and granted too that I have framed the debate in its extreme to make a methological, not logical, point. In studying moral instruction in religious schools, it is important to take the phenomenon of religion seriously and to try, wherever possible, to describe it in terms that are recognizable to believers.

I have presented the religious contradiction in its most extreme form for the sake of emphasis, failing to consider those religious traditions that grant believer and nonbeliever alike the capacity to know and to do the good. This was the position of Thomas Aquinas, the Catholic theologian, who thought that natural law provided everyone with a way to know and affirm the morally correct course of action. Aquinas thought that by understanding the nature of a thing, we can know how to engage it in a morally appropriate way regardless of our religious beliefs. To take a contemporary controversy to illustrate his point: if we allow, as many religious leaders hold, that the purpose of marriage is to procreate or to be open to its possibility, then there are some relationships, no matter how caring, that cannot be accepted as marriage. One of these is a close, loving relationship between members of the same sex.

Still, many secularists rightfully have difficulty with this view and see it as a questionable attempt to ground moral discourse in theological metaphysics. Acorns, as Aristotle properly noted (and with Aquinas's later nod of approval), do turn into oak trees, but whether, as both philosophers believed, this is their *single* "purpose" or whether we can really assign a purpose to them at all is questionable given the appetites of squirrels and other little creatures for the nutrients they have to offer. To many secularists the idea of an essence, planted by God, leads to similar mistakes in reasoning about human affairs.

Thus, religious morality is associated with a set of rules, principles, and virtues that from the inside appear divine but from the outside sometimes appear dogmatic and inflexible, and this reinforces the twin paradoxes. If we take the spirit (if not the logic) of these paradoxes seriously, however, they should lead us to look past superficial claims that are made for religious schools and to explore the deeper conception of the good life that underlies religious educational practice.

A Philosophy of Religious Education in a Democratic Context

Students in religious schools may do better or worse than students in public schools on standardized tests; they may be more or less disciplined in some conventional sense of the term; they may be more or less committed to advancing the good of other people. These are all important indicators of educational progress, but they do not tell us much about the *religious* character of their education and just what, if anything, might distinguish it from more secular forms of education. Granted, we can list some of the surface differences—prayer and devotional exercises, bible classes, and the like—but as important as these are, they need to be examined for something deeper and more powerful, some aspect of our lives which is difficult to understand simply as a part of our individual psychology or of our social life. To see what, then, is *religious* about religious education and how it colors moral education comprises the first task of this book. Religion must be given its due not as just an interesting sociological or psychological phenomenon—a subject for specialists in these fields—but as part of the lived experience of human beings, not just psychological, just social, or just cultural, although it is all of these as well.

The spirit of the double paradox mentioned earlier hopefully will set the tone for the discussion that follows by constraining it in two ways. First, consistent with pluralism and the need to let "a thousand flowers bloom," it must be generous. In other words, it must allow strong differences, even inconsistencies, to be held across faith communities regarding the most important questions of human existence. Second, consistent with the requirements of liberalism, it cannot be laissez-faire about the merits of religious education to the point of permissiveness. This means that religious *education* must address standards for a reasonable education as these are defined in part by the interest of liberal, pluralist democracies in the development of an informed and critical citizenry.

Maintaining this balance is not easy because this dual paradox presents educators with a serious dilemma. If one takes the insider's view, then a complete moral education really is impossible without religion. Even Aquinas, in allowing the spark of reason to us all, Catholic and heathen alike, held that it was the divine purpose that defined the good and that God in his wisdom has provided us with the capacity to grasp that purpose. To be taught "the good" without knowing its source—God—is surely, then, an inferior form of moral education.

But if one takes the outsider's view, then *religious education* is an oxymoron. To emphasize the *religious side* is to block reflection and encourage the development of an overly confident, overly narrow, and too absolute view of the moral universe. It is, then, to encourage habits that limit the critical inquiry required by liberalism and to inhibit the recognition of multiple conceptions of the good that is so important to pluralism. This tension sets the framework for the book—how to engage belief in such a way that a capacity for critical reflection is nurtured.

Requirements of Liberal Pluralism

Briefly, liberalism is the political philosophy that emphasizes the right of each individual to choose, within broad limits, how to live his or her own life, and pluralism is the view that holds that society must embrace, again within broad limits, many different kinds of beliefs and communities. Educational pluralism holds that because no single religious or nonreligious worldview is adequate to encompass, to the satisfaction of every reasonable person, everything that is valuable, we should appreciate the value of the many different kinds of religious (and nonreligious) schools, even though these may not be the values we choose to hold. Educational liberalism holds that children need to develop the critical skills required to reflect upon their own socialization and to revise their own conception of the good. Pluralism and liberalism pull in somewhat different directions when it comes to evaluating moral and religious education. Pluralists[11] want a generous evaluation that will allow a "thousand flowers to bloom." Philosophical liberals[12] insist that the evaluation maintain certain standards of rational reflection and, therefore, that it not be permissive.

A generous evaluation of religious education appreciates the uniqueness of religious experience and religious claims and does not try to reduce them to something else, such as a social impulse or a psychological drive. For many people, but certainly not all, the religious experience is best expressed in an organized faith community, which is defined by a set of practices and beliefs about the sacred and their relationship, as members of this community, to God(s).

A nonpermissive reading recognizes that more is at stake here than the desire of adults to pass on their religious beliefs and practices to their children, although there is very good reason to give parents the benefit of the doubt. It recognizes as well that children fit a special class of human beings, those who are vulnerable to one-sided presentations and who have not yet developed the filter of doubt that guards against premature and self-defeating commitment. Given the characteristics of this class, whatever freedoms we may grant to adults worshippers to self-education do not extend through them to their children without qualification. Children are not the property of their parents or of their parents' religion, and thus their educational interests go beyond reproducing in them their parents' religious beliefs.[13]

The Special Case of Children and the Limits on Parental Rights

One mistake that is often made is to think of children and religion in the same way that we think of adults and religion. While we might desire dialogue, mutual understanding, and enrichment, ultimately freedom of religion for adults does not demand anything but the thinnest notion of respect. I may believe that your religion promotes a false God and that if you continue to worship that "God," you will burn in the fires of hell and suffer the fate of eternal damnation. And, in the attempt to save your sinful soul, I may take any steps short of becoming a public nuisance or a threat to encourage you to see the light and convert before it is too late. And I may believe all of this without knowing very much about your religion or your beliefs. This thin notion of respect only requires that I not follow you into your house of worship, physically force you to worship my God, or restrict your movements in some other way.

Some people argue that this right extends unadulterated from parent to child[14] and that because I hold these beliefs I have a right to pass them on, unfiltered by any competing information or perspective, to my child. The right to express one's beliefs unadulterated to one's own child in one's own house or church is not the issue, although even that right is not absolute if it results in aggressive acts. Nevertheless, the tradition of free speech and a reasonable conception of parental rights are sufficient to protect this transaction between parent and child. It is, however, inappropriate to use the instrument of education to inculcate children into the beliefs and practices of one religion in such a way as to deny them the possibility of autonomy as future adults through systematic misinformation about other belief systems.[15] This speaks to a division of labor between the home and the school, where partiality is tempered to a greater extent in the latter than in the former.

Religious schools cannot be expected to be impartial about the merits of their own faith, but we might expect that ultimately a religiously educated person will be partial in ways that are reasonable and fair-minded, that do not systematically distort the beliefs of other religions, and that are open to the merits of other systems of belief. There are ways to encourage this openness short of a self-defeating "state-mandated tolerance order"—more contact between educators from different traditions, required courses for religious school teachers in child development, and, in the social role of education, required competence in world religious traditions are a few of the ways that might be considered. For the state to exert a reasonable influence on the education of an adult teacher is much less intrusive than insisting on mandates for the child.

In a democracy everyone has a moral responsibility for the education of all children, wherever they are schooled, even though that responsibility is limited and constrained by other important concerns, such as the special obligation I have to my own children. The educational problem is to find a way to respect religious teachings while reproducing in each generation the values, attitudes, and dispositions guaranteed by and for a liberal democracy. Anyone who believes this to be an easy task, and who believes that religion is either perfectly compatible with or irrelevant to liberal pluralism, might think about the attitude of some religious denominations toward the status of women or gays, or about the way in which some religious educators denigrate competing religious belief systems or nonbelievers, serving thereby to lock children into antiliberal attitudes. While it is critically important for children to have good relationships with their parents and it helps to develop an affinity with their parents' religious beliefs, the key issue, as Bredo notes,

> [h]as to do with who experiences the consequences of their education or miseducation. Since children will experience consequences long after their parents or teachers are gone they have a somewhat separate set of interests. Parents should not get confused about whose life it is. Insofar as I try to impress my life and my preferences on my child without allowing their responses, thoughts, and choices to affect this, I have gotten confused about this issue. This is especially problematic because they are vulnerable to things I might do to control or manipulate them. But the core issue is that one should not get confused about whose life this is, which is the same as thinking that the parents or educators are the ones experiencing all of the consequences of the education, when they only experience some of them.[16]

All education, including that which occurs in religious schools, needs to be constrained by this consideration.

Religious Education and the Real World

My task in addressing these issues is made somewhat easier by the fact that religious teachers also work in *this world*. For the most part those whom I have observed and interviewed belie the negative stereotype of doctrinal or inflexible ideologues. They are people who care about both their religion and the well-being of their students, and they have much practical experience and wisdom in negotiating the everyday issues that arise. They must instruct children who come from divorced homes, even if the official teachings of the faith teach that divorce is a serious sin; they must come to terms with children from mixed religious backgrounds where the purity of the faith has already been diluted; and they work in a social environment where sexism is challenged, gay marriage is openly discussed, and feminism is embraced by male as well as female congregants. How these teachers balance religious doctrine with the cultural climate of the time—how some of them attempt to square this circle—is a large part of the story told in this book. Some of these teachers creatively open up possibilities for renewal, while others work gallantly to save the doctrine in its traditional form, as they understand it. In other words, when religious education enters liberal, pluralist societies, new pedagogical possibilities open up—some choose to take advantage of them, and others do not. The educational theorist's responsibility is to enhance the work that educators do on the ground by giving expression to these possibilities and by finding ways to explore, evaluate, and develop their implications.

Religious Education and Democracy

Most of the arguments for religious education in recent years have been advanced in the context of questions about the public funding of religious schools. However this question may be decided, the more fundamental questions are as follows: how should citizens understand the proper aims of a religious education in liberal, pluralist democracies, and what do religious schools have a right to expect from the public in terms of their right to transmit their core beliefs, practices, and habits of mind?

These questions are as critical today as they have been at any time in our history. We are living in the midst of an amazing religious revival. Unlike past revivals that involved exclusively Christians, this one is taking place among all the major religions. It is reflected in the unprecedented growth in full-time religious schools of all kinds—not just Catholic but also fundamentalist Protestant, Jewish, and Islamic—and it is taking place in the midst of a new immigrant stream from Muslim, Hindu, and Buddhist areas of the world. Nevertheless, while the growth of religious schools may be the occasion for asking the question about expectations, it is a question that has been neglected all too long, as if somehow the general citizenry had no interest in the education of children in religious schools and thereby must give these schools a pass when it comes to critical appraisal.

As I mentioned above, a partial but problematic response in some localities has been to hold these schools accountable for meeting minimum academic standards but to allow them a free hand when it comes to the teachings of the religion itself. This approach incorrectly assumes that a strict separation can be established between that which is religious and that which is not. Given this separation it is thought that the religious part of education should be free of the interference of the state. The problem with this argument is that it is often impossible to separate the religious part of education from the nonreligious part.[17] A fundamentalist school, for example, may prefer not to teach about Darwinian evolution, but if there is a state standard that requires that Darwin be taught, then it must do so. Fundamentalist schools often drill their students on the most effective creationist response to scientific evolution with the purpose of inoculating students from evidence supporting evolution. The problem here is not that students cannot answer questions about evolution correctly if they are asked to do so on a test. The problem is that they have been taught to assume that the answers that evolution gives to the question of species development are wrong and that those provided by creationism are right. The students are not scientifically illiterate, but they are scientifically misinformed.[18] It is one thing to be taught that a community holds beliefs that are in conflict with the consensus of the scientific community and to be taught the reasons for those beliefs. This is a condition of pluralism. However, it is quite something else to be *inoculated* against the evidence that supports a scientific consensus and to teach as *scientifically* true claims that the scientific evidence does not support.[19]

Children are not adults, and there are times when they need protection even against the best intentions of their parents. Whether or not the state is the best vehicle to provide this protection in most cases should be an open question, and my own inclination is to limit state interference in any direct sense to the more egregious cases of physical, psychological, or educational harm. Yet without intervention, there is an even greater need for the basic principles to be understood and infused in the culture of religious schools, and, on a different level, state interference should not be confused with state incentives. The political question—what can or should states do regarding religious schools—is a different question than the educational ones: what can people reasonably expect from a religious education, what standards should be used in evaluating it, and what steps could be taken to supplement any deficits that arise?

In this book, I will argue that, ideally, congregants have *prima facie* reason to ask that citizens respect their religious identity and their right to advance that identity in their children. And I will also argue that citizens have reason to ask that religious education respect the fundamental requirements of liberal pluralism, requirements that include a reasonable degree of individual autonomy, public participation, political stability under just conditions, and intellectual development. One purpose of this book is to articulate these mutual expectations in detail and to show why they are important in the world that we live in. The state may or may not become an active player in this project, depending on various historical and contemporary concerns, but fundamental issue is educational, not political. In my view it has to do with maintaining and increasing the space given to liberal education and the role of reflective examination of one's developed beliefs.

Chapters

I open the book with a chapter that explores the unique values that religious education might offer in distinction from those offered by a secular public school. The chapter is not meant to be a defense of either religious or public school education. Rather, it is my attempt to understand how religious education might be viewed from the inside as adding a special dimension to one's children's education. After this stand-alone chapter the book is divided into three parts. The first offers an ethnography study of a number of different kinds of religious schools but focuses most heavily on Catholic high schools. The second offers an analysis of these practices, and the third offers a critical discussion intended to rethink the enterprise of religious education and the public's role in shaping it.

Chapter 1: Religious Instruction and Moral Education

Chapter 1 speculates about the needs addressed by religion and religious education, and explores the reasons why a person might legitimately believe that there is something of unique value in a religiously grounded moral education.

Part I: Back To School: An Ethnography

This part reports on my observations of religious classrooms, observations that took place over a three-year period. In these interviews, I try to understand the different interpretations that are given to best practice within and across religious educational settings, and thus the schools should not be seen as representing any kind of average or norm. In addition to the Catholic schools[20] that comprise the focus of a number of chapters, the "sample" includes Jewish and Islamic schools and Protestant schools as well. The schools were chosen because of the contrasts they provide within and across given traditions, and they should not be viewed as representing a majority of the schools in a given faith tradition. The goal of this section is to illustrate the various ways in which religious schools relate to the ideas of liberal, democratic society.

Chapter 2: The Construction of Religious Communities

This chapter illustrates religious educational plurality by examining the construction of religious identities in fundamentalist Christian, conservative Jewish, and Islamic classrooms. Special attention is paid to the limits of religious dialogue and to the function that such limits serve in constructing distinctive faith communities. These communities serve as components of the plurality that goes into the formation of a liberal, pluralistic society.

Chapter 3: Criticism and Commitment

Teachers of religion juggle three different goals. They are expected to transmit doctrine, tend to souls, and refine conscience. In these goals we have
the threefold purpose of religious education: to inform students about
their faith (the doctrinal), to attend to their emotional and spiritual needs
(the pastoral), and to provide them with the capacity to make informed
judgments about the good (the intellectual and moral). In theory these
three goals should fit together seamlessly. The well-formed conscience conforms to the doctrinal truths, and doctrinal truths guide soul-craft. In
practice things are somewhat different, and some teachers place a heavier
emphasis on one than on the others as they deal with the realities of classroom life, realities which include girls who have had abortions, sexually
active and homosexual students, and students with divorced parents. For
some of these teachers, doctrinal purity conflicts with their concern to protect the child from messages that assault self-esteem. This chapter explores
the ways religious teachers in Catholic schools modify their teaching to
take into account the needs of these students and examines the ways they
justify their pedagogical interventions.

Chapter 4: Faith and the Pedagogical Limits of Critical Inquiry

This chapter argues that a generous evaluation of religious education is
critical for liberal pluralism. It uses a failed attempt of a high school
teacher to have students reflect critically on formative Christian doctrines
to show that there are justifiable limits to critical reflection in religious
education.

Part II: The Nature of the Public Interest in Religious Education: A Critical Analysis

Part II uses the descriptive material developed in the previous section to
explore the nature of the interest that a democratic public has in the conduct of religious schools. It argues that while pluralism requires a generous
understanding of the work of religious educators, Liberalism requires that
a generous reading not be confused with a permissive one, and Chapters 5,
6, and 7 outline the educational expectations of liberal democracies.

Chapter 5: Safety and the Question of Educational Negligence

Chapter 5 explores the issue of educational safety and distinguishes it from
school safety. Educational safety involves those lessons that students will
need to live a reasonably secure, healthy life. It includes the need for accurate information about sexual practices and orientations. This chapter
shows how some religious educators address this need given the constraints of religious doctrine.

Chapter 6: Intellectual Growth, Autonomy, and Religious Education

Moral development involves tacking between three moments—standard moral theories and their implications, our own moral intuitions, and the possibility for new moral formulations. The most serious concern about moral education in a religious context is that it can overwhelm moral intuition and moral novelty with premature commitments to established moral theories. The concern is less that students will come to adopt an inadequate moral doctrine than it is that they will come to think that moral agency consists only in conforming to the teachings of authority and that their capacity for independent intellectual thought and moral growth will be aborted. This chapter uses interviews with graduates of Catholic schools to analyze the different ways in which moral novelty is approached from within a religious tradition.

Chapter 7: Religious Chauvinism and the Democratic Citizen

Religious chauvinism is one of the tacit goals of religious schools. Religious schools are designed to promote the merits of their own faith community. Religious chauvinism is also an important ingredient in pluralism. Many different conceptions of the good need to be reproduced across generations for pluralism to thrive. Thus by each group promoting its own conception of the good, the interest of pluralism is also served. Yet if religious chauvinism is not to be divisive, another level of learning is required, one that is committed to the plurality itself. In those areas of the world where religion is at the center of instability, this commitment or its transparency is not established. Here I explore the educational requirements needed to construct pluralism out of plurality.

Part III: The Reconstruction of Religious Education: A Pragmatic Framework

In this section I return to the issue raised earlier in this introduction and look at both the opportunity religious schools can provide for critical reflective inquiry and the way in which liberal democratic society can advance this goal. I also explore the legitimate limits that a democratic public might place on religious schools.

Chapter 8: The Challenge of Religious Education for Pluralism

In Chapter 8, I develop a conception of religious truth that will enable religious educators to maintain the integrity of a specific religious formation while helping students appreciate the values served by competing religious claims to truth. I argue for a pragmatic understanding of competing religious traditions and for a conception of religious "truths" that will help students understand competing traditions.

Chapter 9: The Challenge of Religious Education for Liberalism

The challenge of democracy is to promote critical and reflective thinking in religious schools while minimizing state intrusion. In the concluding chapter I suggest that excessive entanglement can be avoided by providing a program of instruction and course work for religious educators that could enhance both their understanding of their own religious tradition and their commitment to the ideals of liberal pluralism. I conclude this chapter with a statement about the role that public secular schools play in providing the larger climate in which religious education can flourish.

CHAPTER 1
Religious Instruction and Moral Education

"I was reminded of an account in Katharine Tait's book, *My Father Bertrand Russell*. The daughter of the celebrated agnostic reminisced about her early days, when her father attempted to teach her certain principles of right and wrong.[1]

When he tried to press a moral imperative upon young Kate, she would protest, "I don't want to! Why should I?"

She remarked that a conventional parent might reply, "But you must. . . . Because I say so. . . . God says so. . . ." But Russell would only say, "Because more people will be happy if you do than if you don't."

Defiantly, she would respond, "So what? I don't care about other people."

"But you should," he would insist.

Katharine again would ask, "But why?"

To which the frustrated scholar would snap, "Because more people will be happy if you do than if you don't."

Tait then concluded, "We felt the heavy pressure of his rectitude and obeyed, but the reason was not convincing—neither to us nor to him" (184–85).

Do skeptics practice morality? Yes. But their "morality," in and of itself, is not defensible. It has been begged, borrowed, or boot-legged from some source higher than they—though such may be denied.

If man may manufacture his own moral standard, then "anything goes"—and no one can say otherwise."[2]

On Religious and Secular Moral Education

Many people believe that there is a crucial connection between religious instruction and moral education and that without consistent and strong instruction in religion, moral education must be inadequate. And to many, such as the author of the above quote, the connection is perfectly clear and seems to need no explanation. Yet why, to turn to the excerpt, should the authority of Bertrand Russell, the father, count for any less than the authority of the father of Abraham, Isaac, Jacob, or Jesus? If moral education is connected to religious instruction in some essential way, then just what is that connection, and is there something about it that is the same for all (Abrahamic) religions? Is there some generically religious conception of morality, and if there is, can it be described in a way that can make sense to those of us who are not especially religious and that can distinguish it from the kind of secular education that is prized in liberal, pluralist societies?

I want to begin here by ruling out one obvious and very popular answer to my question—that the difference between Russell's authority and that of God is that the authority of Russell, the father, extends only to those situations where Russell is present, and once he leaves anything and everything can be done behind his back. In contrast, God is everywhere. He never has his eyes off of us; hence, we can never escape his judging gaze, and we can never get away with anything. The plausibility of this response turns on a certain kind of moral psychology—one that sees fear as the foundation of moral behavior and is captured by an expression such as *trembling before God*.

Yet acts motivated by fear and compulsion are not thought of in moral terms. If, for example, a person holds a pistol to a reluctant doctor's head and forces him to mend a wounded child, the doctor has not committed a morally praiseworthy act. Motivation counts in whether we classify an act that serves another person as a moral one, and fear for ourselves, while an acceptable motive, is usually thought of as morally neutral.

Some religious parents and educators accept this objection, but they argue that if children are taught to fear God early, they will come later to love him, and that whereas once they obeyed God's will out of fear, now they obey it out of love. This seems far-fetched. Victims who come to "love" their abusers are thought of as disturbed, and their "love" is properly diagnosed as false consciousness. If the argument continues that once the children reach adulthood, they will substitute reason for fear, it begs the question, suggesting that "God" is no more than a placeholder, a way to personalize reason; and in the end, it actually denies what it began by assuming—that moral behavior is congruent with God's will. On the contrary, to take this position is to allow that God's will and moral action need not always be congruent (shades of Abraham and Isaac). Yet perhaps the oddest feature of this response is that it actually has very little to do with religion and much to do with the psychology of motivation. It offers a testable hypothesis that children raised to fear God would, in the long run, be more moral than those who are not raised in a God-fearing home.[3] Even if true, it is too close to the prisoner syndrome, where the prisoner comes to identify with and even love his or her captor.

Religion has no monopoly on moral motivation psychologically understood.[4] It is neither a guarantee of nor a necessary condition for moral behavior. And many theologians would agree with this. As mentioned in the introduction, the Catholic tradition holds that reason provides insight into natural moral law and that this allows all human beings—Catholics and non-Catholics, believers and nonbelievers—to know the good. God plays an important role here, but it is in the creation of a universe that is subject to natural law and in the creation of beings who can know this law and use it to determine the morally right thing to do.

One other difference between religious and secular morality that is sometimes suggested is that the borders of secular morality, especially that advanced by liberalism, begin where the self ends and hence cannot speak to the moral harm that I may do to myself. In this view, liberalism allows me to do whatever I please as long as my action does not harm you. My moral obligation begins where my skin ends. Religious morality, on the other hand, is thought to be self- as well as other-regarding. Because God cares about me, and because my very being is dependent on God, self-harm is as much a problem as is harm to other people.[5]

This distinction confuses political with moral regulation. While it is correct that a branch of liberalism, libertarianism, rejects state paternalism and thus will not allow the state to interfere with acts in which only the agent is harmed, it is not true that political liberalism is coextensive with moral liberalism. Political liberalism rejects state paternalism because, among other reasons, it is skeptical about politicians' claims that they know what is best for me. However, this political principle about the limits of government does not mean that liberalism avoids making moral judgments about self-referring acts or about the qualitative difference between going to the symphony and going to the arcade. The preferred limits on state action are one reason why contemporary liberals place so much importance on education and its role in informing children about different conceptions of the good. Moral liberalism has much to do with how we are to develop principles of behavior that are fair and will serve to regulate all of us. Most contemporary liberals would ascribe to philosopher John Stuart Mill's notion that there are qualitative differences among different forms of life[6] and that it is the role of education to enable students to experience this difference.

There are other arguments for the superiority of religious morality. There is, for example, the historical roots argument that holds that, historically, all of our present-day moral understandings have biblical roots. This claim is questionable on two counts. First, it seems to assume that morality is a static enterprise and that unlike, say, physics or biology, moral knowledge does not grow. To allow that moral knowledge does grow would be to acknowledge that while the Bible may offer modest guidance for many of today's moral problems, it certainly cannot fill in all of the details that unanticipated advances in technology require.

The historical roots argument falters also because of the complexity involved in determining whether a particular act falls under a particular command. For example, even the Bible cannot tell us what constitutes killing in an age when breathing can be sustained even when cognitive functions cease. If we pull the plug, are we violating the commandment that tells us not to kill? If we do not put the plug in at all, is that equivalent to failing to hand a person undergoing a heart attack a pill that will save him or her? The argument is inadequate because it assumes that once we know the origins of something—in this case, the injunction "Do not kill"—we then know what to count as killing. Allowing people to die by taking them off of life support because they are brain-dead is not of the same moral quality as withholding a needed supply of oxygen to otherwise healthy people. Even though both are intentional acts, and even though the consequence of each is dead people, the latter clearly is killing and blameworthy, while the former is more complex and, under some circumstances, may be praiseworthy.

Moreover, this argument leads us to oversimplify the actual history of an event and to seek its source in one isolated point in time. Perhaps it is true that one day a gym instructor in Springfield, Massachusetts, decided to entertain his kids by placing a fruit basket on a pole. Was this really the origin of basketball? Or did it begin when the first child somewhere decided to throw a ball (or was it a rag?) into a basket on his mother's head? Or perhaps it really started when the bottom of the basket broke, and the players found that they did not need to worry about the ball bouncing out of the basket. Those who believe that the origins of modern-day morality are to be found in the Bible, and that this therefore defines and exhausts moral action, might be challenged to push their inquiry into origins backward to the different tribes that existed before Moses, whose moral codes were likely incorporated into the Bible (note, for example, that prohibitions on killing and theft were part of the Egyptian moral code), and forward toward the various nuances and interpretations that have colored the way in which the biblical text is understood today. And, of course, they might also be encouraged to examine those biblical passages—for example, genocide in Samuel I—that today we find appalling.

Another argument for a strong connection between religious instruction and moral education holds that love is the marker that distinguishes secular from religious morality. The argument from love holds that reason actually separates the believer from the moral act and allows self-centeredness and a calculating form of rationality to substitute for an identity with the benefactor of one's goodness.[7] To be a religious person, it is said, is to love the good and to do it for others as one would have it done for oneself. Here self-interest is not the motivating force for goodness but the instrument for evaluating the good act. I think that there is something to be said for this view, and I will address it in more detail later in this and other chapters; but, as it stands, it has the same problem as the historical argument—it assumes that knowledge of the good is unproblematic. Whereas the historical argument anchors the good in the truths of the Bible, the argument from love anchors it in a pure heart. Yet here, the same objection regarding moral novelty applies as it did with the historical argument. Unless the conversation with God is extremely detailed, the issues surrounding murder, killing, and letting people die—to take but the most dramatic examples—still require much thought and deliberation.

Arguments for the uniqueness and superiority of religious morality are not easy to make on substantive grounds. We should not need to hang the Ten Commandments on the wall of a classroom for children to know not to steal or kill, and there is no evidence to suggest that when they are hung on the classroom wall, children's behavior will change for the better. Many religious schools have a reputation for discipline and order, and some for providing their students with an especially caring environment, while others have allowed staff to brutalize and abuse children, and children to abuse each other. As with any school system, public, religious, and private, the first are to be commended, and the second condemned.

The Moral Difference

Even though there is no necessary or sufficient relation between being educated in a religious school and being a moral person, there is a distinctive religious tone that Western monotheistic religion (and possibly others) adds to moral action, which comprises a critical, generic aim of a religious education. It is tone more than substance that provides a distinguishing characteristic for *moral* education in a religious context, whether it is Christian, Jewish, or Muslim. Imparting this tone in its students will determine in part whether a religious school (but not a secular one) is successful in imparting a moral education.

To the secularist, moral instruction is successful when it allows social action to take place and enables students, as future adults, to contribute to and receive the benefits of social life. To many religious people the fact that we have the capacity to act morally toward one another is a sign of a loving God who cares about us and whose caring gives our lives significance. This recognition provides a spiritual tone to every (moral) act and acknowledges our dependency on larger forces ourselves. The awareness of this dependency is accompanied by a sense of religious humility and a trust in the ultimate benevolence of the universe. This is expressed in many different ways, the most visible being the vulnerable posture—kneeling, bowing, hands outstretched, hands together, and head down—signifying prayer in all Western religions. And for the religious educator, the foundation of moral *education* involves the acknowledgment of our dependency on the divine source of moral action.

A religious education is aimed at reshaping the child's will so that it will conform to "God's will" and by doing so will return the love of a loving God. Certainly not every child who attends a religious school develops this attitude; it is likely that many teachers in a religious school do not fully understand it. Yet it is expressed in many different ways and serves to guide the school's evaluation of itself. A religious school cannot judge its success simply by the worldly achievements of its students—how many were accepted into Ivy League schools, the average income of its graduates, and so on. It must also judge its success in terms that reflect an awareness of the obligations that a relationship to a loving God entails. Regardless of other differences, this attitude provides a common aim for people of very different faiths when they confront questions of moral education.

Religious Humility

Religious humility, the key to this attitude, arises out of a profound sense of awe and is related less to the psychology of moral development than to the recognition of the ontological conditions required for a moral universe to exist. In the larger scheme of things, conventional morality is secondary to the ontological conditions that it points to. The fear and trembling that Abraham felt as he readied himself to sacrifice his son Isaac are an expression of this awe, a recognition of the conditions upon which conventional morality rests. Abraham's very *love* for Isaac is one of those conditions. God makes Abraham's love possible, and therefore Abraham's love is contingent on God's love. In his willingness to sacrifice his son, Abraham acknowledges that contingency and the deeper forces that make it possible. It is an expression of Abraham's faith that, in the darkness of limited understanding, God will guide his will toward the right and the good. Much like a soldier in battle carrying out otherwise objectionable orders because of his belief in the justness of the war and his faith that the generals know what they are doing, the religiously moral person accepts limitations on his capacity to know the good by himself and seeks guidance through the sacred text and accumulated wisdom of his religious tradition or faith community.

The moral psychology expressed by those who believe that fear is a necessary part of a moral upbringing may be right or wrong. However, this psychological hypothesis has very little to do with the *religious* component of morality, where the ultimate test is not a single act—Abraham is the most extreme expression of this—but the affirmation of the conditions that make moral action possible. Ultimately, religious education is directed toward faith that these conditions will be sustained by a divine source and that the world is, to use a religious term, ultimately redeemable. There are certainly admirable ways to be moral that fall far short of the recognition of this ontology, and there are conditions—inadequate knowledge, weakness of will, self-delusion, and rationalization—where one can appeal to a "divine" source of morality and yet do very immoral things.

In the Abrahamic tradition, faith in the reality of a divinely sanctioned moral order entails the recognition that humans are incomplete or, for those who hold to the doctrine of original sin, flawed in some fundamental way and cannot possibly live up to this order. And love of God allows that, as incomplete or flawed as we are, God still chose to create us and provides the possibility for redemption. This idea is expressed in many different ways in the biblical literature, through the stories of Adam and Eve, the flood, the release of Isaac, and the suffering of Jesus, the ultimate redemption of Israel. To some, this is expressed in the idea of original sin, but even without an Augustinian interpretation of the creation story, the significance that forgiveness plays in most religions is an important acknowledgment of this incompleteness. At its foundation it entails an acknowledgment of the gift of life and its contingency.

People who have survived a catastrophe where many others have died perhaps express this view most dramatically when they cry out, "It was a miracle," or that it was "God's will." To the outsider, especially the nonreligious outsider, these remarks seem self-centered. "Some miracle," we might say. "God let a thousand people die, but saved you! What did God think was so special about you?" Yet, taken generously—and, of course, that is what we should do given a catastrophic ordeal—these words communicate the sense that my survival was not my own doing. Taken on a religious plane, this kind of humility expresses a profound truth. We are all dependent on a seemingly incomprehensible set of circumstances—from the mixture of gases in the air that we breathe, to the distance of our planet from the sun, to the speed of one particular sperm that reaches one particular egg, to all of the very unique experiences that make our life the particular life that it is.

Humility is, of course, not just a religious virtue. People can be humble for many reasons—out of respect for others; because they truly underestimate themselves; because they hate bragging, whether it is done by others or by themselves; or because they believe that human ideals can overrun human reason. *Religious* humility, however, is informed by the awareness of my utter dependence on the unlikely circumstances that resulted in my being the person who I am. It is the virtue that literally informs us of our place. It serves as an expression of our awareness that our very being is contingent and that all could have been otherwise.

To the question "What might religion add to conventional morality?" one answer involves the potential role of humility in directing the moral imagination. Humility as an educational aim can provide a unique twist to moral virtue and eventually to moral action itself. The twist is not, as mentioned above, in the content of moral belief or the object of moral commitment. Religious differences over specific moral issues, for example abortion and euthanasia, can be as intense as those that occur in the secular world.

Religious humility directs us not to the belief itself but to the way a belief is held, recognizing that contingency of being may well extend to contingency of believing and that religious humility promotes recognition not only that we all labor under the possibility of error but also that forgiveness is an imperative because of ontological uncertainty about who deserves to occupy the role of forgiver. When Jesus warned the sinner about throwing stones, he was appealing to a requirement of religious humility. Religious humility need not rule out moral certainty. If it did, then orthodoxy and fundamentalism could not count as religious expressions. Rather, it rules out taking exclusive credit for one's capacity for moral understanding and allowing that the center for a moral world is to be found outside of oneself. Self-centeredness (pride) stands with self-aggrandizement (greed) as among the most egregious sins.

Some theologians like Antoine Vergote also believe that humility provides important worldly benefits:

> Belief in human perfectibility is both a necessary goal to achieve an ever-greater degree of humanity, and an insidious danger. When morality separates from its religious ground and retains the ideal of perfection, that ideal is projected on an historical future defined by reason. If there is nothing beyond human history the ideal of perfectibility has to be sought with the aid of earthly coordinates. Two dangerous possibilities are then possible. Because it realizes the actual imperfect state of things, the will to change is grossly dissatisfied. Tradition is criticized and cast aside, and so is any form of authority, for both are seen as responsible for the lack of happiness and harmony. The dream of perpetual revolution is kept alive, even though no one knows where to go despite the firm desire first to erase the traditional system in the vague belief that a new mankind will arise from the ashes as if from some aboriginal combustion. . . .
>
> The ideology of a perfect mankind . . . necessarily changes society into a Gulag.[8]

The point for Vergote is not whether religion actually works to achieve a virtuous end, but whether it defines for us a unique virtue—whether through religion we might glimpse a stance toward virtue that would be otherwise hidden. He provides some sense of what such a glimpse might be.

> In faith we know that destiny will be a glorious transformation which will complete the perfectibility of man. We know too that the historical effort made by mankind is not in vain: faith is a 'power'. But in confirmed ignorance about perfect humanity, and powerlessness to establish ideal humanity, and trusting in the promise, man relaxes his 'tension', surrenders his exaggerated will to do good, and rejoices at the actual spark of peace, love and well-being that he is able to coax into being. . . . The symbolic power that hope imparts to the world of men frees it from that destructive violence born of a desire to bring about the heavenly Jerusalem here on earth.[9]

One can doubt that Vergote's claim to greater virtue holds for organized religion, given the various crusades, jihads, and pogroms and given the ethnic cleansing and genocide that God seems to order in Samuel I. Vergote, himself, allows that religion can be very dangerous and that things can go terribly wrong. Yet there is more than just a historical claim being made here. There is a claim about the uniqueness of religious value, a uniqueness that organized religions may themselves not always live up to, and for which they can be called to task when they do not. Vergote emphasizes the uniqueness of the value of forgiveness and love. He notes that to love your enemies is the hardest of all the commandments and the most specifically Christian one.

> True forgiveness is the real essence and means of love. Forgiveness refuses to judge and represents an act of confidence in the secret possibilities of the other's goodness. . . . Forgiveness or love of one's enemies implies a refusal of any intention to identify the other with evil. . . . Forgiveness is possible only if man includes in his attitude to his enemy the attitude of the Father who, with infinite discretion, goes out to the prodigal son in order to welcome his return with joy.[10]

Christian love is somewhat more controversial than Vergote might think. Many non-Christians fear that such love will provide an excuse to treat them as a mere means to their own salvation. Sometimes forgiving is a power play, placing the forgiver in the position to define an act as a transgression and grant himself the *right* to forgive.[11] Some worry about placing the moral burden on the victim to forgive and about focusing the ethical attitude of the perpetrator on the self-indulgent request for forgiveness.[12] From the Freudian perspective, such love may be seen as an act of sublimation that inhibits productive attempts to deal with anger, and the fact that Vergote writes exclusively in this essay in terms of the father and the son might suggest that religious virtues are largely a masculine affair.

Nevertheless, there is more to Vergote's notion of religious virtue than these concerns can fully capture. The word *love* may be too ambiguous to express it adequately, but if love is the right word, its source is a profound sense of gratitude for "the world as we find it"; that regardless of our squabbles, we are members of the same family, and that because our "father" loves each of us, in returning that love, we should all care, as he does, about each other.

Given that our love for each other is predicated on and an expression of love for the father, it is arguable whether such love need be accompanied by the strong feeling of affection that one might have for one's wife or child. For many people, this demand is over the top and requires too much from us. Regardless of how this issue is decided, the theme of human brotherhood and sisterhood expressed at least by Western religions is partly satisfied if I become a better, more caring person and if I can help others to grow in the same way. The acknowledgment that we all fall short of achieving this destiny, a destiny that is entailed by the gift of life, is best expressed by the notion of religious humility. It is difficult to say how well any religious school succeeds in developing the virtue of *religious* humility, but as a central educational aim, it allows a distinction between moral education in a religious context and moral education in a secular one.

Education and Humility

To understand the way religious humility works in the classroom, contrast two classrooms, one secular and the other religious. In each of these classes, a bigger child has pushed a smaller one.[13] In a secular school, the teacher might ask the bully who pushes a smaller child, "How would you like it if I pushed you?" and hope that she can establish a sense of reciprocity. In a (Christian) religious school, the teacher might ask, "How would Jesus feel?" hoping to connect the child's sentiments to a wider religious community and thus to center his activity beyond himself. The child is asked to consider his action not from the standpoint of himself but from the standpoint of a loving being who cares about us all. Here we are placed alongside all other people, and the significance of our own standpoint is absorbed into the standpoint of one who, like a loving parent, cares for us all.

While these two moral standpoints can often result in similar acts, they imply different educational aims. In the first, the aim is to evaluate moral action from the standpoint of the self as it is engaged in considering competing alternatives and deciding which one will accomplish best a given purpose. In this evaluation the moral chooser takes a strategic standpoint, evaluating each alternative in terms of maximizing the satisfaction of competing desires, present and future, one's own or those of others. In the second, the aim is to shape the will in such a way that one is compelled to act in certain circumstances as if there really were no other choice.[14] From the religious standpoint, the error of the first is exemplified in the horror and the guilt of Thomas Hardy's mayor of Casterbridge that are the result of his realization that by selling his wife and child, he placed that which belongs exclusively in the second category in the first. In other words, he now understands that when he sold them, he viewed the exchange in strategic terms when it should never have been an alternative in the first place.

The Issue of Obedience

Complications arise because the attempt to align the will of an individual child with the will of God is *always* mediated by a religious community and by those within the community who are designated to speak for it. Thus habits of obedience require conformity not only to God's will but also to God's will as mediated through an earthly agent. I am not ignoring the obvious differences between, say, traditional Catholicism and Protestantism regarding the role of religious authority in interpreting the Bible. The mediation that I have in mind is that which speaks to the beliefs people are expected to hold if they are to be considered members of this religious community rather than that one. And part of the function of these beliefs is to mark off this community and to bind its members together in a *distinctive* communal and spiritual formation.

Religious beliefs bind people together into lived communities that persist across generations, and lived communities are themselves bounded, each requiring markers with which to distinguish it from other lived communities. Belief systems, much like religious symbols and rituals, serve as such markers. Some Western religions seem to add to their exclusiveness by appropriating personalities who have dirty hands and limited outside appeal. Anger management is a problem for many foundational figures such as Moses, Paul/Saul, and Martin Luther, to name just the most prominent examples.

Beliefs that seem to others fantastical can then serve a function similar to that of the practices of circumcision and strict diets (which are also taken as obedience to God's will). They mark an identity with others who proclaim the same beliefs. For example, whatever outsiders may think about Joseph Smith (the founder of the Mormon religion), his proclaimed encounters with angels, and his proclivity for misplacing divinely authored plates, those who believed in his story created a new collective and intergenerational reality, and in this creation new truths are enacted. In their very oddity to others, these *new* "truths" serve as the cornerstone of the community. To be a member of this community is to accept these beliefs, however odd they might otherwise sound to the outsider.

This presents a dilemma for moral education as commonly understood. Moral education requires moral inquiry as well as obedience if for no other reason than the fact that human relationships are not fully predictable and no one is sufficiently omnipotent to adequately anticipate every novel relationship or the moral quandaries raised by every new technological innovation. The problem for moral education posed by the religious mandate occurs when beliefs and practices that are necessary to the formation of the community are placed beyond reasonable deliberation because they are proclaimed to be matters of faith. Thus moral inquiry is constrained.

The dilemma is that moral education, as contrasted with moral instruction or moral indoctrination, requires critical inquiry within the context of public standards of evidence. To advance but one conception of the moral good as superior to every other candidate is something like telling a child that Macintosh apples are the only worthy apple and that none of the others are worth tasting. Before looking more closely at this issue in subsequent chapters, I want to explore in the next chapter the ways in which the initial and generic religious impulse—the sense of awe, dependency, and humility—becomes bounded through religious instruction to recreate distinct religious educational communities.

PART I

Back to School: An Ethnography

CHAPTER 2

The Construction of Religious Communities

Are We Born Religious?

Infants are born with certain inclinations, capacities, and dispositions. They all have the capacity to learn a natural language; some are more passive, others more active; some are more sensitive to sound, others to light. There are those people who believe that our capacity for religious spirituality also comes with the original package and that we seek a relationship with God from the very beginning. And it certainly is possible that the initial bundle of awestruck protoplasm that eventually becomes a religious adult seeks out a spiritual life upon emerging from the womb.

What is unlikely is that that original bundle seeks out one form of religious expression over all competitors. You are not destined to be a Buddhist, and I a Jew. The pope's DNA did not predestine him at birth for the priesthood. Neither the intensity of adult belief nor the depth of adult devotion allows us to infer any infant predilections toward one faith rather than another. The Orthodox Jew had at birth no preference for avoiding pork and eating kosher food. The intensely religious fundamentalist Christian was not destined to believe that the world was literally created in seven days. While religiosity may or may not be a natural inclination, Jewish religiosity, Catholic religiosity, or Islamic religiosity is learned as a part of the bargain that children make with adults for meeting their material and psychological needs.

There is, as the Darwinian would tell us, survival value in taking on the specific beliefs of those we must depend on for material goods and psychological nurture. Yet once a child is placed in one religious tradition rather than a different one, or for that matter in a nonreligious tradition, perspectives are set, horizons shaped, understanding circumscribed, boundaries constructed, epistemic foundations established, relational possibilities circumscribed, roles marked off, and a collective identity stamped. And while it is to some extent simply a matter of religious luck where an infant lands, he or she will take on many of these practices as second nature and may find those of other groups to be alien or incomprehensible.

From an external point of view, aspects of these systems are incommensurate with each other. While there are certainly points of contact, there are other points where the reconciliation of differences seems impossible. This irreconcilability is in fact a condition of religious pluralism. It is where dialogue must end and plurality begins. This chapter focuses on two schools—one Jewish, the other Lutheran—and analyzes the formal and informal instructional moves that result in two very different religious communities with two very distinct ideas of obedience to God and two different approaches to modernity. At the conclusion of this chapter, I also consider how one teacher in an Islamic school works to reconcile her religion's concern with piety and obedience to God's word, as understood by the Prophet Mohammed, with the requirements of modern science.

The Production of a Religious Identity: Orientation toward Truth

Religious identities are reproduced systematically and formally in Sunday schools, Hebrew schools, or religious day schools. It is in these places, as well as at home and in houses of worship, where students learn the practices, rituals, beliefs, and commitments that distinguish their religion from others, and where they take on the identity of a specific faith community. They learn to be Catholic, Jewish, Lutheran, or Muslim. But just how do they learn this? And just what does it mean to be taught to have a Jewish or a Lutheran or a Muslim identity, and how are such identities developed? This is the topic of this chapter.

I focus on two contrasting educational experiences, Jewish and Lutheran, and on classroom episodes where some critical feature of a religious identity is at stake. I chose the first because it is familiar in a familiar way—I know about it, and I have experienced it—in some sense, it is mine. And I chose it also because the experience has surely influenced some of the ways in which I think about religion. I chose the second because it is familiar but in a very different way. I know *about* it, but it remains foreign, indeed alien, to me. It is not mine. I selected them together because the contrast illustrates some of the ways in which a religious school builds an identity and how through it society develops and reproduces a religious plurality.

The Production of a Jewish Identity: The Cognitive Dimension

Moses Jewish Day School, with its carpeted corridors, well-paid staff, boisterous students, and engaged parents, is located in a well-off suburban area and attracts students away from some of the best suburban schools. Its student body is restricted to Jewish students, although there are a few boys and girls from mixed religious backgrounds. It is largely white, although there are sprinklings of children of color who have been adopted by Jewish families. In some respects the school is very different from the Hebrew school where, as a youth, I spent three days a week studying Hebrew after public school for a seemingly endless period of time. Here Hebrew is one of many academic subjects, not the only one, but it is taught every day of every year. In my school Hebrew was some sound system you studied on the way to your bar mitzvah. Here, Hebrew is taught as a language of religion, a language of rabbinical scholarship, and a language of a modern nation. Because girls were not bat mitzvahed in my temple, the student body was all boys. Here the student body is coed. Most importantly, children at Moses Jewish Day School attend this school *instead* of, rather than *in addition to*, public school, whereas I attended Temple Ohabei Shalom Hebrew School only after my public school classes were over. Yet despite these differences, this school is familiar to me in a way those of other religions are not.

True, in Catholic and Lutheran schools I am a welcome guest, often greeted with warmth and openness. I recognize most of the rituals, but I do not participate. In the Islamic school, things, while still friendly, are a bit more formal and strange. The head of the foundation that runs the school feels that I need to be instructed in deportment. "Try not to look women teachers in the eye; glance a bit to the side," I am politely told before my observation began. And then again, before a workshop where teachers from a number of the city's Islamic schools participated, I was requested to sit with the male teachers. Had I been raised an Orthodox Jew, some of these instructions would not have been so strange, but I was not. Moses Jewish is, however, Conservative, not Orthodox, and while I was expected to don a yarmulke, the directions in the Moses Jewish Day School were minimal. The names of the teachers I was to visit and how to find their classes were all that was required.

In the Catholic masses I knew only enough about the rituals not to try to participate in the communion. In the Lutheran service I had to wait to take my cues from others, and in both I felt the need to remain silent when a prayer to Jesus was said or to stay seated as others knelt. It is perhaps a tribute to American pluralism that no one seemed disturbed by my presence or by my minimal level of participation. In the Jewish school, I knew the routine and felt no hesitation in participating in it, even though my synagogue attendance is restricted to invited weddings and bar mitzvoth and occasional bouts of unexplainable guilt. I knew to place the yarmulke on my head before entering and found that the words, the rhythms of the services, and the prayers were all still familiar, though I have forgotten what little Hebrew I ever knew and need to use the transliteration to pronounce the words.

I should reiterate that this degree of familiarity and comfort may have something to do with the fact that Moses Jewish Day, like the one I attended, is located somewhere along the Reform-Conservative axis. Things would not be this familiar to me in an Orthodox or ultra-Orthodox setting. Granted, there are features of the school that mark the generational distance. The picture of Martin Luther King, Jr.—or of any other person, black or white, with the name *Martin Luther*—would not have adorned the halls of my school as it does here. Nor would the doors have been locked, a common practice in religious as well as public schools these days. All of the classrooms in my school were arranged in rows. Here there are various formations: clusters, circles, as well as rows—progressive education has made quiet inroads even in religious schools.

Familiar, too, is the controlled level of chaos—students go in and out of the office with seemingly little rhyme or reason, and there is sometimes the sense of a classroom almost out of control, but not quite. Recognizable, too, is the way in which identity is marked, horizons of understanding developed, and narratives structured. While this is in most every respect a superior school, one where students lack very little and where teachers are paid well when compared to many religious schools, Jewish and non-Jewish alike, it has much in common with Jewish schools that operate on a shoestring as well as with the Hebrew school that I attended over fifty years ago.

Method of Instruction: Order Out of Chaos   If there is something called *Jewish energy*, it refers to a certain kind of interaction, a surface level of disrespect, a kind of chutzpah (Yiddish for nerve or gall) that is associated with being Jewish. I may have a lower tolerance for the emotional intensity associated with "Jewish life" than some of my friends, possibly because I was brought up with an excess of it. Nevertheless, I can still appreciate the special form of Jewish chaos that I associate with my life growing up in a Jewish family.

Of course all of this is a stereotype. There are in this school some well-ordered classrooms with children working together, reasonably well mannered and appropriately obedient, by traditional standards indistinguishable in deportment from students in hundreds of other schools, public or religious. Yet these classes are not suggested to me when I tell the principal that I would like to see the best that he has—a request that I make in every school I visit. The class that he selects is a seventh grade class in Jewish history where order is hidden below a surface chaos. It is the kind of class that might fail nine out of ten inspections and where the teacher would be regularly upbraided for failing to keep order and discipline. Here there is disorder, but it is not your everyday, run-of-the-mill disorder. I occasionally wonder whether it takes a Jewish eye to understand just how special it is.

In even the most orderly of schools, anarchy may be close to the surface. A strict teacher is absent for a day, and the students "eat her substitute alive." Children who walk up and down the corridors and stairs of their school in neat and quiet columns go on a classroom field trip and become as difficult to keep together as a herd of cats. Disorder can occur in any system, even those that have a reputation for high levels of control. A former student of mine who spent two years working in a Japanese middle school wrote to me about the reign of disorder and chaos that ruled the school—kids smoking, breaking windows, and interrupting classes to the point where the teacher cannot continue with the lesson. If Japanese schools, touted by Americans for their no-nonsense approach to education,[1] have their anarchistic moments, no system is home free. And while the classrooms in Catholic schools that I visited were generally well run and respectful of both teacher and student, there are exceptions. One former student now at a university describes her reaction to the religion class taught by a priest: "I just wanted to say something to kids who were taking apart desks with screwdrivers when he wasn't looking." While chaotic schools can be found in many unexpected places, chaos itself is viewed as an aberration. It is a disruption in the normative expectations. It is not the right way to do things. Orderliness is a condition of learning.

Jewish education has similar expectations. Memory work and recitation were (and still are) a large part of traditional Orthodox Jewish education. Moreover, there is a vision of a larger order behind the workings of a traditional Jewish upbringing. As one teacher of Torah explains to me, the traditional Jew lives his whole life in anticipation of the Sabbath.

> Some people even date the days of the week in relation to the Sabbath, so Monday is like the fifth day towards the reading of the Torah. In the large assembly the children read a little portion of the Torah reading for that week to give them a taste of what's to come. In the Orthodox tradition all of this would be reinforced in the home, adding order to order.

He laments that in the Conservative tradition, home reinforcement varies from student to student.

The Torah teacher explains to me that his goal is to inject into the student the desire to pray when he is not there and to add a level of spirituality to their lives.

> So I would want them to want to put on their prayer shawl and then say the Shamah or the prayer that declares that God is one. I want for them to build a Jewish space in their secular world—a sense of Jewish order. I would want them when they go away to school to try to keep kosher to some extent. And I would want them to join Hillel to see what Jewish people are up to, to join their group. To socialize with the Jewish person as well as with a non-Jewish person—maybe to date a Jewish person. And they could be involved in Jewish activity when they go to college.

He is not unique in his desire to promote an ordered life of piety, obedience, and Jewish identity. While the piety may take different forms in different religious communities, it is difficult to see how an education could be called religious if it did not promote a pious relationship to God.

Yet there is another part of the Jewish tradition in which God is in conversation with man and where even the voice of God can be questioned.[2] This part provides a model for a more chaotic education where argument holds center place, where disagreement even with the highest authority is part of the moral order, and where elements of chaos are built into the very conception of education. It is not anarchy *or* education! It is anarchy *and* education! The Torah teacher explains how Jewish education can allow both. He describes a model class in the Yeshiva that he is trying to copy in something that he calls *cooperative learning*. The class promotes heated arguments about the meaning of passages in the Bible and the historical rabbinical commentaries. Students are paired off against one another, and there is a lot of back-and-forth shouting, finger shaking, and interruptions. And all of this is encouraged.

He says that if the text is of sufficient importance, one need not worry about polite niceties. He tells me that given a total involvement with the text, people *should* interrupt one another as they try to get their points across. When I ask him, "So what's so great about that?" he says,

> It's not yelling like "sit down and shut up." It is not a negative yelling. It is a positive yell. It is a reinforcing of opinion where each one is trying to convince the other that his take on the text is

correct, but based on prior commentary that is based on prior commentary, that is based on prior commentary. So there is a whole lineage of thinking and they're each trying to represent their opinion based on a variety of sources that speak to the text. This is important because there is a lot of interpretation since the Torah was written. After Sinai [Moses], everything is pretty much interpretation. So even the great rabbis are interpreting text. So the yelling is really a spirited engagement or discussion in which each one is trying to understand the best way to understand the text. They are almost like lawyers in a courtroom trying to state their cases, if you will.

I ask whether the arguments can be reconciled. He says, "Usually, but sometimes there are arguments that go on for three pages in the Talmud and in the end it says this argument cannot be reconciled. And we must wait for the coming of the Messiah who will answer all questions." He then gives an example:

When God says to Moses, "*Go* to pharaoh," the Hebrew word is really best translated as *come* to pharaoh. What he was saying was come to pharaoh, in other words come with me to pharaoh. I will be there by your side, so it won't be just you talking; it will be me too. No matter what you think from your human standpoint, it is going to be OK. God took us out of Egypt. It was not Moses alone.

He observes that the text says that God "hardened the heart of pharaoh," and at this point I am drawn into the spirit of the pedagogical lesson and ask, "Why?" He responds that we believe that man has a free will up to an extent. He says that in this case, "God hardened the heart of pharaoh to set the whole thing in motion." I find his answer unsatisfying and tell him so. He promises to have a more complete answer next time when he has time. However, he reiterates that the short answer is that "God set it in motion in order to propel the exodus from Egypt. In other words he [i.e., pharaoh] had to say no in order to get the plagues started, and then in order to get the Jews to leave." He then says, "It wouldn't have made sense for God to stop them and soften pharaoh's heart and have him let the Jews go." I ask, "Why not?" and he says, seeming to shift the point of view from what God might want to what pharaoh needs, "Because they were an asset to pharaoh." But I point out that the text says that God was the one who hardened his heart, meaning that God was the one who got pharaoh to say, "No." He says, "Right, I know it's complicated, but I promise you that there's a reason for that and I will let you know next time." We're now figuratively toe to toe, shaking our fingers at one another just like the students in the Yeshiva, although we do not literally get out of our chairs. It ends by him promising to let me know next time.

I found his responses extraordinarily fanciful and, on the cognitive level, completely unsatisfying. Nevertheless, on the pedagogical level he had succeeded in illustrating the way in which a totally engaging relationship can be formed around a text and in which finger wagging and shouting can function to develop a total commitment to the enactment of an immediately present interpretive community. There was a way in which, at that moment, we were both being Jewish on his terms. While Moses Jewish Day was not an example of his ideal, one could see elements of it in some of the chaotic, highly charged, yet powerfully intellectual activity in some classes. A good teacher can override the chaos without threat of punishment or bad grades if he or she is able to engage the students fully in the text.

In the Beginning: Order out of Chaos   As I enter the seventh grade class, Michael, a lanky, blond seventh grader who I had encountered during my last visit, strides up to me as I open the door, hand extended as if he is expecting to take ownership of my visit, and declares in a voice that anyone paying attention could hear—"My man from the university is here!" Few were paying attention to anything quite as focused as our exchange. I disappoint his hand and beckon with my eyes for him to take his seat. He does a sharp about-face and strides, with gusto, back to his desk. I finally spot the teacher, Rabbi C, an intense but warm, friendly, and scholarly man well concealed among the many students. His voice is rising from a mild whisper to a shout: "I'm getting angry, real angry!" A few students glance up, curious about the interruption; there is a brief moment of silence, more curious than fearful; and then the anarchy resumes.

The teacher, giving up on any direct attempt to maintain order, continues with the lesson, speaking to anyone willing to listen. He is trying to describe what Orthodox Jews believe (he is Conservative). He says they believe that "if the whole of the Torah is given by God, then it is remarkable chutzpah for me to want to change it." So it would be chutzpah for me to say that one man should be treated differently than it says in the Torah.

"So the writing we are studying," he continues, "says that men are required to put on tefillin[3] but women are not. And the Orthodox follow this." He then offers an alternative, less absolutist view of interpreting the text by suggesting that the rabbis who wrote down the words that they were reading were influenced not only by the word of God but by their time as well.

There is still a lot of gratuitous talking, but other students, working with the teacher, read and translate from the Hebrew script. A student translates, "The law says both men and women are obliged to have candles in their home." And then the teacher says, "But we know that today only women light candles. Why is that?" A girl shouts out, "Because it is woman's work and men would burn down the house!" The teacher says, "But men light Hanukkah candles."

The teacher then yells at a girl who is talking to her neighbor. He then says quietly, with more exasperation than anger, to another girl, who has spilled nail polish remover, "I am furious." The class quiets down as the odor of the nail polish remover wafts through the room. Iris, a rather energetic girl who would much rather visit with her friend across the room than pay attention to the teacher, responds to the candle question, "Women are found in the house." The teacher agrees: "The Mishnah [the legal codification of basic Jewish law] says the reason women light candles and men don't is because women are in the house."

A girl then says, "Now there are men who stay home and women who go to work." The teacher agrees, explaining that assumptions about home and work have changed. "So perhaps, just perhaps, our ideas about lighting candles may change." A student asks who has the authority to make this change. Iris is out of her seat, visiting a classmate on the opposite side of the class. The teacher tells her directly, "I've had it!" She returns to her seat. Then, answering the boy's question, he replies to the class, "You have to realize that the Jews have always differed with one another. There always have been differences among Jews." At this point three boys leave the class, seemingly without asking permission. As the door is closing, Michael shouts out, "Leave the door open so we can get the nail polish smell out. It stinks in here!" The teacher mumbles back, "You have survived worse!" The translation continues. The student who spilled the nail polish remover apologizes to the class. The teacher says, with an edge to his voice, "That's OK—we don't have to spend anymore time on that!"

He then says, "I am trying to ask how these laws are influenced by history and society." A student asks him what he believes. The teacher responds that he believes in change, he does not believe women's place is in the home, and both he and his wife have taught both of their children, a son and daughter, to light candles. Iris is up again, visiting friends in the back of the room. A few minutes pass, and she is back in her seat. The students are now engaged in the question of who should light the candles and say the prayers. The teacher says to me after class that the student who spilled the nail polish remover is one of his best students.

It is easy to be blinded by the chaos of the class. Indeed it does not even meet the orderly Yeshiva chaos described by the prayer teacher in which the focus, ideally, was on the debate and not on the nail polish. Nevertheless, the school prizes Rabbi C. As I mentioned, he was the one teacher who the principal singled out as the best possible model for my study. Clearly, there is a model of education at work here that does not assume that a good education always requires an orderly classroom. It is one that allows that out of chaos, a kind and persistent teacher can do remarkable things educationally. In this case, students are translating a difficult text from Hebrew to English, and they are engaged in a deeper philosophical issue about moral judgment.

The teacher is telling the students that he believes that there is a core of morality represented by the laws but that the expression of this core may change depending on historical and social circumstances. While lighting the candles is a way of signifying devotion perhaps, who lights the candles is a matter of historical circumstance. The deeper message is that laws are in part human products and that there needs to be some flexibility in the way in which we interpret them. Thus while this is not an "anything goes morality," it is a morality that allows for adjustments depending upon circumstances. His remarks that Jews have always disagreed, which legitimizes disagreements and debate. The controlled chaos in the classroom, although not necessarily typical, indicates that the boundaries of this disagreement are indeterminate and that the teacher has to win the student's attention away from the many possible distractions that classroom life provides.

Narrative Structure   The task of building a religious identity involves constructing a location—a center—from which events may be viewed and present and future events judged. For Jews the center is the historical exodus and the story of national construction and survival that accompanies it. The exodus from Egypt is, for many Jews, one with the establishment of modern-day Israel. Both are stories of humiliation, devastation, and resurrection, with the latter being read in terms of the former. While some Jews disagree with the presentation of modern Israel as part of the historical destiny of a people, as Jews they must engage with that story from the inside. Even those who do disagree must allow that they are connected in an essential way to those who tell the story as if it were God's own truth.

There are other possible stories. The Egyptian records show a very different reading of Moses' people—one where Jews defy the Gods.[4] There is the story of Abraham and Ishmael as well as the story of Abraham and Isaac. But to the Jews Ishmael offers no center, and it is the story of Isaac that matters. About the others there is silence. The preferred version provides a window through which the trajectory of Jewish history—indeed, all of Western history—is to be viewed. This forms the narrative framework for not just ancient history but modern history as well.

Consider, for example, the way in which the French Revolution is taught in Moses Day School. In public schools, if students learn about the event (given the unfortunate decline of the teaching of Western history, this may not be a given), its effect on the Jews may not even be mentioned. In Moses Day its role in the formation of the modern Jewish identity is central, as is the significance of this construction to the eventual formation of the modern state of Israel. In an interview the teacher explains his goal in teaching about the French Revolution:

> Once I get them to understand what it means to be a modern citizen, then I can get them to look at what it means to be a Jew in the modern world. Here the Jewish question asked by the French—whether to give citizenship to Jews—is a prelude to the French question asked by the Jews:

> Once the Frenchman have answered the question "Are Jews our brothers?" then Jews have to ask, "Are Frenchmen our brothers?" What is our loyalty towards France? Judaism? What is Judaism? It's a religion? Is it being a member of the people? These are questions that had never been asked before because Jews had never separated out nation from religion.

And the questions asked by the Jews of the French will now have to be asked again by these students as part of the process of shaping their Jewish identity. This is more than a historical lesson. The teacher takes the identity of these students for granted. They must address the question as Jews for whom the answer has a personal significance. And, by the very fact of taking their identity for granted, by voicing no doubt that the answer to this question is essential to their identity as Jews, he also stamps that identity. He calls upon them as Jews, and by calling on them as such, their identity as Jews is enacted as part of a process whereby they become Jewish. No argument is needed that they should be Jewish or that they could choose a religion other than that of their parents. And in the very silence, their identity as Jews is fixed and the issue is defined not as "whether Jew" but as "In what way Jew?"

> I want them to understand that being a modern Jew involves a number of choices. And ultimately they will be asking some of the same questions that have been asked since the French

Revolution, and they will begin to understand some of the forces that have shaped them. Obviously the growth of anti-Semitism in the 19th and 20th century is going to affect our sense of who we are. The question is "What is the answer to the Jewish question?"

So I want them to explore the issue of Jewish identity . . . and then to locate themselves religiously, nationally, or however they want.

A history thus exists ready-made for them. Jewish history is *their* history, and their task is to have it tailor-altered to suit their own shape and size. As Rabbi C sees it,

The nature of being young people is that you do not have a con-text, you don't understand history, you don't understand your own history. You don't understand your own psychology. You're reacting right! The reason you study history is to get self-aware-ness. Disagreement is a natural part of this shared history, but it is by engaging with the same questions that membership in a shared faith community is shaped, and by understanding how other Jews might choose differently than they. It is this debate that shapes the character of the Jewish community: regardless of the position that I have and the position that you have on Jewish identity—on any issue, we are going to have differences of opinion—but we are in a community.

It is significant that he says "the nature of being young people" rather than "the nature of being a young person." In his mind, the young person is coming into being as a member of a people. Thus to engage the question "What kind of people are we?" builds commitment to this commu-nity—an identity with this kind of people. Asking the question to these students in this setting is a part of a larger series whereby this people is reconstructed through the enactments of its newest members into its history. For the rabbis, thinking about the question "What does it mean to be a Jew?" is critical to being a Jew.

The Construction of a Christian Identity: Missouri Synod Lutherans (MSL): The Cognitive Dimension

Not far away, in a different city, a different enactment is occurring and a very different religious community is reproducing itself. The Lutheran Church in America has two distinct branches resulting from a split between traditional and progressive elements that occurred in the 1970s.

The Missouri Synod, the more traditional branch, broke with (what is now called) Evangelical Lutherans over such issues as the inerrancy of the Bible and the acceptance of shared communion with Roman Catholics. Evangelical Lutherans allow that the Bible is a historical document and needs to be reinterpreted in light of the times, while the MSL adopt a "literal" reading of the text.[5] The differences between the two branches are obvious in their official Web pages, with Evangelical Lutherans emphasizing social issues such as peace, hunger, and dialogue, and the MSL emphasizing doctrinal issues and right belief.

Saint Martin, a Lutheran K-8 school with about two hundred students, is physically and spiritually attached to an MSL church. The school is located in a midsized community of about a hundred thousand people. Upon completion of the eighth grade, most of the students attend a local public high school, although a few continue at a nondenominational Christian school with strong fundamentalist leanings. Although the community in which Saint Martin is located has a minority population of about twelve percent African Americans and Hispanics, the school has no black or Hispanic students, and the vast majority of the students are white and Lutheran. A few other Protestant denominations are represented, and, at the time of my visit, the school had one Muslim student. The school gives tuition breaks to Lutherans and an additional break to children from their own congregation. There are many pictures of Jesus hanging on walls throughout the school. He is always white. Ironically, unlike the Jewish Day School as well as an inner-city Catholic school, where a picture of Martin Luther King, Jr., was displayed in a prominent place, I could find no such picture of *Martin Luther* King in this Lutheran school. However, flag and faith coexist every morning in every class as the students pledge allegiance and follow it with a prayer.[6] Children are well behaved and obedient; teachers promote harmony and discourage tension and discord.

Students at Saint Martin are instructed in the "literal" truth of the Bible and taught to distinguish themselves from other religious faiths, especially Catholicism. Perhaps because the Bible is taught as the literal word of God, memory work is a heavy component of the school's curriculum and especially in the religion classes. Religious teachings in the classroom are reinforced by sermons and song in the chapel. Students rarely ask for explanations; issues are not debated. In a typical religion class, the students will be instructed in Luther's Small Catechism, and the teacher might follow with a brief explanation to clarify the doctrine. Words might be defined and spelled for the students, but the doctrine remains unchallenged by both students and teacher.

The senior pastor teaches an eighth grade religion class where he distributes cokes and jokes about students falling asleep without their caffeine jog, providing them with a comfortable setting. While students are expected to memorize passages from the Bible for their confirmation, considerable care is taken to reduce the tension that has been connected with the event in the past. For example, confirmation used to be held before the entire church congregation, but now the audience consists largely of the children's immediate families. While memorizing biblical passages is still the major part of this rite of passage, considerable thought has been given to reducing the number of embarrassing errors a student might make. The school has increased the recitation sessions from one to three a year, thereby decreasing the amount of material that needs to be memorized for each one.

The basic Christian message of the school is also transmitted in artwork, in the pictures of Jesus on classroom walls, and in the posters and cartoons that adorn the classrooms. In a science classroom there is a bumper sticker with a picture of Darwin's grave and the statement "Right now, even Darwin is convinced,"[7] thus reinforcing the school's creationist teaching.

The Construction Lutherans: Christian Love in the Classroom   In an early morning fifth grade classroom with a blond Jesus overlooking the children from over the blackboard and a streamer that says, "Each of us matters to God," displayed prominently, students begin the class with a training session in Christian love. Class begins with a child going to the front of the room; a candle is lit, and a passage from the Gospel is read. The teacher then reads from a book about how to make a rainbow with a hose and says that "the rainbow reminds us that the spirit of God is working through our hearts to make us faithful because we're weak and do not keep our promises. God always keeps his promises. Let us pray."

An emphasis on human weakness and sin pervades the curriculum, and the pastors offer themselves up as examples of sinners with their own struggle to overcome sinful desires. In this way they reinforce the message that all people are sinners. Each class period is initiated with a prayer that serves to remind the children that their faith binds them together in Christian love. The prayer also helps to calm the class down and to provide a moment when the class can remember teachers or classmates who are ill or have lost family members. It functions, among other things, as a transition from quiet chatter to class work.

As the class begins, the teacher asks the class to think about their families and what they're going through. After a short silence he blows out a candle that he had lit and says that one of the most loving things you can do for your classmates is to pray for them.

The teacher tells them that "one way we can show love is by being kind, compassionate and forgiving. We can be forgiving because Christ forgave us." The teacher says that "for the next three weeks we will be studying peaceful problem solving, how to get along with one another, how to make the most of life, enjoy and forgive one another and we all know that all of this comes from Jesus." He then divides the children into three groups, saying that the activity they are about to engage in is intended is to help them learn to be positive. "It involves listening carefully to each other, no trashing each other, respect what the other person says, no negative body language or sarcastic statements," and then, handing each group a ball of yarn, he tells the boys to each roll the yarn to a girl and the girls to each roll the yarn to a boy while always holding on to a small piece. Each time they roll the yarn, they are to say something positive about the intended receiver. The teacher concludes his directions by telling them, "What we want to do is to show real connections with our ball of yarn." One student asks, "Can you also say what you don't like in the person?" The teacher answers, "No, make it positive," explaining that the purpose of the exercise is to show acceptance of each other. "We are trying to show that everyone is important."

The students in one group get a bit rambunctious with the yarn as one boy, seated like the others, throws the ball briskly to another group member and follows it with a softly spoken "Sorry." When everyone has rolled and received the yarn, the generally soft-spoken teacher raises his voice slightly to quiet the class, which is not hard to do, and asks, "What has been created?" He then answers his own question: "A web." Then he asks, "What does a web have to do with friendships?" In a louder voice, he says, "You are all connected. Sometimes when we are friends we only want to be with one or two people, but that is not good. We want to accept everybody and to be willing to include everybody. Sometimes we have a tendency to not want to talk to someone, but one rule is to accept everyone." One group of students has begun to gently rock while holding the webbed yarn. Turning to the group, the teacher says, raising his voice for the first and only time, "Let's not be pulling on the web; that creates tension. We don't want tension." In the end, a girl in each group is left the task of winding up the yarn.

Christian love, the governing pedagogical ideal in this classroom, is very different from the idea of creative tension that governed the classroom in the Jewish school—not that the rabbi would not have appreciated a little less tension. Here, the idea is to avoid tension—not to build on it. Thus, negative feelings are suppressed, and positive ones are given central place. Children are to mention only positive qualities and to suppress negative ones. The admonition "Don't pull on the yarn" should be taken literally as well as metaphorically. Tension is not wanted in here. In the end neither the teacher nor the rest of the class notices that it is the girls who take on the task of winding the yarn without any complaint. Tension is eliminated, but the rabbi, no matter how much he might envy the orderly calm, would see a high cost in this largely unnoticed conclusion—gender inequality.

Education as Countercultural   The acceptance, if not conscious promotion, of *gender inequality,* a term the staff of the school would likely redefine as *gender differentiation,* is an important aspect of education in MSL schools. Children are taught that women should be submissive to men, and wives submissive to their husbands. This is part of a larger picture of hierarchy, harmony, and acceptance. The Bible is the word of God, and, unlike the pedagogical ideal expressed by the Jewish prayer master, all is not interpretation. Hence the whole idea of an education in this school, according to the senior pastor, is to be countercultural—to use "God's word" as corrective to the cultural movements of our time. As the senior pastor explains to me, "We want children to know that there is an objective truth and that it's given in God's word."

The school teaches its students to take both the New and the "Old" Testament literally. They learn that God really did part the Red Sea and that Jesus really did raise people from the dead. Students are directed to "take God at his word" that "when he said that he created the world in six days he means six twenty-four hour days—not long epochs." As the pastor tells me, "The Hebrew word for day, *Yom,* is indicative of a 24-hour period." He continues,

> We believe that if you call into question the story of Adam and Eve, you can also call into question some of the things that Christ said. We believe in the Mosaic authorship of the first five books of the Bible even though we may allow that Joshua added a little bit [of] tone of those books.

The teachers anticipate the challenges that will arise when the children graduate and attend a public high school, and Saint Martin works to prepare the children to meet the onslaught of unfriendly theories like Darwinian evolution. Science education is appropriated to inoculate students against the errors of false science. Science teachers rehearse students to meet the challenge that the school expects they will face when they take biology in a public high school. And religious education is appropriated to protect the students against the appeal of false religions such as Mormonism, Seventh-day Adventism, and especially Catholicism. The expectation is that once they graduate, students will be well armed against both the errors of science and the errors of religion.

"Reading" the Bible and the Construction of Religious Difference In the Jewish school, interpretation occurred all the way to the top of Mount Sinai, and the student's identity was shaped within a context of ambiguity and difference. As the rabbi commented, "Only Moses spoke to God. The rest is interpretation."

Things are different at Saint Martin. Here identity is shaped around certainty. The Bible says what it means and means what it says. Trust in the Bible as the "literal" word of God, and you meet all of the criteria for being a Lutheran of the MSL persuasion. Yet just what does it mean to take the Bible literally? For example, the pastor never points to a passage in the Bible that says that infants must be baptized, quite a big issue in this school; and since Jesus was already an adult when he was baptized, it might be argued, as some Christian communities do, that baptism should only be performed on adults. The Bible does not give directions on how we should read it—it does not say, "Read this passage as having but one and only one meaning," nor does it say what to do in places where it is silent. This suggests that a literal meaning begins with an inference, that is, "Read these words as if they had one and only one meaning and as if the meaning they had described the world as it is." And then, for MS Lutherans, a subsequent rule: "Where the Bible is silent, consult Luther's Catechisms."

Whatever a "literal" reading of the Bible may entail, the idea of such a reading marks the boundaries of MSL. These boundaries are shaped in three distinct ways by MSL. First, there are those groups who do not accept the full content of the Gospel's message and therefore cannot be saved until they see the light. These include Muslims and Jews. The MSL's official doctrines are uncompromising about the requirements for salvation, even denying to present-day Jews their historical identity. The official Web page of the MSL puts it bluntly: "It is the people who believe in Jesus as the Messiah sent by God who are the true Israel. In that sense, Israel is God's chosen people. It is not the nation or the race as such, apart from faith, which are God's chosen people."

Lutherans are advised to pray for the conversion of Jewish people who do not know Jesus as the messiah, the savior, "just as we pray for all others who do not have that faith."[8] The senior pastor, in one of our meetings, spontaneously assures me that Jews could be saved as long as they come to believe in Jesus Christ.

The second boundary exists between true Christians and pretenders. These people may accept the Bible—indeed, they may even believe that it is the literal word of God—but they simply misconstrue the message. Here, the two groups that are most prominently mentioned are Jehovah's Witnesses and Mormons. Jehovah's Witnesses are described in an official publication of the MSL as "anti-Christian" and "heretical."[9] Mormonism is then described as an anti-Christian cult that uses many of the same terms as Christianity "but give[s] them entirely different meanings."[10] There are also important distinctions that are drawn in official doctrines and elsewhere between MS Lutherans and Evangelical Lutherans; in the eyes of the former, the latter have strayed from basic Judeo-Christian ethics, especially when it comes to the issues of women in the church and sexuality.

A third boundary line exists between MSL and other Christians who accept the basic message of the Bible, and especially the Gospel—Jesus is the son of God, he died and was resurrected—but who allow their message to be tainted by doctrines that express the sin of pride. Evangelical Lutherans commit this sin in their willingness to reinterpret the Bible according to their own liberal views and in their failure to condemn women's ordination and homosexuality. Catholics, who equate the salvic power of faith with good works, commit this sin by assuming that they can help to author their own salvation. Safely on the other side of these different boundaries—failure to read, failure to read correctly, and failure to follow the correct reading—is to be found the core religious identity of the MSL.

The senior pastor explains to me some of the critical differences between Lutherans and other groups, with the emphasis on the distinctions between MS Lutherans and Catholics. I am told that in contrast to Catholics, MS Lutherans believe that there are only two sacraments, baptism and the last supper. Also, Lutherans are taught to reject the ideas that you can appeal to saints for your salvation and that salvation can come through good works. He also tells me that some Protestant groups make a similar mistake when they emphasize personal conversion rather than God's gift of grace.

> We believe in salvation through grace alone. We believe that God's free gift through Jesus Christ is 100% God's doing and that even his turning our hearts to that works only through his exposing us to his message and then his spirit working in our hearts for us to believe that. And so we want the children to understand that other Christian groups would inject the idea of human works and human cooperation as being an intricate and important part—like God does his part and we have to respond by doing our part, that kind of approach we are quick to point out is a mistake.

He distinguishes his group from others that insist on a literal reading of the Bible by the respect and humility which they are expected to give to people of opposing beliefs. It is the job of Lutherans to know God's high standards, but humility, he tells me, prevents them from holding others accountable to those same standards.

This could be read as either a lesson in patronizing and condescension or as a lesson in tolerance, depending on whether one believes they do have exclusive access to God's truth. Whatever the preferred reading, it serves to mark off a MS Lutheran from others and to give their students the message that they have special access to God, while allowing that this access must be practiced with humility. When the message is translated into a classroom lesson, it has an edge to it. As the pastor tells his eighth grade religion class,

> Greek Orthodox and Catholics pray to saints. The Scripture does not recommend this. If you want to pray to someone, ask God himself, not a surrogate. Another thing that has grown up with this is the belief that if someone is extra good, for example, Mary, some people believe that she has extra merit with God and can pray for me, using some of this credit. We believe that you can't save yourself. No one earns or deserves it.

As he puts the same point in a private conversation we have later in his office,

> We don't want people to dislike Catholics but we do want people to steer away from that faith. A relationship with God is based upon Grace, which we see as God's purely undeserved love and choice to save us. We believe that Protestants run into some of those errors too when they talk about the idea of conversion as if it were a human choice to declare for Jesus; we believe that that, too, detracts from the gift.

I mentioned in the last chapter that I thought that one of the generic features of religion is a certain kind of cosmic humility. From the inside, the content of the MSL message suggests exactly that. Since people can have no effect on their own salvation, they must trust God to achieve it. Yet from the outside it is difficult to hear it that way, since the implicit substance of the message seems anything but humble—they are wrong, and we are right.

I am not sure what the supposed cost of these errors of Catholicism is. Are they counted as just simple mistakes, not serious enough to disqualify a Catholic from salvation? Or, are they like the mistakes of Jews and Muslims, serving to disqualify a person from the saving grace of God? At this point, the theology gets too convoluted for me. Yet it seems as I listen to the pastor that there is a performative contradiction in warning that salvation requires faith in Jesus Christ alone and in then holding that there is nothing that we can do to effect our own salvation. If a warning means anything, it is as an admonition to act in order to avoid some undesirable consequence, for example "Believe in Jesus or be damned!" However, if we cannot do anything to effect our own salvation, then *choosing* to believe in Jesus as the source of that salvation should have no more effect on our future in heaven than choosing to do good works. Indeed, if we do *decide* to believe in Jesus *in order to* avoid damnation and to achieve salvation, then how is that different from doing good works *in order to* achieve salvation? Both seem to fit the Missouri Synod's notion of the sin of pride.

A Condition of Religious Pluralism: Limited Understanding across Traditions

There seem to be two logics that can be applied here—theirs and mine. Theirs follows the reasoning of the words all the way down to its ultimate conclusion—if we are sinners through and through, then grace is all we can rely on and gratitude is the only proper response to this grace. Salvation is taken out of our hands. My logic, however, emphasizes the contradiction between the meaning of the word and the fact of its utterance. Mine is bred of skepticism. Theirs is the result of faith in the power of the "Word" and its ability to stand up to nonbelieving skeptics. Why this suspicion? Why that faith? To respond to these questions can open up for inspection the fault line that separates one religious tradition from the other, and it can tell us something about an important condition of pluralism—the limits that traditions place on understanding.

Suspicion and faith are themselves boundary features—the first can be defensive, a response to likely incursions from an outside tradition. The second can be benevolently paternalistic, seeking to advise those who do not know about salvation how to achieve it. One seeks to maintain walls, and the other to tear them down. The impasse is unlikely to be overcome, but it can be followed as a way to understand how these two conflicting logics enable both a tradition to be maintained and an identity to be stamped.

Logic of Maintenance

It is possible to look at both Conservative Jews and MS Lutherans as minorities, struggling to maintain their different conceptions of the good.

This may be somewhat obvious with Jews, although there has been a significant movement into mainstream ideas on the part of Reform and Conservative Jewry in recent years. Nevertheless, there are a lot of things about being Jewish that are different from the Christian mainstream in the United States. Of course, MS Lutherans are a part of the Christian majority in this country, but they are a small minority of that segment, indeed even a minority among those who profess the Lutheran faith, and their ideas are considerably beyond the mainstream. Theirs is not a religion that is designed to make a lot of friends in other denominational groups.

Yet the external reading of the logic need not correspond exactly to the internal reading, and there is no single conclusion that logic alone requires. When I hear that only those who accept Jesus can be saved, I conclude (bracketing my reservations about the whole idea of salvation) that this is a harsh and exclusive religion that would deny salvation to innocent people who might never have even had the chance to hear of Jesus. The MSL member, however, might conclude that there is a need to support missionaries all around the world, set up clinics, introduce the word of Jesus, and give everyone an opportunity for both health and salvation—hardly the mark of a cold and harsh religion. Furthermore, in response to my criticism that there is a performative contradiction in *warning* people that God is the only source of salvation, there are likely a number of responses. The believer could answer that Jesus, not the words, is the source of faith. The words are not a warning but a way of opening a person to what is already present. None of these responses are convincing to me, in part because I do not know what they might mean, but from their point of view this signifies that I am still closed off to their message. I cannot penetrate their logic with mine, and they cannot penetrate my logic with theirs, and this is ironically the first condition of normative pluralism—logic and evidence alone are not sufficient to resolve questions of faith. Yet one of the conditions of pluralism is the plurality that, together, these different logics create.

Plurality and the Limits of Religious Dialogue

There are limits to religious dialogue, and the extent to which a religion may maintain its own identity if it is too open to ideas from the outside is limited. Just what this limit is will differ from religion to religion, but respect for the limits of dialogue is as much a part of pluralism as is dialogue itself. Plurality depends on these limits, but as we can see from a "discussion" about the status of women that I held separately with both the rabbi and the pastor, even the permissible boundaries of dialogue are contestable. While the discussion starts over a difference about the status of women, it ends with a difference over the legitimate limits of truth and dialogue.

The senior pastor explains the biblical framework that requires them to teach children that women should be submissive to men. He allows that

> in the new order there's neither Jew nor Gentile, neither you know, slave nor free, nor neither man or woman but all are one in Christ. As Christians we live with a foot in both worlds, in the world that is and the world that is to come. I think you can make some arguments that Jesus elevated the dignity and status of women. For instance, they're the first eyewitnesses of his resurrection and very much around him and his circle of ministry and influence.

But he continues,

> And yet there is this old way [of] doing things [established in Genesis], and as long as we're in this world there still has to be some credence given to that. Paul still honors the old order, which would include recognition of submission.

I sensed considerable hesitancy and vacillation in his remarks. The old order, the order of Genesis, places women below men in the chain of command. The new order, the order of Jesus, raises their status. Yet in this world, the old order has to be given its due—and thus the submissiveness of women in this world is to be maintained. In a discussion of the MSL objection to the ordination of women, the pastor throws up his hands and admits that he wished God would give him a good reason for this policy.

> The Missouri Synod takes an approach that we believe is historically accurate to Christianity. It does not ordain women. And that is a real struggle for a lot of our women. That comes up often, and people express their views. And I try to explain the position as best I understand it. And, frankly, I wish God would come down and explain this to me [laughter], but I suppose that the community holds on to some beliefs, not necessarily that one, in such a profound way that prolonged debate on it would be contentious.

Given that the ordination of women was one of the issues in debate when the split in the Lutheran Church occurred in the 1970s, he may well be speaking out of a collective experience. Damage had been done over this and similar issues. Nevertheless there are times in our conversations when the pastor confesses that he would like a more convincing reason. At one point he mentions that since women are more naturally caring and sensitive then men, perhaps God reserved the ministry for men to teach them sensitivity and care, and he calls on the episode where God called on the stutterer Moses to suggest that this might be possible. However, he does not seem all that convinced by his own argument. In the meantime his faith, and perhaps an unexpressed desire to minimize discord, allow him to support the church's position, and Saint Martin school does just that.

I confess that just as I was not convinced by the Jewish prayer master's appropriation of Moses, I was not convinced by the pastor's either. However, unlike my response to the prayer master in the Jewish Day School, I do not feel that a debate is called for. There seem to be more answers here than questions, and as an invited guest, not a member of the family, I am not comfortable entering into a theological debate about why God chose Moses—although my best guess would have to do with his status as a member of pharaoh's family and not because he had a stutter, but who knows?

Dialogue at a Distance

At one point, when the minister was presenting the MSL's views to me about the subordination of women, I brought up the discussion that I had observed in the Jewish Day School about the lighting of the candles. I mentioned the rabbi's suggestion that in light of changes in the working conditions of men and women, we might consider the need to change the rule about candle lighting. The minister responded by rejecting the idea that God's law is time bound.

> These principles are timeless, and there is something morally valuable in a culture rethinking its position in terms of the word rather than vice versa. We wouldn't *tell* women how they should behave specifically to be submissive, but we *would* point to certain passages in the Bible, such as when God says to Eve, "Your desire will be for your husband's place yet he will rule over you."

The passage that the minister cites is from Genesis Chapter 3, as God speaks to Eve upon her expulsion from the Garden of Eden, and the pastor has taken the passage to mean that God has decreed that women are obliged to be submissive to men. Yet is this the literal meaning of the passage? And does the passage even have a literal meaning?

I later asked the rabbi, an expert on the Hebrew language, about the passage from Genesis; he responded that the Hebrew is unclear about whether the passage was descriptive or normative, that is, whether it was describing the world as it was or whether it was promoting a normative standard about the way things should be. However, he allowed that there might be passages from the Christian Bible that would provide a more definitive reading for Christians. He also replied that he would not begin to tell Christians how they should interpret their texts as long as they did not tell him how to interpret his tradition, and, he adds, as long as they do not challenge the historical right of Jews to the Land of Israel. The response suggests that for the rabbi, the boundaries that comprise a religious identity are also strong markers, setting off "ours" from "theirs" and allowing for a plurality of religious and moral truth. In other words, a boundary marker is just that. It comes with a "no trespassing" sign. I will not tread on your tradition if you do not tread on mine.

This view is consistent with an understanding of religious truth as emerging out of a partnership in which God and humans are in a cooperative venture toward truth. It is not, however, consistent with inviting into the discussion someone who is convinced that they already have the truth in hand. A few days later, when I asked the pastor about the rabbi's response, he allowed that it might be possible but that there were also passages from Paul that advanced the same idea of submissiveness. He did not, however, reflect upon his previous statement, noted in the passage above, that Paul, in trying to meld the old with the new, may have misconstrued the old or that he might have displaced Jesus' message about equality with his own about the need for women to be submissive.

Is It Good for Pluralism?

Different communities develop out of different historical traditions, and these traditions provide each with different horizons that set limits to the way in which they understand the other and the way in which they understand themselves. Both Saint Martin and Moses Day give students a place to stand, and by standing in that place and not some other, it is hoped that they will learn to preserve those things that are unique to this particular religious tradition and to understand a good part of the world through the horizons that it sets. Students are taught to see themselves as a part of a larger historical community, a community extending both backward and forward in time, and a community reaching across national and other borders. The web that the children at Saint Martin's weave together as they toss the yarn is representative of the life that they hold with others in the name of Jesus. And the text that the children in Moses Day struggle to translate brings them into contact with a historical community that extends into antiquity and provides a foundation for a connection with

Jews all over the world. In each of these schools and in many others, the elements of religious plurality are reproduced in the beliefs, the rituals, and even the comportment of their various students.

The identity work carried on in Saint Martin and Moses Jewish Day, when taken together, is an illustration of the way in which religious plurality is constructed in liberal, democratic societies. It is also an illustration of the way in which boundaries are set, and understanding and dialogue across religious traditions are constrained, by radically different notions of religious truth. Together they provide an example of the points of radical incommensurability that can exist between traditions, where even the conception of evidence and rationality cannot be agreed on. For example, truth is constructed, at least from the rabbi's point of view, within the boundaries of tradition. The rabbi's tradition tells him one thing about gender equality; the pastor's tells him another; and here, at least for the rabbi, the discussion must end. The rabbi does not feel he has the right to tell the pastor the right way to think, nor, of course, does the rabbi feel that the pastor has a right to speak the truth for the Jewish tradition.

The pastor has a different idea. When I told him about the rabbi's response, he allowed that the rabbi could be correct about the meaning in the Old Testament, and he was also correct that there are additional passages in Paul that speak to the issue of the submissiveness of women. However, the rabbi was wrong to think of this truth as tradition bound. It was and is a part of God's will. God has ordered a universe in which children are to be submissive to parents, women to men, wives to husbands, and all to God. The order of things was made not just for Christians, but for everyone, Jews included. They may choose to ignore these truths if they wish, but that does not make them any less true.

From the rabbi's point of view, this is an incursion, another example of the hegemonic impulse of some forms of Christianity. From the pastor's point of view, the rabbi's understanding represents a challenge, another domain where the light of the Gospel has yet to penetrate. From the point of view of pluralism, these two views represent the kind of radical incommensurability that pluralism helps to accommodate. Together they contribute to a society where many different conceptions of the good may flourish.

Thus, the identity work carried on in Moses Jewish Day and in Saint Martin's Lutheran would seem to be good for pluralism. It provides the curricular material for different faith communities to persist and to reproduce themselves across the generations. However, reproducing the elements of pluralism is not exactly the same as reproducing pluralism.

The reproduction of pluralism requires an additional level of commitment, one where citizens understand and accept the reasons for the principles that sustain the plurality of religious and nonreligious traditions. The commitment to pluralism requires a certain ability to distance one's self from one's primary commitment, to grant a certain contingency (if not to one's own beliefs, then to the fact that one holds them rather than some other set) and to allow that regardless of "the truth" of one's own beliefs, others have an equal right to hold conflicting beliefs. These understandings are not intuitively obvious and, indeed, are not practiced in a significant part of the world. Thus democratic pluralism cannot be indifferent to the internal quality of the pluralities that comprise it. When schools simply reproduce the Old World values, as for example Mecca Secondary School, an Islamic high school, does when it forbids students from talking to the opposite sex, describing it in its handbook as "conduct that is serious or illegal and is potentially life or health threatening,"[11] the intersubjective understandings required to sustain pluralism are at risk. Students here are taught that the normal interaction between men and women that occurs in most every group in the larger society is a violation of the values of Islam.

A condition of democratic pluralism is a society in which there are many points of contact between individuals—cultural, economic, religious, political, and so on. Contact can, although it need not, soften the hard boundaries that primary group affiliation often creates, and it may allow friendships to form across differences. Friendship is an important source of the civic glue that holds a society together. Moreover, contact across differences allows individuals to form alliances with one another on many different grounds, enabling them to have some leverage over each one of their group affiliations, thus maintaining some level of individual autonomy.

A second related condition of democratic pluralism is a society in which a person's identity need not be exhausted by membership in a single group. An identity that crisscrosses many group boundaries is an advantage. It can contribute to political stability; it can serve as a source of just relations and as a condition of individual freedom. Political stability is aided because each individual has to consider his or her advantages from multiple standpoints. A disadvantage from one standpoint may serve as an advantage from another, providing material for critical reflection and reasonable compromise. This complex identity serves as a source of just relations to the extent that it provides an imaginative connection to members of different communities, thus extending empathy beyond a single narrow group. As a condition of individual freedom, it gives people an opportunity to reevaluate commitments and to shift the balance of loyalty from one source of identity to another. These two conditions mean that democratic pluralism will favor certain kinds of schools over others. It will favor those where contact between individuals from different kinds of groups is encouraged. It will favor those that allow for porous boundaries. And it will favor those that encourage students to explore their different identities.

Because religious schools have a doctrinal responsibility to promote a certain kind of identity, some separation is required if the religious doctrine is to be preserved in a reasonable way. Separation for the purposes of advancing a given religious identity needs to be distinguished, though, from isolation where the object is to limit all forms of contact that might serve to complicate identity. In this case religious authority works to close off as much contact as possible with the external world in order to establish a monopoly on a person's identity. Consider, for example, an incident that was reported by a former teacher, herself a Muslim, to have occurred in Mecca Secondary School. An American Muslim woman asked one of the other teachers whether it was permissible to buy a turkey and a pumpkin during the months of October and November, the months of Halloween and Thanksgiving.

> The teacher had responded by saying that the Imam had said it was impermissible to do such an act; however as soon as those months pass it would be okay to do so. The woman who had asked the question inquired further and asked, "Well, what if they are cheaper during those months, then what?' The teacher replied, "No, it's a haram!"[12]

There is, of course, nothing inherently problematic about dietary rules, except that Islamic law does not mention anything about buying a turkey during October and November, and the rule is most likely intended to discourage participation in the non-Muslim world on a cultural level. This is in sharp contrast to the tone of another Islamic school, Medina Preparatory School, where the message was Islam *and* science, where science is a stand-in for modernity.

On the wall of the corridor outside her science classroom, and down the hall from the large mural of Mecca on the intersecting corridor to my right and from the school mosque on my left, this religiously devout Muslim science teacher posted a chart that she had meticulously drawn showing the major points of evolutionary theory from the formation of the earth to the appearance of *Homo sapiens*. Paralleling each of the entries, she had written the official Muslim position on the topic, which showed that Islam is open to every plank of evolutionary theory from the creation of the earth to the ascent of human beings and is in explicit agreement with many of them.

The left side of the chart might hang in any public school. Freestanding, it would be a statement about evolution alone. However, its placement between Mecca and mosque is a statement about Islam as well as evolution. It seems to tell children, "Islam is a religion that embraces modernity, and you have permission to embrace it too." It provides a sanction beyond science for students to believe in the authority of science. Moreover, respect for the public evidence of science adds a level of commitment in addition to a commitment to Islam. This "second-order" commitment is not about doctrine but about evidence and openness to other views, and it serves as a condition for the reflective critical thinking and autonomy that are needed for liberal democracies to flourish.

Pluralism: A Second-Order Commitment

Whether or not a religious sanction for the study of science is consistent with a truly scientific attitude it a complicated issue. However, the important consideration from the standpoint of pluralism is that the chart on evolution may serve to open children up to an additional source of authority and provides a possibility for the second-order commitment that pluralism requires.

Pluralism is served when citizens can count on schools that promote a second-order commitment to (1) the conditions of democratic pluralism, such as multiple points of contact and complex identities; and (2) the conditions of liberalism, such as reflective critical thinking and openness to evidence. This second-order commitment is not an automatic outcome of education—religious or otherwise. It requires a systematic effort to provide children with the capacity to appreciate other faiths and other kinds of first-order commitments. For religious schools, the balance between educating for a particular faith and educating for appreciation of religious (and nonreligious) plurality is a delicate one. Neither first- nor second-order commitments come naturally. In the next few chapters, I explore how different Catholic schools address these two commitments.

CHAPTER **3**
Criticism and Commitment

One of the most commonly expressed concerns about religious schools is that they shortchange critical thinking and autonomy. This criticism reflects in part the stereotypical Catholic parochial school of the 1800s and early 1900s, where students were expected to memorize set answers to religious questions and where the schools were designed to "protect" children from outside influences and to teach them to submit to the authority of the bishop. The Baltimore Catechism, first published in 1891 and used for many decades after, warned Catholic children in no uncertain terms about the costs of believing in another religion:

"The Roman Catholic Church is the . . . only true Church."[1] Recognition of this fact is critical for salvation.

> Anyone who knows the Catholic religion to be the true religion and will not embrace it cannot enter into Heaven. If one not a Catholic doubts whether the church to which he belongs is the true Church, he must settle his doubt, seek the true Church, and enter it; for if he continues to live in doubt, he becomes like the one who knows the true Church and is deterred by worldly considerations from entering it.

> In like manner one who, doubting, fears to examine the religion he professes lest he should discover it falsity and be convinced of the truth of the Catholic faith, cannot be saved.[2]

To many critics of religious education, the sharp tone of the catechism is but a reflection of a deeper problem: the inherent incompatibility between (1) the goal of critical thinking that autonomy and democracy require, and (2) the promotion of an early, uncritical commitment to a given set of beliefs, practices, and dogma that religious education promotes. For these critics, the problem is broader and deeper than the past teachings of the Catholic Church. It is an inherent part of religious education itself. The teaching of creationism at Saint Martin, while a softer, gentler version of this antagonism between religious and democratic education, is a modern example of the unreflective absolutism to be found in the earlier Catholic catechism. Just as the Baltimore Catechism armed students against other religions, Saint Martin arms them to ward off any evidence in support of evolution. Commitment to a preconceived belief trumps critical thinking and evidence.

However, it is questionable just how far this criticism should extend. The Islamic science teacher at Medina Preparatory School suggests a more complex, more ambiguous possibility. Is her chart comparing evolution to Islam designed to provide children with *permission* to believe in evolution. and, if it is, is she implicitly endorsing religious authority over science? Is she reinforcing critical, reflective thinking? Or is she doing both?

The problem with this criticism of religious education as I have expressed it above is that, like the religious schools it purports to criticize, it takes an a priori and absolutist stance. It assumes that all religious schools function in the same way and that commitment means the same thing in each of them. In this chapter I take a closer look at this assumption and explore the shape that commitment and inquiry take in different religious schools. Because Catholic schools have been so influential in shaping the stereotype, and because there have been significant liberalizing changes in them during the last fifty[3] or so years, I concentrate on commitment and critical thinking in Catholic high schools, showing the very different forms these may take even within the same religion. I focus also on those classes where students learn about their own religion because it is here that the opportunity to advance religious commitment over reflective critical thinking is likely to occur.

Three Goals of Religious Education

Teachers of religion juggle three different aims. They are expected to transmit doctrine and shape belief, to craft souls, and to refine consciences. In these goals we have the threefold purpose of religious education: to inform students about their faith (the doctrinal); to attend to their emotional and spiritual needs (the pastoral); and to provide them with the capacity to make informed judgments about the good (the intellectual and moral). In theory these three goals should fit together seamlessly. Ideally, the well-formed conscience conforms to the doctrinal truths, and doctrinal truths guides soul-craft. Practically, some teachers will place a heavier emphasis on one than on the others.

This difference arises because educators vary in their interests and abilities, and because some are willing to take into account individual student's needs more than others. It also arises because the press toward doctrinal obedience is moderated to some extent by interpretive possibilities that some teachers take advantage of. For example, in cases where a strict interpretation of religious doctrine could assault a child's self-esteem, psychologically astute educators find ways to teach the doctrine that minimize the harm. This tension between the religious ideal and the practical needs of teachers and students is played out most often in Catholic schools, the largest private educational system in the United States, in a dynamic interplay between the center of the faith, located in the Vatican, and those tasked with transmitting its official doctrine—the teachers in each individual school.

There is a similar tension between the emphasis on teaching Church doctrine and the task of developing a mature conscience. The development of conscience, or the self-governed tendency to seek and to serve the good, entails the development of judgment and is quite in line with the goals of critical thinking. In order to develop students' ability to judge well, educators need to provide students with higher-order reasoning skills and the information required to make up their own minds. Yet, if teachers work honestly and intelligently to help students develop their consciences, they must allow that conscience may lead the student in a different direction than doctrine would suggest.

Catholic Schools in Three Registers: Traditional, Modern, and Liberation/Feminist

Some Catholic teachers stress the fixed nature of doctrine as defined by the authorities in Rome. Others emphasize the role of the individual conscience in deciding moral issues and also guard the self-esteem of individual students, such as homosexuals, from doctrinal assault. Still others view doctrine as flexible and open-ended, and use the interpretive opportunities it presents to develop a personal transformation and a commitment to aid the poor and oppressed. For the sake of convenience, I call the first *traditionalists*; the second, *modernists*; and the third, influenced as they are by both feminism and liberation theology, *postmodernists*.[4] This inevitably means that teachers will differ from one another in their view of the moral authority of the Church hierarchy and the emphasis they place on critical thinking.

Tradition-minded teachers tend to be pleased with the leadership of the last two popes and their attempts to reaffirm the primacy of the official Church over matters of faith and morals. They often express the view that the reforms undertaken following the Second Vatican Council (1962–1965) called by Pope John XXIII have now gone too far toward "a feel-good, anything goes, touchy-feely brand of Catholic education." They are suspicious of a Catholic education that bends to the cultural norms of the time, and they believe that it is part of the Church's job as a cultural critic to stand apart and to critique modern culture when it strays too far from the authority of God as reflected in the teachings of the Church. They worry that too many contemporary Catholic schools bend to popular excess, and they want instead to reaffirm the authority of the Church. Reaching out to other religions as Pope John Paul II did is to be admired, but students should not take these gestures of friendship as signs of theological equality. These educators teach that all papal teachings, even those that have not quite risen to the level of infallibility, are sacred and absolute truths, and they want their students to treat these teachings as absolute moral obligations.[5] They guard against errant interpretations of Church history by students who will take the opportunity to dilute their own moral responsibility by arguing that the historical Church has in fact changed many of its ideas.

They counter adolescent skepticism with the observation that any change in doctrine is not a sign of the relativity of truth but rather an indication that the earlier teachings of the Church may be complemented and completed by later teachings. Traditional educators are more likely than their modern or postmodern counterparts to teach apologetics (a branch of theology devoted to defending Christianity) in the hope that it will help students defend the Church against external criticism. They reiterate Church doctrine on matters such as divorce or sexuality unconditionally; they are reluctant to teach about other religions, stressing the need to defend the Church against challenges.

Modernist Catholic educators hold a different view of the role of the Church, the pope, and Catholic education than do their traditionalist colleagues. They take their model from the Second Vatican Council, which emphasized the Church's ecumenical mission to other Christian faiths, the importance of dialogue with non-Christians, and the sacredness of the individual conscience. They are not enthusiastic about courses in traditional apologetics, preferring a capstone course in world religions, and may even encourage students to visit mosques and temples, and thereby to inform themselves of different religious traditions. And they are especially concerned to soften the impact of morally charged Church doctrines when they would reduce the psychological well-being or lower the self-esteem of their students.

Modernist teachers tend to have personal reservations about a number of the Church's positions and will, if pressed hard by their students, express some of them, but they will do so with considerable hesitation and respect for the authority of the Church. If they fear a position of the Church will damage a child's self-esteem, they will distance themselves from it in class without explicitly rejecting it. While they will generally not *initiate* a critical discussion about the Church's positions on birth control, divorce, or homosexuality, if students raise the issue, they may allow a free discussion, informing the students of the Church's positions but without personally endorsing them.

Modernist educators express respect for John Paul II and the present pope, but their deepest love and affection are reserved for the reformist pope, John XXIII. They worry that the Church's absolute stance is often blind to the complexities of modern education. Although they will justify the Church's stance against relativism, or the idea that the individual or the culture is the measure of truth and morality, in class they also allow for the complexity of individual cases and stress the need not to judge others. As one teacher told me when I asked about the discrepancy between her teachings on sexuality and the pope's, "Well, he's there and I'm here." The remark, while forthright, was not disrespectful. She was merely expressing the fact that she has to take into account particular and local considerations that will weigh differently on each individual student, and that these considerations were more complicated than the universal principles advanced by the pope.

Because they place a great deal of emphasis on the self-esteem of each student, modernist teachers want to respect their opinions and choices. They speak of original sin less in terms of judgment and more in terms of equality. If we are all sinners, then only God has the capacity to know what is in our hearts and to judge us. Human judgments—even those of priests, bishops, cardinals, and popes—are tentative and revisable, although, on the whole, they are the product of the best deliberation we have available. They allow that this century's heretic may be next century's saint.

To them, the pope is a wise teacher, and the Church is at its best when it serves as an embracing and forgiving parent. Yes, the pope is infallible when speaking ex cathedra, but his wisdom is illustrated by the very fact that he claims this level of infallibility so sparingly. Much like their liberationist colleagues, they are most at ease when teaching about the Church's commitment to social justice and least at ease when trying to defend traditional moral doctrines on sexuality and reproduction against the Church's critics. The modernist teacher shares some ground with his or her traditional counterpart in that both understand Church doctrine in similar ways, only one wants students to accept it (even if unquestionably) and the other places a higher priority on allowing engagement, dialogue, and reflection.

The postmodern teachers, influenced by feminism and liberation theology, hold many of the sentiments of their modernist counterparts but use doctrine in quite a different way, often providing it with a radical critical spin and encouraging students to criticize the Church whenever it serves power, privilege, and patriarchy. It is not just the alleviation of poverty that they stress but also the complicity of the developed world, church and state alike, in benefiting from the structures that maintain oppressive conditions of poverty. They do not reject the teachings of the Church, as they understand them, but they will diverge from traditional interpretations to the extent that a revisionist version is plausible and could be appropriated to serve "the least among us." They use the doctrine of the Church to mobilize resistance against oppression and domination, and to challenge political, economic, and ecclesiastical authority, taking advantage of textual openings and reshaping traditional interpretations to do so.

In terms of the blueprint for change, the postmodern teacher has a lot in common with the premodern traditionalist. Tradition is important to both, and change must be in accordance with the guidelines it establishes. In contrast to the traditionalist who uses Church authority to shed critical light on secular authority, the postmodern teacher also holds a critical light up to the practices of the Church and will criticize government or Church when it finds either one supporting oppressive policies. The postmodern Catholic teacher uses doctrine and Scripture to open up meaning, provide insight, and relieve suffering. The ultimate test of a good interpretation of doctrine for them is whether it works in the service of human beings.

Papal High and Teaching the Tradition

Papal High,[6] a new coeducational school located in the rural area of a diocese known for its conservative bishop, draws its students from the surrounding urban and farm communities. At the time of these observations, it had a hundred freshman and sophomore students and expected to grow to four hundred within two years. Its mission statement emphasizes its faithfulness to the teachings of the Roman Catholic Church as interpreted by the bishop of the diocese. The tuition of four thousand dollars was for the time considerably lower than Catholic schools in larger cities, and local parishes have signed on to help any student in need who wishes to attend the school. Since the school was only in its second year of operation when it was observed, it had not yet graduated a senior class, but the intent was to require four years of religion, including a course in apologetics, where students would learn to defend the basic ideas of the faith.

Papal High wants students to live the faith as well as learn its doctrines. Its handbook spells out in some detail the service requirement and the types of activities, from feeding the hungry to visiting the sick or burying the dead, that will serve to meet this requirement. The school wants this activity to take students beyond what is "known and comfortable." While students are not expected to wear uniforms and have some choice in their dress, there is a dress code that emphasizes modesty and neatness. Girls can wear one earring in each ear, but jewelry, crosses, dog tags, and medals must be worn inside the shirt, and hair must be a natural color. Mass is held each morning before classes begin, and both students and parents are invited, but not required, to attend. There are other church-related activities that are held during the year, including field trips and retreats as well as an optional summer trip to Rome for students who qualify.

The school follows the diocese's requirements for religious education. These include units on the Old and New Testaments during the freshman year; a semester on the sacraments, prayer, and liturgy during the sophomore year, as well as a semester course entitled Introduction to Morality. In the junior year, students take a semester on Church history and a semester on Christian vocation and evangelization. This is followed in the first semester of the senior year by the course on apologetics and advanced theology, which includes, among other things, the topics of human sexuality, justice, and poverty as well as a survey of medical ethics as understood through Catholic doctrine.

Father D Father D is the young, energetic, full-time religion instructor and pastoral counselor in the school. He studied in Rome for five years and wants his students to understand that "everything ultimately gets consumed under religion and points to God the creator." He explains to them that "God is the source of all truth." He hopes that the school develops in a way that "every class would be able to integrate in one capacity or another the reality of God." For him, these include the sciences such as chemistry, biology, and physics, where "you're simply studying the creation of God. He created these physical laws of the universe and the chemical elements."

Father D believes that the theological perspective needs to be reflected in every classroom, and he expresses concern to me that only fifty percent of the teachers at this point are Catholic. While he is pleased that thirty percent of the student body are not Catholic, thinking that it suggests that the Christ-centered nature of the school appeals to many of the parents, he is concerned that very few students come from working-class or poor backgrounds.

Sex and Sin   According to Father D the percentage of sexually active students in his school is the same as that of their age group, and a number come from divorced parents. In his mind these are both serious and objective sins. There is no coddling here to appease the surges of adolescent hormones or parental indiscretions, such as divorce—at least not within the formal classroom. Sin is real. It is an objective transgression against the will of God. Divorce is a sin. Homosexuality is a sin. And birth control and abortion are sins. In the classroom his position is uncompromising, but he is young and approachable, and some students do come to see him when they are troubled by the implications of his message.

It is in these private sessions where the tension between his doctrinal and his pastoral duties is most obvious. He struggles with ways to talk to students whose parents are divorced. In one of our interviews, he describes the problem and the way he handles it:

> We have to look at what our Lord said without watering it down. You try to discuss sin objectively, divorce objectively, without allowing the subjective realm to enter in. Inevitably a hand will raise and the issue will come, "Well what if this one woman left her husband and remarried? Is she going to go to hell?" Well, eventually they're talking about their mother. And you know that, and they kind of know that, and everyone else knows that. Now I immediately respond, God only knows the eternal salvation of a soul. I don't. We know from Scripture and from the church what God's design for marriage is.

> Nothing can terminate that marriage except God. So I try to discuss it in the objective realm. And keep the subjectiveness away. They will reach their conclusions on their own and try to work it out.

> I had a girl last year, when we were talking about it. After my class she was kind of in tears. And she said, "Well my mother was in a very poor marriage and she had to get out, you know. I don't think she's bad."

> Well of course that is very difficult. I immediately said, "Well I'm by no means saying your mother is bad. I'm by no means saying she's sinful. I'm only speaking about what God's intention for marriage is."

> As an adult we can easily make those abstract distinctions in our minds between objectivity and subjectivity. But for them it's

immediately united to something subjective. Divorce is wrong. They immediately think of someone who's divorced. And so I have to, as a teacher, remember that with adolescents. And that is the challenge.

I found the distinction somewhat difficult to grasp, but operationally it seemed to involve the difference between Father D's self-initiated discourse in class when advancing a general rule and the discourse as it was softened, sometimes in private consultation, when confronted with the particular concerns of a child for a parent.

In class, however, the distinctions are not as complicated, and Father D orchestrates the students so that little doubt is likely about what is and what is not a sin. For example, he begin's one sophomore class if there are certain laws in society that violate divine law. The students respond,

"Abortion!"

"Homosexual rights!"

Father D agrees and likens homosexuality to being a diabetic—the condition is not your fault, but there are certain things you ought not do in order to live right. The students continue,

"Divorce!"

"Prostitution!"

Here, Father D is fully committed to the doctrinal positions the Church takes on matters of personal morality. In this exercise there is no compromise and no complexity involving objective and subjective sin. In some instances, he is even more hard-line than the official position of the Church.

For example, whereas the Church allowed at that time for the legitimacy of a homosexual "orientation" as distinct from homosexual action, which it disallowed, Father D, when discussing priestly scandals, placed the blame on homosexuals and, in contrast to his earlier remark likening homosexuality to diabetes, made no distinction between orientation and action, and suggested that homosexuals should be barred from entering the priesthood. He told the students that homosexuality, not pedophilia, is the source of the recent scandals in the Church. He allowed that both practices are "evil" but offered a feeble defense of the Church by noting that "there's a difference between a ten-year-old and a seventeen-year-old," thereby incorrectly implying that all of the victims were seventeen years or older. He then blamed the sexual revolution, homosexuality, and psychiatry for the misdeeds of these errant priests. "In the 60s and 70s the sexual revolution permeated the seminary and seminary education. A group of active homosexuals came into seminary, and no one challenged them to be holy." He then adds, "The devil loves to bring down priests."

A student asks, "If the Church knew, why didn't they do anything?"

Father D answers, "Most bishops dropped the ball, probably because they didn't know what to do. They did what they thought was best. [Boston Cardinal] Law sent him [a deviant priest] to a psychiatrist who said he was fine." The implication of this remark is clear. The fault lies not with the innocent bishop but with the psychiatrists who failed to adequately inform him.

The same student asks, "If he did it once, wasn't that enough to get rid of him?"

Father D responds, "These priests are like children of the bishop. You get them help and you think they are healed." He says that now the Church is unlikely to let in homosexuals even if they don't act on it.

A girl, following the distinction that the Church makes between inclination and action, asks whether it would be right to bar homosexuals who do not act on their inclinations from becoming priests. Instead of exploring this distinction, Father D responds that "one of the roles of the priest is as the groom and the Church as the bride, and this is not compatible with homosexuality." His response bypasses the question, and he fails to tell the other student why the Church continued to assign repeat offenders to parishes where they continued to abuse children.

In class Father D teaches doctrine unadulterated by concerns about damaging self-esteem. It does not seem to occur to him that he might actually have gay or lesbian students in his class. Indeed, for him it may be that if some students are inclined in this direction, then likely they need these lessons more than anyone.

Yet as we saw outside of his formal teaching role, D is kind and sympathetic when confronted with individual cases. He cares deeply about his students, arranges to take some of them to Rome during the summer, and when not discussing matters in the general moral categories of the Church can show considerable understanding and sympathy. It seems that the formality of the classroom is taken as a cue requiring that moral evaluations be delivered in an undiluted, categorical way. Once class is over we see another side.

One day when students were waiting for the dismissal bell, a girl came up to his desk and asked D if he knows her uncle. He says that he does, and then she says that the uncle is getting divorced. "From his young wife?" Father D asks. The girl responds yes. Father D says that it is "too bad," and then asks her what happened. He goes over closer to her, and they talk about the situation quietly. His tone is one of interest and concern, but he doesn't say anything about it being wrong. He says that he knows of four marriages that are "crumbling" right now, and it's "too bad." Regarding one of them, he says that they do not have to get it annulled because they never got married in the church. He doesn't say this with any particular derision but matter-of-factly with kindness and sympathy in his voice. Then the bell rings.

Political Action: Taking Sides   Unlike public schools that are often restricted from taking an overt political stance partly because of competing interests within their communities, religious schools have greater license to take positions on controversial issues, and Father D encouraged his students to be active agents for the Catholic point of view. Here religion is commitment and commitment is shaped through both the formal and the informal curriculum by the way incentives are structured, in the kinds of rewards that are provided for being "a good student," and, as illustrated in the segment below, in the way classroom discourse is guided.

One morning Father D announces that a pro-life march will take place in Washington, D.C., in January. D says he wants to take "a select group of sophomores and juniors" (about fifteen to twenty people) to D.C. with him to attend this march. The trip would coincide with their postsemester exam break, so that they would only miss one or two days of school. D passes around a preliminary sign-up sheet for anyone interested.

The majority of the students sign up, but one girl who doesn't sign up says quietly and with a defensive tone in her voice to the girl next to her, "I don't know if my parents will let me go." D continues that if there were more than fifteen or twenty interested students, he would probably ask them to write a one-page essay explaining why they wanted to go and then choose those with the most compelling essays. He indicated that he wants students to go who are "convicted in their pro-life position, understand the need to voice their position in the political scene, and are serious in their faith."

The girl who did not think her parents would allow her to sign up asks Father D a question about the abortion debate. She mentions that she was watching something about it on television and heard that before abortions were made legal, there were people doing coat hanger abortions in alleys and people dying. Father D responds, "That's the pro-life argument—if they're going to do it anyway, they should have a safe way to do it." Before he can continue, a male student in the back says, "Yeah, but people are going to do drugs anyway. Should we make that legal? People are going to kill people anyway; should we make that legal?" D follows up, "That's the pro-life argument." There seems to be a consensus, likely reinforced by the prospect of the march, that this is the correct argument, and the girl who has asked the question nods and is silent. While Father D allowed her to question the pro-life position, he did not need to defend it because the students themselves policed dissension within their own ranks. After this exchange between the students, Father D pulls out his overheads and begins presenting a new section of material on "the Virtues." He promotes a theocratic conception of civil law.

> Legislators ought to be instructed by eternal law—to lead us to our ultimate goal. But it doesn't always happen. People have different definitions of the human person. Some of our civil laws contradict natural law: laws that allow abortion, the laws that made slavery legal, laws that contradict liberty and free speech. If we don't agree that there is natural law, then laws are someone arbitrarily imposing their laws on me. In order to have a good society, civil law needs to reflect eternal law.

While Father D mentions the fact that people differ about these matters, he does not mention that different religions differ about them as well or that the liberal alternative is intended to accommodate these differences. The impression that students are left with is that there is a correct answer to these issues and that it is the job of the civil society to conform to this answer.

Thus the official Catholic view is reproduced through directed political action, through students who police the borders of dissent, through the teacher who neglects to consider religious or liberal alternatives, and through extracurricular programs that channel rational debate to fit within the boundaries of Catholic dogma. Father D plans to initiate a debate team. The debates will begin with the revealed truths of the Church. The question to be debated will not be whether there is a right to life for the fetus but how best to protect it.

Saint Dillon: The Modern First Alternative

Saint Dillon is a coeducational Catholic high school which until the late 1980s was an all-boys school. It is among the most prestigious high schools—public or private—in the state. The school is located in a fortress-like five-story building that occupies almost an entire square block. It contains a small, lovely chapel with original stained-glass windows that were designed in the 1950s before the liberalization of the Church by the Second Vatican Council. The school also has a new, Olympic-sized swimming pool. The doors to the building are locked, as is the case with all but two of the schools visited, but entrance is easily gained by signing a visitor's sheet and explaining your business to the friendly woman who guards the entrance.

Dillon is located just outside of a large city and draws students from many different communities with what the principal describes as "significant economic diversity" (about three percent of its students are below the poverty line). In 2001 it had an endowment approaching $4 million, charged $7,000 tuition, and provided needy students with a total of about $600,000 worth of financial aid. It is located in an affluent, progressive, largely white community that is separated from a much poorer black area by an interstate highway. It draws students largely from upper-middle-class and professional families who live in the metropolitan area and its surrounding suburbs. About five percent of its students are African American, and another five percent are of Hispanic origins (about three percent are Asian).

St. Dillon has received recognition as one of the nation's outstanding high schools in a national survey, and its students frequently win state competitions in both athletic and academic contests. When I was there its teams won first place in state contests in engineering and science, basketball, and water polo. Its graduates include a Pulitzer Prize winner, a Heisman trophy winner, an Olympic gold medalist, and an astronaut. It sends virtually all of its 1,150 students to four-year colleges, many of them to elite and Ivy League schools. Almost half of the student body attends out-of-state colleges and universities. Admission is highly competitive, with the school accepting only about half of the six hundred students who apply each year.

Dillon is proud that fifteen percent of its students come from other religions, a fact that it advertises together with the relatively high SAT and ACT scores of its graduates, to parents of prospective students on its handsomely embossed recruitment materials. Parental surveys indicate that more parents choose the school for its high academic standards than for its religious climate. The curriculum reflects the heavy academic emphasis of the school. Students are required to take four years of a foreign language, four years of English, a minimum of three and a half years of math, and at least two years of science. Students also take theology for a total of seven out of eight semesters. The principal tells me that it is called *theology* rather than *religion* to emphasize that it is an academically rigorous course and not to relegate it to second-class status. He describes the theology classes as rigorously academic in contrast to some of the "touchy-feely, feel good about your faith, give the kid an A" courses that he says are to be found in other Catholic schools. He laments the fact that the accrediting association will allow only the course in world religions to count toward meeting the social studies graduation requirement.

While the school has a strong academic culture, there is a considerable attempt to maintain its Catholic and its Dominican character. The parent-student handbook speaks to the importance of the Catholic tradition and the Dominican heritage as important parts of the school's philosophy, mentioning the importance of grace and theological development. The handbook stresses the importance of God in the life of the school, and it affirms that a Catholic graduate should continue to participate in the sacramental practices of the Church and that non-Catholics can use their understanding of Catholicism to reflect on their own faith traditions. While it does not mention whether Catholics are to have this advantage as well, the fact that the school continues to require a world religion course and does not offer an apologetics course, where students traditionally were expected to serve as defenders of their faith to critics, suggests that it does not see reflection as just a one-sided gift to non-Catholics.

The Catholic character of the school is built into its physical structure and its daily routine. The four stunning stained-glass panels mentioned earlier, each depicting a saint, frame one side of the school's chapel. A statue of Mary guards the staircase that I ascend to attend theology class. Every day begins with a communal prayer said by a student over the loud-speaker system, and every class begins with a student reciting a prayer. All students, regardless of their religion, are required to attend a liturgy mass at least once a month. Despite the efforts to maintain the Catholic charac-ter of the school, some of the religion teachers feel that its highly charged academic climate interferes with its Catholic mission, and the theology teachers lament that too many parents view the Catholic side of the school as less important than its reputation for academic excellence. Nevertheless, moral development is an important part of the Dillon education.

Moral education in Dillon occurs in both the informal and the formal features of a school—in the classroom, on the playing field, in the retreats, and in the disciplinary rules and the way in which they are enforced. The disciplinary regime is labeled JUG, or justice under God, and student behavior is monitored inside school and outside, at parties and other events. Infractions are reported to school authorities that administer the appropriate punishment. While every teacher and administrator is, in principle, responsible for the moral education of the students, theology teachers provide formal instruction about the moral teachings of the Church.

Mr. P's Class   Mr. P is a highly respected teacher at Dillon and was rec-ommended to me by both the president and the principal of the school as one of its very best teachers.[7] His thirty students sit in neat rows, as is the case in all but one of the Catholic high school classrooms I observed. The girls wear knee-length plaid skirts the same color, depending on their year, and plain blouses and sweaters. The boys wear chino pants, long-sleeve shirts, and ties. Mr. P is in his mid-thirties. He is married, as are many teachers in Catholic schools, with two young children, and he considers himself to be a devout but somewhat revisionist Catholic who had once considered entering the priesthood. He graduated from a Catholic high school seminary and continued his studies for one year at a college seminary, at which point he abandoned his desire to be a priest and finished his studies at a local Catholic university. Interestingly, he describes his experience in the college seminary as the only time in his life when, as a heterosexual male, he felt like a member of a minority.

P is a gifted although not dynamic teacher who maintains the students' respect through his clear presentations, his willingness to listen, and his authenticity. He is open in discussing his strong faith with me, as well as some of his reservations about Church doctrine. He wants his students to learn not only about their own faith but about others as well, and during my visits he asks me to help him arrange for an expert on Judaism to talk to the class.

In the first semester his students are introduced to the biblical and historical foundations of Catholic moral teachings, while in the second semester they discuss the application of these teachings to issues of social justice. The course also includes a forty-hour service requirement, such as volunteering in a hospital, a soup kitchen, or a homeless shelter, and a report on the experience.

P's class combines lectures with questions and answers, and while P is usually the focal point of questions and responses, when discussions get lively the fixed desks do not get in the way and students bypass him to address one another directly. His classes are almost always informative, and he provides his students with a systematic presentation of moral doctrine. He feels that it is his obligation as a teacher in a Catholic school to present the doctrine as the Church intends, even in cases in which he may have some reservations. He does not volunteer these reservations to the students, although he does share them with me. His reservations are not about the importance of the principle, but rather he fears that if he teaches certain doctrines as absolute truths, he will undermine his pastoral effectiveness and will compromise his ability to care for his students' well-being. It is when P thinks about the pastoral mission of the Church that he becomes uncomfortable with its doctrinal absolutes:

> It's very important to me that I honestly try and present coherently the Catholic faith to them. At the same time, I think one needs to have a pastoral kind of awareness that some of the kids in here are sexually active. A few of the girls I'll see during the day I'm sure have had abortions. You know, a number of them come from divorces and remarriages, okay, where according to the

official teaching of the Church, if you're divorced and remarried, you should not be receiving communion. That's kind of, if you will, the rule of the Church. So you have to be very careful how you approach things.

Or, an issue we'll talk about is *in vitro* fertilization and you know, the Church is opposed to [it]. And a couple of years back, we were talking about it, and one kid put up her hand. A real nice girl. And she was talking about how her younger sibling had been conceived that way. And I'm like, "Whoa, okay." And again, I realize that in a few years, I'll probably have somebody sitting in front of me who was conceived that way. And so again, a tension in that exists kind of in the church is between faithfulness to the church's teaching and freedom of conscience.

P is deeply troubled by the conflict that this likelihood will create—assuring a child that the Church accepts her as a member in good standing but rejects the only possible way in which she could have come into being. To address this problem P looks back not to doctrine but to history, where, he tells me, "If you look at the history of the church, some of the people proclaimed as saints of the church have been persecuted during their time as members of the church."

P's teaching reflects the tension that he feels between the doctrine of the Church and the need to develop and follow one's own conscience. This issue comes up repeatedly in different ways—through P's openness to his student's views; through his willingness, if pressed, to express a reservation here and there; through the sympathetic treatment that he gives to lesbians and homosexuals in a self-chosen unit on prejudice; and through his usually generous treatment of other religious traditions.

In our private conversations P confesses a certain tension between his responsibility to teach the doctrine of the Church and his growing reservations about the adequacy of some of those doctrines. He holds very strongly to the "primacy of conscience" and believes that the Church does too, although he is also aware that conscience and doctrine do not always fit neatly together. And there are times when his students force the choice.

A Sample Class   P introduces the teachings of the Church hierarchy not as an ultimate authority but as a guide to thought and action. He tells his class, "From a Catholic perspective, there is a special authority, the Magisterium, or the teaching authority of the church, that's vested in the pope and the bishops." He says that conscience, as judgment, is what is called

Command Conscience Interestingly, he does not tell them that they need to follow this as a command but that they do need to consult it. P then applies the idea to the issue of premarital sex, and this prompts students to begin to test the authority of the Church.

P asks, "Where does the church say sex belongs?" A student responds, "In marriage." But then the student adds, as a quiet aside and to the laughter of the class, "But that's not what I believe." In contrast to Father D's absolutism, P softens the Church's message by telling the students, perhaps in response to the aside, that this is more a teaching and less a command, and he advances an image of a Church that is less enforcer and more counselor and guide:

> But some people say it's not realistic, when today people don't get married until after gradutate school. But when people say the church should change its rules, they are mixed up. It is not the rule; it is the church's teaching. That is, it is the church's best wisdom. The church feels it is in the individual and the society's best interest to only have sex in marriage.

He continues,

> The role of the church, then, is as a teacher. Catholics believe that the Church is guided by the Holy Spirit. That doesn't mean that the Church is always right or that Christians can't do some terrible things. But it means that the Church is guided by the Holy Spirit.

While he tells them that he doubts that the teaching on sex outside of marriage will change, he informs them that the Church doctrine is sometimes revisable. "Now there is some precedent to change. For example, there were once married priests. But on those things that have always been there from the beginning, like sexual abstinence, those are much less likely to change."

P stresses the need for a balance between the authority of the Church and the authority of an individual conscience, warning his students against both blind obedience and extreme permissiveness. He concludes that Catholics must take very seriously the Church's teachings, but ultimately "if I do the best job I can informing my conscience, then I am not guilty of sin." Once I form my conscience I have to follow it, but that only applies to me. I have to be faithful to what I believe is right, and you have to be faithful to what you believe is right. "The education of conscience is a lifelong task." At that point the bell rings and the class leaves.

Protecting Children from Church Doctrine: Distancing Modernist teachers can feel a deep conflict between their role as purveyors of Church doctrine and their pastoral role as protectors of student self-esteem and psychological well-being. For example, a teacher, concerned about the damage to a student's self-esteem might present certain doctrines as simply the "Church's position," much in the same way as she might present the beliefs of Confucius to her class as the "Confucian tradition." The effect is to gain reasonable distance from the Church's position without completely renouncing it. A principal of a parochial K-8 grade school illustrates this technique when she describes to me her efforts to protect a child from Church doctrine about the sinfulness of divorce. (Note: I provide letters to the relevant paragraphs in order to refer to them later in the analysis.)

a. In one class a boy raised his hand. The book must have said something about divorce, divorce is wrong, marriage is forever. But he said, "But they say you're excommunicated"

b. I knew his parents were divorced. So you have to explain it in a way that doesn't hurt the child.

c. I said, "You have to understand where the Church is coming from. If you are going to get married, if you are going to bring children into the world, they would like it to be for life." When I was a kid, there was less divorce.

d. Now there is more, so I went into explaining the Church's teachings. They don't want people getting divorced, and they don't agree with it because they want what is best for the family.

e. Divorce now is quite in, and you have to just say it so that you are not offending anyone and so that you are not just saying that the Church is saying that divorce is OK. So it is a very fine line, but I feel that in that kid's life, his parents are divorced, and if I am going to stand up and pontificate and say, "Yes they are excommunicated, or they are going to go to hell," or whatever, it's totally not helpful to that child.

f. So I have to say something that is still the Church's teaching but maybe give it a historical twist and try to take care of the kid. A lot of us feel that way.

g. I had a Sister who worked for me who was wonderful, and she had a spaghetti dinner cooked by the kids and her for the parents. She came to me one day and said, "This little girl wants to bring her stepmother but I said no." And she saw my face and she said, "But it's not right, her mommy's coming and I don't think her stepmother should come." And I just looked at her and said, "Sister, in that kid's life she has a mother and a stepmother, that's the reality of that."

    h. Now, Sister was a good soul and she came back the next day and said, "I should not have done that." It was sort of old school, but it was also built into her and no one had ever called her on it.

    i. The reason I confronted her was not because I am wonderful, but because I was divorced. I know what kids go through.

    j. I could say it to her, and she could go home and come back the next day and say she should not have done that. She was a good soul.

The principal uses a number of different strategies to work through this moral dilemma. On the one hand, the Church has a certain position on divorce—marriage is sacred, and divorce is a sin in the eyes of the Church. As a representative of the Church, the principal is obliged to also represent its position on divorce. She cannot just pick and choose as she likes. She is also aware of the vulnerability of her students and of the fact that some will understand the Church's position as an indictment of their divorced parents. As an educator, she is aware of the psychological and social cost that children pay when the school authority finds moral fault with their parents. The principal resolves her dilemma by shifting the Church's discourse from a religious, judgmental frame to a historical, explanatory one. She justifies this shift to me by asserting as her cardinal principle, "[Don't] hurt the child" which, as we will see, she interprets in a certain way. Once the dilemma is established in lines a and b, and the cardinal principle established—"Don't hurt the child"—she switches the explanatory frame from a theological discourse on sin and excommunication to a historical and sociological one. Thus in line c, she reports telling the students, "You have to understand where the Church is coming from." And the original discourse on sin is altered to a discourse on preferences—"They would like it to be for life." And the *we* of the Church is turned into a *they*, distancing the judgment of the Church from that of the principal.

Yet the hold of the Church on moral behavior is not completely abandoned, as in d where it is explained that the Church wants "what is best for the family," and the assumption is allowed to stand that the Church might know better than the family itself what is best for it. Yet d succeeds in switching the tone from moral framework to an explanatory one and distances teacher, parents, and child from the official judgment of the Church. In e and f she shows that she is aware of the way she has altered the official message and why she has done so. "So it is a very fine line, but I feel that . . . if I am going to stand up and pontificate and say, 'Yes they are excommunicated, or they are going to hell' . . . it's totally not helpful to that child. So I have to say something that is still the Church's teaching but maybe give it a historical twist and try to take care of the kid."

Then, in g and h, she confronts a more traditional understanding in the person of the Sister and describes how her (the principal's) understanding gets promulgated to the staff—through looks, body language, and discourse. Then in j she describes the transformation that she believes occurred in the Sister and the way the ongoing life of the school was renewed, and in h and j she reestablishes, through the appropriation of religious language, "She was a good soul" through her own communal affiliation with the Church. In this instance the dialogue is set against the background of the formalized understandings, as these are represented through the Sister's behavior, and (earlier) through the pedagogical material in which the child first learned that divorce is an offense calling for excommunication.

Even the vocabulary is embedded in competing theoretical understandings. Consider the way in which the principal uses the concept of hurt in b and the way in which an alternative use of the same concept shadows her primary discursive frame. In this discussion, the notion of hurt forms the end point of two competing doctrines. The first is theological. Here hurt is imbedded in concepts like sin, soul, salvation, and so on and suggests a falling-away from God's will. The second is psychological. It is embedded in concepts such as self-esteem, choice, and autonomy. In this discourse the hurt to the child develops by lowering the status of his parents in his eyes. Given this notion of hurt, the discourse tracks to theories about the importance of role models in the development of self-concept and self-esteem.

Thus the principal, in weaving together the discourse of modern psychology and the discourse of dogma and theology, gives priority in this instance to the former but allows the latter to shine as relevant, not to the case at hand but as informing the more general, more abstract, but less pointed question—what might a good life look like in the eyes of the church?

Protecting Children from Church Doctrine: Historicizing   The requirement to present an accurate account of the Church and its beliefs together with the educational requirement to maintain opportunities for the development of student insight and the sharpening of their interpretive and critical skills provide the religious educator with an additional challenge: how can all of this be done without undermining faith? P speaks to me often about this challenge and to the way he tries to work it out. Here he tells me his own doubts:

> The pope has said there are no reasons that could ever justify the
> use of contraception, and I'm saying, "No, well, if your doctor

tells you, you know, a pregnancy is going to kill your wife, you know." Or again, if you're in the Third World, and you are poor, not poor in the sense of what we might consider poor. I mean, you know, I'm not convinced of the absoluteness of that.

P explains the Church's position to his class as "the Church's teachings." He neither endorses it nor challenges it, but allows the students to debate the issue and provides them with relevant historical documents such as Pope Paul VI's Encyclical Letter[8] upholding the Church's position on birth control.

When a student questions the Church's stance on contraception, P places its present position in a historical perspective, providing his students with a sense of the Church as an evolving institution. He tells them that for a long period in the Church's history, the Church would have rejected the idea of natural family planning that it accepts today, and Church fathers such as St. Augustine would have said, "No, that's wrong." But that family planning has been embraced only within the last fifty years. Given the question his response could well be taken to allow that in the future, the prohibition on condoms and other means of contraception may be ended.

His goal, as he explains it to me, is to provide students with a historical understanding that "the Church, and the Church's rules and practices, did not fall out of the sky somewhere." He wants them to understand that there is a history to moral theology as well as to the sacraments and other Church practices. For him these changes indicate that the Church is open to change, and he wants his students to understand it in that way. He explains that there is a perennial tension between conservation and innovation in all religions. For Catholicism he believes that there is one essential truth that is at the top of the hierarchy of beliefs—the idea that Jesus Christ is fully God and fully human. He objects to the idea that other proclamations such as the Church's stand on birth control should be placed at the same level as this core belief, and thus he feels that it is quite appropriate for his students to debate the issue and to come out with different answers. In the distinction that he draws from them between teaching and dogma, he provides an essential instrument for thinking critically about the importance of different features of Catholic doctrine, and sometimes students ask whether a given norm is to be thought of as dogma or teaching, perhaps thinking that if something is placed in the latter category they have permission for debate and challenge. Yet the meaning of dogma remains unchallenged, and in the end students are forced to either agree or disagree with a given ruling of the Church, and doctrine remains interpretively closed.

Liberation and Feminist Approaches

Liberation High   Liberation High School is a new school that is receiving considerable attention for its innovative financial aid program and for its remarkable success in sending a very significant percentage of its students to four-year colleges. When compared to the public high school down the block that has a dropout rate of well above fifty percent, Liberation High, with ninety-one percent of its students going on to four-year colleges, is a rare success. While many of the students choose to attend college near their home, an increasing number are going out of town, and during the year of my observations the school sent its first graduate to an Ivy League school.

The opening of this Jesuit high school was the result of a long series of conversations between the Jesuits and the local, largely Mexican and Mexican American community regarding the way in which the order might best service the community's needs. Because of the high dropout rate and the problems of many children from Mexican families in adjusting to the public high school, it was decided to build the school as an alternative to the public high school.

Tuition at the school is relatively expensive—seven thousand dollars for the year 2001–2002—and were it not for generous financial aid coupled with a unique work-study program, most students would not be able to attend. However, the school has lined up commitments from many of the businesses, law firms, banks, and other financial organizations in the city to donate at least one full-paying job to the school. That job is then divided up between five students, each one of whom works for one day out of the five and uses his or her portion of the paycheck to go toward tuition. For those who need more, the school raises money through dinners, auctions, and various events throughout the year. At the event that I attended (an auction), about five hundred people attended and it raised over one hundred thousand dollars. During the five previous years of the school's existence, the priest who serves as president of the school raised over 18 million dollars, a remarkable amount, paying for the physical plant, among other things.

Unlike Dillon and Papal High Schools, Liberation is well integrated into the local community. For example, before becoming a teacher in the school, Father J, one of the religion teachers, served for a number of years as a pastor administering to the spiritual needs of the community; and he, like most of the other teachers in the school, is fluent in Spanish—the dominant language of many of the adults in the community. The fact that he learned Spanish while serving peasant communities in South America adds to his legitimacy in the eyes of the students. The school serves the community in many ways, holding health fairs, distributing flu vaccine to community members, and helping recent immigrants, some undocumented, find the services they need without any questions asked. Counseling services are provided to the students through the full-time staff as well as through an outside service that includes a Jewish rabbi.

Prayer in Liberation High is a moment for connection with parents, community, and relatives back home. The school celebrates many Mexican holidays. On the Day of the Dead (November 2), celebrated with a special all-school mass, students are encouraged to tell *their* stories, to pray for *their* departed relatives and friends, and to receive communion. In class, when students are asked to pray for others or to tell their stories, it is not at all unusual to hear of friends or family members who were murdered. Others pray for friends or siblings who are involved with gangs, and still others thank their mothers for finding the strength to support the family when fathers were seeking work outside of Mexico.

For many the school is credited with implanting the idea of attending college and with inspiring them to use their education to serve their community. Below seniors describe the way the school works for them and the strong sense of connection that it helps them weave between their past, present, and future.

Student 1: "Our classes are focused on history and on our background. At the same time we study general education, we also study ourselves, our background, our spirituality. We develop our dreams from that. My dream is to help my culture to get equal rights. I want my family to know that we're not as the media depicts us."

Student 2: "What I love about the school is that we all help each other. . . . It gives me confidence. I get to know a lot about people's personal lives."

When asked about their plans for college and how it will help them achieve their goals, student 3 responds, "It helps us to achieve our parents' wish for us to get ahead. And it also will help us to grow personally, to get outside experiences, to get rid of the obstacles that help keep our people back."

When asked about the obstacles, some respond, "Money, immigrant status, language barriers, fewer educated people in the neighborhood." Yet ninety percent do go on to college, and many receive financial aid.

The school is committed to preserving the Hispanic culture and language of its mostly Mexican population. The "Anglo" Sister who serves as principal speaks in terms of linguistic genocide when describing transitional bilingual instruction that uses the mother tongue only until the students can understand English, and then ignores and devalues it. She holds that this stunts the mental development of students as they try to learn both a new language and new content. In the end, the traditional approach to English shortchanges the students' culture, language, and skills. Here, she tells me, students continue to learn academic work in their native language as they are introduced to English, and then instruction is carried on as both languages are used.

While English is the dominant language of instruction, teachers shift from English to Spanish and back to English, and students may respond in either language, although students are encouraged to improve their English. Frequently the teacher writes on the board in Spanish, continues the discussion in Spanish, and then switches back to English. Some students who seemed to have more trouble than others in reading aloud from the English text do better when reading in Spanish.

Father J and the Theology of Transcendence: A Sample Class   Father J is an inspired, charismatic teacher who teaches the courses in religion, morality, and social justice to the students at Liberation. To him the Bible is a modern text that speaks to the lives of his students. For example, he begins one class by asking his students, "Let's look at Cain and Abel. Do you think that such people ever existed?" and then, quickly answering his own question, he says, "Probably not, but they symbolize a dysfunctional family; now let's talk about dysfunctional families," and the discussion then turns to sibling rivalry. To Father J the Bible is about abusive relationships, dysfunctional families, and machismo, and it is also about commitment, compassion, hope, and love.

He teaches that self-centeredness is the fundamental sin and that redemption is no more or no less than working to overcome this self-centeredness and to add more love to the world. For a group of inner-city seniors living in an area of high crime rates, undocumented aliens, and unemployment, and who have been encouraged for four years to attend college, there is an understandable temptation to escape and to use their education as a one-way ticket out of poverty. Father J works hard to remind the students of their debt to their parents and to encourage them to view a college education as an asset not only to themselves but to their community as well. This seems to ease their separation anxiety and to give them a concrete and visible reason for wanting to continue their education. He gets this message across as often as he can and in doing so provides students with a sense of themselves, each one of them, as future liberators.

In one class J tells the students a story about a professor of philosophy who holds up a mayonnaise jar to his students, and he fills the jar with stones. And then he asks the students, "Is the jar full?" And his students say, "Yes." And then he takes pebbles and he drops them into the jar, and they fall between the stones, and then he asks the class, "Now is the jar full?" And the class says, "Yes, now the jar is really full." And then he takes sand, and he drops the sand between the stones and the pebbles, and then he says to the class, "Now is the jar full?" And the class says, "Yes, now it's really full." And then the professor explains that if he had dropped the sand and the pebbles in first, he could have never have gotten the stones in. But the stones represent the building blocks of a person, those things that are most important in their life—family, self, Church, and a relation to God. He tells them that the pebbles represent other things that are important to them but not essential, like college education and so forth. Those are the things that'll serve as means to more important ends. And then the sand just represents everything else. Thus, if they concentrate too much on the things that are not important in their life, they'll miss the important things. Right now, he reminds them, they are writing their applications for college. J explains that while those applications are important, they are a means to something else—they are a means to serving other people in their community eventually.

The theme of overcoming self-centeredness through service to others and spiritual transcendence is then carried through in the discussion of the Gospels that follows. Most of the class period is taken up by talking about three parables and a case study. He has them look at Mark 6:35–44. "The Feeding of 5,000" is the subtitle. The student reads. The story is about the loaves and the fishes, and how Jesus multiplied them to feed 5,000. And the teacher asks, "What does this story mean? How many people were supposedly fed? Well," he answers, "5,000." And then, "Why were 5,000 people there?" he asks. "They were there," he answers, "because Jesus was teaching them. They were all hungry for the truth, like we're all hungry for truth. So 5,000 people are a lot of people. And the disciples start to get worried. What are they worried about? They're worried about feeding these people. Well," he then says playfully, "Thank God Mexicans don't worry about food." And then he adds as an aside, "I've never been to a Mexican party where there hasn't been a shitload of food." He continues,

> The focus is not on the people but on the disciples. If the people are not fed, they, the disciples, will get in trouble. So they come to Jesus and ask him to solve their problems. But what does Jesus do? He puts it back on them. "How much do you have?" he asks. "Five loaves and two fishes." And what do they do then? They share it. And when they share, there's a miracle. That is, there's more than enough.

So Jesus' ethic is that if we share what little we have, even if we share it out of poverty, we're generous people. And we will have enough. So we can't get into this idea of help me. We can't get into these applications to college and say, "Oh, I can't do it. Help me, help me."

And he goes into a parody of the anxiety the students are feeling about their college applications. J then continues the discussion of self-centeredness and transcendence by having them look at Mark.

"Okay. Now let's go to Mark, Chapter 10, about the rich man." After a student has read the passage, J squats at the student's desk, crying out, "Jesus, Jesus, what am I going to do to get into eternal life?" And then standing, he says, "Now let's think. Who am I focused on when I asked that question?" And the students say, "Me." Then the teacher explains, "After Jesus says, 'Keep the commandments,' he says, 'Sell your things and follow me.' And that's when I say, 'Oh shit.' Jesus is saying that life is loving and giving, which is the opposite of the American dream that life is receiving and taking."

Then J asks the students to open up to Luke, Chapter 19. And the students read about a tax collector. J explains, "The tax collector is a sinner. He's taking money from his people to give to the Romans. So Zachariah is a sinner in his society. Now he wants to see Jesus. But there's a big crowd, and he can't see Jesus because he's short. Now being short, the teacher explains, is more than just height. It means he has obstacles to seeing—obstacles to converting or believing. Like I have," and now J goes into his act. "Like I have five applications, okay. And one, I'm overwhelmed. So what am I going to do? I go and I watch the *Survivors*. But these applications, they're still there in the morning. Oh my goodness. I'm a loser. I'm a real loser."

Returning to the text:

So what does Zachariah have to do? He has to work. He has to run. He has to go climb a tree. So you have to work. You have to work to see God. So when I work to see, I see a little better. That's what prayer does. So where is Zachariah when Jesus sees him? In the tree! So Zachariah is probably thinking, "Oh shit, he is looking at me, and he says I want to be with you." So he opens his heart to Jesus, and he decides to give to the poor, to be generous. People who are with God tend to be generous.

J then hands out a case study about a man dying of AIDS who returns to his estranged family.

J:	What's happening?
Student:	He's dying. His friends have abandoned him. He's worried about whether his family will abandon him too.
J:	He feels ugly. He has warts on his skin. He's thin, sickly. Why did he not want his family to see him? He was embarrassed. What kind of place did he grow up in?
Student:	Well his father was angry with him. He didn't talk much to him, and he didn't talk much to his sister.
J:	Now she didn't comment on his lifestyle. "So does she accept me?" he's probably wondering. Now why do you think he left his small town?
Student:	Well, his lifestyle.

And then J asks, "Who is Jesus in this study?" And a student responds, "His sister, who came to accept him. She hugged him, she kissed him, and she ran to him."

| J: | In my experience, when I was young like you, I found it hard to be with dying people. But you know, touch is so powerful. Sometimes when I go home and my mother is on oxygen, I just sit there and hold her hand. I think Max felt good when the whole family accepted him. Are there black sheep in your family? Don't we have them at our parties? In my family, Tommy, my brother after me, was the black sheep. He'd always be asked, "Why can't you be like J? Why can't you study?" Who are the black sheep, and who did Jesus walk with? I hope that, my prayers when I grow up, and I'm still a kid, you know, is that like the sister in the story, I would want to touch people and hold them. |

Self-centeredness but not homosexuality is the theme of this class and, using the Church's language of "forgiveness," I asked him about this:

| Interviewer: | You focused on the sister's forgiveness of her brother, a homosexual dying of AIDS. But you didn't at this point say anything about the church's teachings on homosexuality. My sense is that you and the Church's teachings are going to have to part company on this. |
| J: | I would say that yes, kind of in a quick broad stroke. But I think, the Church says this for this reason. That homosexual behavior is nonprocreative. Therefore all sexual behavior, according to official Church teaching, is to be procreative. The value is that it's not about me simply. As a pastor here in this |

neighborhood for six years prior to coming to the school, I had a number of people come up and whether it's parents talking about their gay son or daughter or the gay person themselves, saying, "What do I do?" On a pastoral level, I explain, "This is what the Church teaches." Now in this relationship, especially if it's a relationship that is somewhat faithful, [lasts] how is your relationship giving more life to you and to your capacity to love others, not simply your partner? I mean, to get into that type of reflection is. . . .

I: So you see the way to evaluate it is not just by the physical act of procreation, but it's a sense of life as infused in a community.

J: Right.

I: And if this relationship gives you the power to infuse more life into a community, then it has a different quality to it.

J: Right, right. It's not self-centered. It's giving of yourself to others. Think of marrying people who are beyond [the] age of having children. It's kind of a similar situation. Technically, if they're not able to procreate, they're not to get married. Well, priests are marrying them.

Father J and the Seven Deadly Sins   Catholic religious teachers follow a similar script, many of the texts are officially approved, and the biblical topic will be similar from school to school. Considerable variation is found, however, in the way the topics are approached. Father D approached the teachings of the Church as detailed rules to be disobeyed at a person's peril. Mr. P treats them as guides to the formation of conscience and allows for considerable debate and probing. Here students are allowed to engage the teachings of the Church as grist for their own intellectual development. Father J treats Church teachings as occasions to engage the students in critical reflection about their own personal experiences.

In a class on the seven deadly sins, he begins by asking, "What do you value most?" The students talk about living in Mexico with their mothers and grandmothers for many years while their fathers worked in the United States. They speak of many siblings and very little money, of waiting for years for their families to reunite. One speaks of the school and how it helped him to escape the gang culture in his neighborhood. Father J concludes this early discussion by collecting the students' journals and asking, just as the formal class begins, "Who should we pray for?" As if to respond to the student who saw the school as an escape from the gang culture, a boy says, "My friend's father, who was shot yesterday." Others add to the list, and then the students join in a prayer that is said in Spanish.

Now the class begins. It is on sin and virtue, a lesson that I had experienced earlier at Dillon, where Mr. P spent a number of days teaching his students basic definitions and distinction, for example mortal from venial sin, and the relationship between habit and character, character and choice, and choice and community. Father J covers some of the same ground, but his approach is more direct and personal. He begins with a rapid-fire series of questions and answers, somewhat reminiscent in form to the discussion Father D had about sin when discussing divorce and homosexuality, but the substance of the questions and answers differs dramatically. Father J begins,

J:	What is paradise?
Student:	Union with God.
J:	What is sin?
S:	Loneliness, death, suffering.
J:	What is the consequence of paradise?
S:	Harmony, peace.
J:	Do you think paradise only happens when you die? What is hell for you?
S:	When we are lonely, despair.
J:	So you are saying hell is not only when you die. Heaven and hell begin here. I know people who live more in hell than here. I know people who live more in paradise; where do you make your bet?
J:	Sin is an attitude. It is more than an action. Robbing is more than just an act. It is selfish. Is it a sin for someone to steal bread to feed her kids?
S:	No.
J:	Why not?
S:	Cause she wants her kids fed.
J:	So sin is not just an act. It is an attitude.
J:	What is another capital sin?
S:	Pride.
J:	What is wrong with pride? I am proud to be Irish.
J (answering his own question):	It is when pride blocks the ability to love. What other examples of pride are there?
S:	Machismo.
J:	Sure, you know, father comes home, tells wife she did a shitty job of cleaning and so had to hit her. Sin is an attitude where you are the focus of attention.
J:	Does anyone know what gluttony is?

S: Overconsumption.

J: What are eating disorders—bulimia, anorexia? I think that these are gluttony because it focuses on the self. Who is beautiful according to the media? In my life, I am gluttonous? I overeat. [He has the slim body of the long-distance runner that he is.]

J: The fourth sin is greed. Wanting more and more. Are you greedy, Chris?

S: Yes.

J: How?

S: For money, oil.

J: Yes, there are five Jesuits who work here [living in the same home], and how many cars do we have? Five! Or, how about kids who say it is cold in here [a number of students made the complaint at the beginning of class on a late September day]? We like oil because we want comfort. I recall when I worked in South America, it went down to forty-five degrees and we wore sweaters.

J: Jealousy! Are you ever jealous?

S: Yes, of other people.

J: Do people look at us and say, "Why us?" [Meaning, "Why are we so lucky?"] When people say to me, "Mexicans should stay home," I say, "Come with me and see how people live." Sure it would be better if we could distribute the wealth of the world equally. I never knew anyone who left Mexico without tears.

J: The sixth vice is lust. What is lust?

S: Obsession.

J: Is it bad to be horny? What is the difference between being sexually alive or, in Jose's case [gesturing to a boy in class], being frustrated? Lust is trying to possess the other as an object, a pleasure. The problem is it is selfishness. Wham bam, thank you ma'am! Lust is when you walk down the street as a female and boys whistle. If I were a female, I would be angry. I am not an object for your desires.

J: The last is anger. We all lose our temper, but this is different than someone who goes through life bitter.

The teacher then hands out a case study (in English); it is about the wilding incident in Central Park. New York, some years ago, where a gang reportedly raped and beat a woman jogger senseless after attacking a number of other people.

J: Is there sin here? Hurting people for no reason. What pre-
        ceded that in their heart; what might be some of their
        motives?

S: Boredom.

J: So who is the focus? Me!

S: Anger.

J: Why anger?

S: Cause they were beaten.

J: But why beat someone on the head? [He asks for a general
        reaction, prodding.] Have you ever seen such activity in this
        school?

S: Yes, in the gangs in our neighborhood.

J: Have you ever found yourself asking later, "Why was I a part
        of that?"

S: Kids who make fun of other kids.

J: When I look back on my life, there were too many times
        when I was silent. What happened to M [a young black boy
        beaten senseless by a white gang in another part of the city]?
        He was beat up. Who beat him up? Where did they go to
        school? They went to Saint Catholic High School (name
        fictitious). It is kind of scary when you think that people
        who had been taught values were able to do that.

Social Justice: Two Responses   Students at Liberation High are responsive to
these messages, and when it comes to concerns about social justice will
often go beyond them. They identify the lives of poor and oppressed people with the lives of their own family members; they are quick to spot
injustice and respond to it, sometimes collectively; and they are willing to
organize to address an injustice. This contrasts to many other Catholic
high schools such as Dillon, where the emphasis is on individual service
projects where the students might work in a hospital or a community
center where they do what they are told by the staff and then report
back to the school how they benefited from the situation. At Liberation
High, many students are inclined toward collective as well as individual
remedies.

J begins the class in Spanish, saying, "I hope we all get knocked off of
our horses once in a while because that keeps us humble." Then he brings
up an assembly that the school had on the Nike sweatshops overseas,
mentioning in an apologetic tone how much he really likes his Nike sun-
glasses. They don't fall off when he runs, and they stay on his nose. Then
he asks in a pleading tone, "What do you think I should do with them?
They were a gift—I didn't even buy them." One student responds that she

got from the presentation that as long as you have your reasons for wearing glasses, like protecting your eyes, it's okay, not just because it's Nike.

The teacher then asks, "What was your reaction to the Nike assembly?" One boy says, "Guilt, because I have a lot of Nikes." J then asks, "Why would Nike go to Indonesia to build up their company?" A boy says, "Because that's how they make their profits, through cheap labor." A girl says, "Because they don't have the labor laws, like a minimum wage." "Another student responds, "Well, environmental issues, like they're burning rubber, and they don't have to control for the environment." The teacher says, "Yes, we have environmental laws that prevent pollution. So where do we then send our toxic waste?" And he responds to his own question, "To Mexico. Don't you think that some people in Mexico and Indonesia are making money, a lot of money, a payoff? Now, what is going on in Argentina these days?" A student responds, briefly describing the bankruptcy problem in Argentina and its conflict with the World Bank.

Father J asks, "Well, how did the presentation make you feel? We're all talking very intellectually," he mockingly asks, "but what was your feeling?" A student says, "Well, both good and bad. Good because there are things that I can do, I think." A student then asks him, "Father, will you go and protest with me in front of the Nike store?" The teacher says, "That is very challenging. Perhaps we can organize that. We could get flyers that we could pass out." He goes on to say, "The next senior assembly is next week. We can make an announcement. And you can get service credits for that, not, of course, that that is why you are doing it".

Protest is not unusual in this school. A year before I came, students organized a trip to Georgia to protest the School of the Americas, a U.S. government institution intended, in the words of its critics, to train dictators and torturers.

Father J uses his understanding of the interpretive possibilities of doctrine to reorient the behavior of his class—to lead them to think of Jesus, of exclusiveness, of suffering, and possibly of homosexuality in different terms. The object of reflection is their own attitudes and personal behavior.

He does not, however, share his interpretive challenge—for example, his understanding of the reasons for the Church's rejection of homosexuality as resting on an overly constrained view of procreation—with his class. His interpretive framework serves to justify the lesson by keeping it within what he can accept as a more adequate interpretation of doctrine than that which is the official one. Yet he does not provide his students with all of the theological insight to enable them to go on and to intelligently reflect on the interpretive possibilities that J personally believes can be found in Church doctrine, and hence he does not provide his students with all of the tools required for interpretive discourse. Unlike D's doctrinal orthodoxy, where matters of the heart are reserved for the informal, after-class discussions, J brings matters of the heart front and center in his class-room, but, in contrast to the feminist example below, the students are not encouraged to acknowledge the fact that there are interpretive differences or the reasons for preferring one over another.

Sisters of Struggle and Hope   Sisters of Struggle and Hope is located in a modest white neighborhood of a large metropolitan area. Students come from a wide swath of neighborhoods within the city and are academically tracked. The school is only one of the five remaining all-women's schools on this side of town and only one of three that does not have plans to admit boys within the next year or so, reflecting the considerable financial and enrollment pressures that Catholic girls' schools have been subject to in recent years. These pressures are intensified if, as is frequently the case, a previously all-boys school decides to admit girls, hence increasing the competition for the limited number of girls wishing to attend a Catholic school.

While Sisters of Struggle and Hope has but a modest endowment of about two million dollars and charges a comparatively low tuition of less than six thousand dollars, its strong commitment to women's education and to a feminist curriculum is an important factor in helping it maintain its single-sex mission. The school has not had an easy time of it within recent years, and the clash between traditional Catholicism and feminism has at times been intense. The relatively new principal experienced these conflicts as a former teacher in the school and describes her vision for the school.

> We walk a very fine line—how do you teach women to feel good about women, what women have accomplished in the world with-out being extreme feminists? You know, my belief is that God created men and women to be partners in the whole creation of the world. And that's what we need to be able to teach our young women to do. It's not better if you're replacing Nazi feminism for the reverse, sexism.

The reference to "Nazi feminism" was uttered with the recent history of the school in mind and the practice that if you referred to God as *He,* you got points taken off of your reflection paper, and the Theology Depart-ment had exerted pressure to drop "In the name of the Father, the Son, and the Holy Spirit" and change it to "In the name of the Creator, Redeemer, and Sustainer of Life." "You didn't say the 'Our Father.' You just said the 'Hail Mary'. You could not mention God as *He.*" Students were discouraged from marking themselves with the traditional sign of the cross since that represented the father on one side and the son on the other, with the Holy Ghost in between. The principal explains that all of these innovations were recently changed because they did not meet the idea of a "good Catholic" held by many students, parents, and faculty who felt that their faith was being disrespected. Now they have a variety of ways of addressing God, from the Father, the Son, and the Holy Ghost, to the Creator, the Redeemer, and the Sustainer of life, to just plain "Dear God."

After a curriculum review the feminist emphasis was toned down, but it was not lost. Electives that once focused on women's issues alone became incorporated into a required general course that includes sections on woman's issues and women in biblical literature. A person from outside the school replaced the twenty-year veteran chair of the Religion Department who was perceived by some as taking feminism too far. However, her replacement was no shrinking violet. She had recently been arrested in a demonstration against the School of the Americas, the same school that the students at Liberation High protested against; she too had strong, progressive, feminist values; and the school still maintains its feminist commitment.

Ms. G's Class on Church History   Ms. G has taught religion at Sisters of Struggle and Hope for over thirty years. She views the present Church as an institution both of beauty but also of domination and patriarchy. In her class on Church history, she traces the history of patriarchy, and by placing patriarchy in a historical context with a beginning, she allows her students to imagine that it will end. She tells them that patriarchy is a social system whose primary characteristic is domination and subordination. And once the system of domination is named, it can then be related to other systems of domination, such as "racism, sexism, homophobia, hunger, poverty, and militarism." Jesus then becomes the historical embodiment of dominance transcended, while the historical Church is presented as a culturally infused institution.

She teaches her students that the very early Church, the Church immediately after Jesus, was not patriarchic, and even the early teachings of Paul stressed equality. She recites, "Remember when you are baptized into this community, there is no Greek nor Jew, nor slave nor free, nor male nor female. All are one in Christ Jesus." But she explains that as the Church becomes more embedded in existing norms, it falls further away from its egalitarian beginnings, and so by the time Augustine comes on the scene, the idea of gender equality has been completely lost and Catholic theology begins a long tradition of minimizing and belittling the role of women.

She tells me that she is careful to keep these critical remarks in perspective so that her students will not become disillusioned with the Church, and she explains to them that patriarchy is but one small part of Church doctrine.

> I always say that if Thomas Aquinas's work the *Summa Theologica* was a whole tapestry, what we're going to look at here with his stance on women is one thread, but that it has significant ramifications. That's why the Church won't ordain women. They're not ordainable material. But we know, now, that the biology that Thomas began with is incorrect.

Sometimes Ms. G needs to explain to her students why she remains Catholic when other Christian communities have rejected this false biology and treat women and men as equals. She tells them that there is a struggle for justice within her Church and that "no one is going to take it away from me." To her the Church is much like a family, and it is not to be renounced because some members have strayed from the correct path. She tells her students that she "loves the Church, in its sinfulness and its beauty." And she hopes that they will do the same.

The Role of Women in Church History   Given the scandals that were occurring at the time of these interviews over the sexual abuse of children by priests, many teachers felt that change was in order. Traditionalists like Father D felt that the problem results from the leniency of the Church in ordaining homosexuals. Progressive reformers suggest that the problem lies in the all-male, celibate priesthood. Some argue that priests should be allowed to marry, and others that women should be ordained as priests. Most of the teachers I spoke to thought that the ordination of women would be difficult to square with Church doctrine. Some felt that the Church had more leeway in allowing priests to marry than it had in allowing the ordination of women into the priesthood.

People who argue in this way believe that precedent has been established in each case. The historical Church did allow priests to marry at one time, and if it did it once, it could (if necessary) do it again. They classify the celibacy of priests as not a matter of doctrine, but a matter of discipline, and conclude that if necessity requires it, disciplines can be changed. The male priesthood is viewed differently. Here the argument goes that because all of Jesus' disciples were men, all subsequent priests must be men. This is seen as doctrine, not just discipline. These arguments are thus based not on biology alone but rather on an appeal to historical precedent that may or may not have been grounded in biology.

Ms. G takes issue with the dominant view about the ordination of women and teaches her students to be critical of this argument and of the view of Church history that it rests on. She reminds them that the earliest Gospel, Mark, was written thirty to forty years after Jesus and for specific communities, and that each one takes on some of the coloration of that community. She tells them that in the Jewish community, for instance, twelve is a very significant number, for example the twelve tribes of Israel. So twelve people get named in the Gospel, and the twelve would have to be men for the Jewish people to understand the level of authority. So twelve men get named.

She continues by saying that these men were, of course, close to Jesus, but they were not the only ones. There were women as well, and she mentions Joanna, Mary of Magdalene, Mary, and Martha. She also tells them that there were numbers of women who were disciples as well and who were at the Last Supper. But we have this vision of da Vinci's last supper in our head, and we see the twelve men. All Gospels agree that after the resurrection, Jesus first appeared to Mary Magdalene and she went to tell Peter, James, and John, "all those guys, who are now hiding because they're so frightened."

Responding to the argument that women cannot be ordained because the Church is the bride of Christ, she clarifies the point: the reason she says is the belief that Church women cannot image Christ because "Christ was Jesus and Jesus was a male," But she adds with "as if his Christness had anything to do with His maleness. The fact that He was Christ had nothing to do with the fact that He was male. It had to do with His compassion."

Sisters of Struggle: The Obedient Catholic versus the Good History Teacher
There have been attempts by the Church hierarchy, according to Ms. G, to muffle discussions of the ordination of woman, but she finds these inconsistent with her responsibilities as a good history teacher. A few years ago, the pope "declared that the ordination of women was not a topic for discussion," and a previous principal "reminded" them that they should not discuss the ordination of women in class. Ms. G believes that to follow this order would be to violate her standards as a teacher of Church history, and so she continues to teach that the early Church was perfectly equalitarian. "Women were equal to men; they did anything and everything that the men did, on the basis of their giftedness." And this included preaching. She explains that the practice of ordination did not get formalized for many years after that. However, in response to the culture around them, they began to erect a more defined division of labor between men and women.

To help her students appreciate the initial equality of the Church, she has them read the biblical material in the context of the times and suggests that Paul's injunction to wives to obey their husbands should be seen as a response to the outsider's view of the Church and to the persecutions that developed. And she also has them read the earlier writings from Galatians 3:28 and explains,

> "In Christ Jesus there is no Greek nor Jew, nor male nor female, nor free or slave. We are all one." That was a baptismal formula. So as someone was baptized into this community, remember, this is how we operate together. There is no hierarchy here. We are all one in Christ Jesus. And our celebration, and we share our resources and our gifts. So if there is someone among us who is particularly good at bread baking, that's what they bring to the community. Someone among us who is a good preacher and remembers some stories of Jesus, that person offers that gift. Someone who's, maybe the lady (sic) of the house that we're meeting at, she's going to preside over the whole service. So there was that kind of egalitarianism. I always teach it as the most egalitarian time in the history of the church.

In Ms. G's class the Church itself has fallen away from this original ideal community, but the students learn that there is also the hope of resurrection, a hope that is reinforced by the responses of her students. She reports that they tell her, "It's my responsibility. If I call myself a Christian, then my responsibility is to continue the work of Jesus, to overthrow and to help transform oppression, wherever it is.' Whether we're talking about sexism or racism or poverty, or people or the church as discriminating against women.

And Ms. G sees in the resurrection the template for this hope:

> Even when Jesus appears in the gospels to Mary Magdalene, his closest friend, she doesn't recognize him until he speaks her name. . . . So obviously there didn't seem to be this physical reality here. Some kind of physical reality, but they didn't recognize him. So I would teach resurrection as new life. There's always new life, that the spirit of Jesus did not die. It's a victory over death, as a matter of fact. It is not the end. And that's the Christian mystery—life, death, and new life. And even in our own daily living, when we experience death of some kind, not necessarily our own physical death, the Christian promise is there's always new life. So the death of a relationship, for instance, there's always new life that comes.

In contrast to Father J, who informs his teaching by the interpretive opportunities he finds within the tradition but who shares only his conclusions with his students, Ms. G shares with her students the textual and historical evidence that she believes supports her revisionist ideas.

Summary: Critical Thinking and the Challenge for Liberal Pluralism

These four schools display different elements of critical thinking. In the traditional school, Church doctrine stands as a platform from which to gain distance from and to critically examine the norms and practices of the larger society. The Church doctrine is itself presented as unchanging and absolute truth, students are discouraged from criticizing it or exploring its interpretive possibilities, and the class is orchestrated in such a way that dissent is policed and silenced, often by the students themselves. One of the signs of "successful" teaching here occurs when the students rather than the teacher serve to uphold the doctrinal standard. When the girl in Father D's class hesitantly raises an objection to the pro-life position, the student's rebuttal, not the teacher's, silences her. The teacher has primed the pump, but the student rebuttal allows the class to continue to plan the march without the distraction of a debate on the merits of the pro-life position. Here criticism reaches outward to the society at large and to values that the Church views as permissive and sinful, but it is constrained in its scope, and reflection on the institution of the Church or its doctrine is discouraged.

Mr. P, the modernist Catholic teacher, is more open to the critical initiative of the student, although he is often reluctant to initiate such criticism himself. Still, he wants to protect his students from some of the harsher implications of Church doctrine and will soften the Church's message in certain places by distancing himself from it. Students are *encouraged* to see the Church less as a dispenser of absolute truths and more as a wise teacher and an evolving institution where discussion and debate are healthy features of a truly religious life. For Mr. P and other modernist teachers, student self-esteem is critical, and they will not harm students by shaming them, either directly or indirectly. The Church's positions on homosexuality or divorce must, then, be handled with great care and taught in such a way that they do not serve to assault or undermine the student's self-esteem.

The limitation of this approach is that it remains at the psychological level and does not provide the students with the insights that could be used to reconcile mind and heart—dogma with moral intuition. The vision of the Church as an evolving institution, if shared with the students, would help serve this reconciliation, but a vision is vulnerable without the opportunity to reflect on the doctrine itself and the interpretive possibilities it may provide. Whether students will ever learn to go beyond the vision and to probe the possibilities that Church doctrine itself presents is uncertain. Without such an opportunity, the modernist must yield doctrinal ground to the traditionalist who will *magnanimously* allow that we may love the *sinner* but hate the *sin.*

Father J has more than a psychological reason for departing from the traditional interpretation and often cites specific textual sources for his deviation. To procreate means to add more life, not just to have more babies, and he believes that it is therefore possible for both homosexual and heterosexual couples to procreate. Yet while Father J uses his somewhat unique interpretation of Church doctrine to guide his pedagogy, his students are not instructed on the theoretical considerations that enable him to do so. In this sense, they remain well intended and of good heart but somewhat defenseless, theologically speaking.

Ms. G, in her questioning of the reasons behind the all-male priesthood, is critical of many Church practices and encourages the critical voice of her own students. In appealing to the meaning of the text, as reflected in the life of Jesus, she shines a critical light on the shortcomings of both society and Church, and in the process provides her students with interpretive and theological material that they could use to analyze the more traditional, male-dominated perspective.

From the standpoint of liberalism, the more critical thinking, the better; and hence on the liberal scale of things, there is a progression from the constrained thinking of Father D to the revisionism of Ms. G. The latter is reflective and *self-critical,* whereas the former is not. Yet from the point of view of pluralism, both are within the margins of allowable pedagogy; and, again, from the point of view of pluralism, when taken together they provide real choice for Catholic parents and their children.

These two standpoints—pluralism and liberalism—set the challenge for a democratic philosophy of education that is committed to both. How much critical reflection is enough to satisfy liberalism, and how much difference is sufficient to satisfy pluralism? The challenge for a democratic philosophy of education, then, is to provide a generous reading of religious education, one that will satisfy the needs of pluralism but will not be so permissive as to infringe on the requirement of liberalism.

CHAPTER **4**

Faith and the Pedagogical Limits
of Critical Inquiry

Toward a Generous Reading of Religious Schools

Some features of life are so much a part of us that we take them for granted and have difficulty examining them in any careful and systematic way. The process of maturation involves extending those taken-for-granted features of life to encompass larger commitments and wider communities, which to varying degrees are incorporated into our evolving selves. The child becomes a parent, the student a teacher, and so on. Maturation also involves the capacity to distance some of these commitments and to examine them in light of other possibilities. As Martha Nussbaum explains, endorsing the Socratic task of education,

> The central task of education . . . is to confront the passivity of the pupil, challenging the mind to take charge of its own thought. All too often, people's choices and statements are not their own. Words come out of their mouths, and actions are performed by their bodies, but what those words and actions express may be the voice of tradition or convention, the voice of parent, of friends, of fashion. This is so because these people have never stopped to ask themselves what they really stand for, what they are willing to defend as themselves and their own. They are like instruments on which fashion and habit play their tunes, or like stage masks through which an actor's voice speaks.[1]

The idea of critical reflection that Nussbaum presents involves the development of the skills of rational argument, but it also involves a personal encounter with one's self—with one's "own" commitments and communities. Indeed the cool technician of syllogisms and truth tables may be quite disabled when it comes to the task of *self* reflection, appropriating these skills to ward off reflecting on the commitments that he has built up over the years and making them into objects for study and examination.

Yet the Socratic ideal—that the unexamined life is not worth living—to which Nussbaum gives her own allegiance is unclear about just how much of a life needs be open to critical examination. As Charles Peirce pointed out, we require a certain stability of belief in order to critically assess other beliefs that we hold.[2]

Faith and Reason

Religious belief is a problem for those committed to an unyielding view of critical reflection. Few deeply religious persons have done the kind of research that would speak scientifically to the rationality of their commitment to a single religious community. They have not surveyed the world's many religions, nor have they tested their beliefs against those of others, and they have not weighed the evidence in favor of God to the evidence against. Very few people take on religious commitments in this way, and those who do often choose to reject religion altogether. Indeed, it would take an extraordinary act of theological sophistication to address the biblical gaps and contradictions that young students are expected to overlook. In the beginning, there was the conundrum—where did Cain and Seth's wives come from? Was there a second Adam and Eve, a second Garden of Eden? And without these wives, who would have begotten those who begot us?

Yet the critical thinker is looking in the wrong place if he or she thinks to measure sacred texts in terms of the consistency of their logic or the surface credibility of their claims. It would be better to first understand the functions that religious doctrine serves before dismissing it as irrational, incoherent, or incredible, and, given these functions, to ask whether there might be a wider conception of rationality than the one commonly associated with critical thinking that can engage religious belief. In the absence of a more generous notion of inquiry, there is little about religion that could live up to these rational standards.

Take prayer as an example. When people pray, it sometimes looks as if they are petitioning God. Given the petitioner view of prayer, we should be able to discern the relative merit of different religions by comparing their effectiveness in producing certain results. Controlling for difficulty we could, say, have Mormons and Catholics pray for different sick people to get well and then see the frequency with which a healthy person gets well. Mormonism will be superior to Catholicism if their prayers yield a better rate of recovery. Although many people do pray in the hopes of influencing God's will, this petitioner understanding of prayer misses the point. Among other things prayer is a way of being with other people, of establishing connections while acknowledging our common vulnerability and dependency.

From the standpoint of the unyielding critical thinker, the greatest danger is premature commitment where children are forced to accept a belief long before they have the capacity to assess it. For the believer, however, the greater danger is that critical reflection will go too far, too soon. For teachers committed to fostering both religious commitment and critical thinking, their awareness of these twofold dangers creates considerable anguish, for they see limited grounds for compromise. They feel caught between an unyielding conception of rationality and an equally unyielding conception of faith. Most stay with faith, but a few brave teachers make attempts to reconcile the two.

Mr. S and the Nicene Creed: Limits of Critical Inquiry

One of the foundations of Catholicism is a doctrine called the Nicene Creed. The document strains logic because it seems to violate the rule that one cannot be both an X and a not X at the same time. The creed holds that mutually exclusive categories—human and divine—are not really mutually exclusive in the case of Jesus. It reads, in part,

> We believe in one Lord, Jesus Christ,
> the only Son of God,
> eternally begotten of the Father,
> God from God, Light from Light,
> true God from true God,
> begotten, not made,
> of one Being with the Father.
> Through him all things were made.
> For us and for our salvation
> he came down from heaven:
> by the power of the Holy Spirit
> he became incarnate from the Virgin Mary,
> and was made man.
> For our sake he was crucified under Pontius Pilate;

he suffered death and was buried.
On the third day he rose again
in accordance with the Scriptures;
he ascended into heaven
and is seated at the right hand of the Father.

He will come again in glory to judge the living and the dead,
and his kingdom will have no end.

Virtually every child who goes through a Catholic school is expected to be able to recite the creed, to accept it as true, and to use it to guide moral action. Yet historically the creed came to be accepted only after a strong challenge by an alien belief system, the Arian Creed, and only as a result of a decision at the Council of Nicaea in 325 CE to adopt the present creed and declare the alternative a heresy. In many ways the Arian Creed seems considerably easier to accept from a commonsense standpoint than the Nicene. The Arian Creed holds that Jesus was just a man—made, not begotten. Yes, a model of kindness and goodness, but not a god—"just a man." Most devout Catholic schoolteachers take on the Nicene Creed as second nature, and students are expected to know it by heart and recite it on appropriate occasions. Teachers who have reservations about many other features of the Church, such as its stand on birth control, homosexuality, and divorce, will often say, "But the core of Catholicism is that Jesus is both fully divine and fully human"—the basic principal laid out in the creed.

In my observations, only one teacher, Mr. S at Sisters of Struggle and Hope, encouraged high school students to question the creed in the classroom. He asked them to revisit in a nonpartisan way some of the historical criticisms of it. S wants his students to understand the creed historically. As he explains his somewhat unorthodox teaching method,

Church history is just a series of arguments over the last two thousand years. And the way the church is now is just because one side of the argument won. And so what I like to do is just try to get us back to that argument. And the kids are amazed that, for instance, when they say the creed every Sunday at church, they're taking a side of an argument that is long dead to them, but they're taking a side still. And what I do [is] I bring in the other side of the argument, and then we talk about it. I mean, the creed is about who is Jesus. And we talk about who is Jesus. Because the other side of the argument, the one that lost, the Arians, they had pretty much just as Christian a position as the Nicene fathers did.

Nicaea said that Jesus is both God and man. And the Arians said, "That's a crazy thought," because, taking off, that matter and spirit cannot dwell within the same substance, that Jesus was man but Jesus was not God, not fully God. And what they were trying to do is preserve the holiness of God. And they saw the Nicene people as trying, sort of corrupting the nature of God.

I asked how the students responded.

S: Well I think, on the one hand I think they like it. They like being given the freedom to think for themselves about these matters of religion. Because religion here in this area is hugely ingrained, and I'm grateful that it is. And these are stories that they've been given. And now they're being able to think about it as young adults. I mean it's really treating them as young adults with growing intellects. However, the downside is that I also sort of ruin it for them.

Interviewer: How so?

S: Well, I sort of take the mystery out of it. It's the first time that they're hearing that biblical literature as we have it was also committee documents at certain points. That somebody put the canon together. It's also the first time that they're hearing that the church is also sort of a committee that is sort of manmade. And so there's that, they get so frustrated, so very upset about it, because they sort of, well, it's just such a shock. I mean, it's like tearing them. I think it's part of the adolescent growth process that they want to be taken seriously as adults in their own right, but it's also a very scary thing. So there is that sort of frustration as, like, then they go all over, the pendulum shifts all the way over to the other side. Where they used to take the church so seriously before, and now they can't take it seriously at all. And I hope the pendulum then shifts back to the center.

Mr. S worries a good deal about the effect of his approach on the faith of his students. He believes that what he is doing is theologically sound although pedagogically dangerous, and he continues to try to strike a reasonable balance. He does not want the students to engage in the historical debates for debate's sake alone. Rather, he hopes that they will experience the respectful reflection that he believes, at its best, religion represents. He hopes the debate becomes more than just an intellectual exercise for his students and results in strengthening rather than alienating them from their religion, but the balance is not an easy one to maintain.

While he believes that his students appreciate his open approach, he fears that by taking the mystery out of faith, it may "ruin it for them."

S: We're reading the Bible, and they realize, many of them, most of them for the first time, that there are two creation stories. And it hurts them, and the classic question is why did they lie to me? And it's hard, at this age, to find that gray area and to explain to them that your priests and your parents and your religious formation teachers, they didn't lie to you. They told you the same truth that I'm telling you now, that God created the world. But now we believe you're of an age to read the text and think, okay, yes I know that God created the world. What does this text say that can further inform this? What do these texts, these two different texts, say?

I: So you fear that by opening up the historical argument, you'll puncture their faith?

S: Yeah. I mean, that has been said as much, that while, high school's a strange age. I think it was for me, and I can say it is. Because it's an age in which you want to grow up, in which you want to be treated as an adult with a mind and a body and a spirit all your own. But when you are given freedoms, it's a scary thing as well. And what I want to do in my classroom is give them freedom to think. But that's scary, too, because it sort of takes the mystery away from the Church, that if I present it as a series of arguments, they just look at it as manmade laws, manmade things, easily dismissible.

I: How do you respond to that?

S: What I tried to do in that class is always present it as "These are arguments about truths which we will never see, but truths which we believe on faith." And I try to make sure that they know that religious truth cannot be proven by any other means but by what we call faith.

There are, then, limits to how far he wants his students to go in the conclusions they draw from these historical arguments, and although rehearsing the historical narrative with them would seem to provide openings for alternative ways of understanding the religious mysteries, he does not want them to reject the religious "truth."

> And I make sure that they are in agreement with me that we believe that there is some kind of mysterious creation of this world. And that mystery we're going to call God. And we're going to believe in and [have] faith that God created the world. That God gave humanity a special place in it, and that it was an act of beneficent love. And so with that, then we go to the text. But even that's not enough to support the discrepancy in the text.

In S's mind, his efforts to engage the students are not empty exercises in critical thinking. They are connected to his own understanding of the nature of the Christian tradition. He holds that the sacred includes not just the text but also the long line of interpreters engaging one another in a historical discussion that extends across generations, and he wants his students to experience and participate in this discussion. Thus, through reconstructing these debates, he seeks to create a bit of the sacred in his own classroom. He believes that as they become aware of these arguments and began to participate in them, in some way they are participating in the very divine legacy that is true Christianity.

At its best, S believes that reliving the arguments can bring his students in touch with their faith and help to personalize it:

> I did Aquinas, and I just took the five proofs, which I suppose is probably the most famous. And in the past years, it's actually worked. I think I got something of the Scholastic in the classroom. Because I started by asking the question "Where and in what ways have you actually felt God to be truly existent in your life?" And a lot of people said, "I was in nature. I was on a hike with my family." And from that discussion, then, it was pretty easy, then, to talk about Aquinas. Because then, you have Aquinas, who is like the thirty people in the classroom, trying to prove in some way that God does in fact exist. So the argument from causality is not some kind of philosophical game we were playing in the classroom, but the argument from causality, then, is "Brenda, does this in fact summarize what you were feeling when you were in the woods that day, and you saw that tree, and you thought that surely there must have been a tree before this tree, and et cetera." And that's the only way that, I mean I guess it goes back to the debate about philosophy, you know. You can have a very technical philosophy, or you can have philosophy which serves the purpose of expressing the truth. And that, you know, that was for me, why, I think, philosophy is a good tool but not a wonderful end.

Pedagogically, however, the balance is not easy to maintain, as S recognizes. Ultimately it is the faith of religion and not the reason of philosophy that sustains belief, and argument can potentially alienate one from faith. Yet argument can also ultimately deepen it, as he tells me:

> God's will is always in a sense inscrutable, but God's will is a little less inscrutable when in community, and when this conversation is going on. So conversation and community bring to a little more self-evidence this mystery that we're all trying to figure out. So it will never be really figured out. In a sense, the catechism and the Bible and all the texts are meant to be sort of fleeting. But the catechism, the Bible, and all these texts, the creeds are products of community, and the results of conversations that have been going on. So in having this conversation, I wonder if there's a way of just being honest and letting the truth come out a bit more. And I don't know how to put that to a sixteen-year-old.

There are somewhat different issues here, depending on whether it is Aquinas's proofs for the existence of God that one is addressing or whether it is the Nicene Creed. One may continue to believe in God even if convinced that the logic of Aquinas's arguments is flawed. Yet it is difficult to see how one could continue to believe in the divinity of Jesus if one found the Arian Creed to be sound.

The balance between rational argument and faith is a very difficult, perhaps impossible, balance to maintain at the level of the Nicene Creed. Hence it may well be that the student's resistance here, and the teacher's fear of the alienation that the questioning of the creed produces, arise because of the very critical role that adherence to this creed plays. It is likely that questioning, debate, and even discussion cannot go all the way down and must end at this place, with this creed. Mr. S is aware of this when he tells me, with some despair, "Attending to historical argument is just the method, but I think I've started to confuse the method with the actual goal."

Two Competing Conceptions of Rationality

Before looking more closely at Mr. S's concerns, I want to introduce two different and somewhat competing conceptions of rationality, which I will refer to as propositional and pragmatic.

Propositional rationality, as I am using the term here, is often associated with scientific inquiry. It insists that a rational true belief be consistent with other true beliefs, that there be convincing evidence for such a belief, and that the belief correspond to a real external state of affairs as determined by publicly verifiable evidence. In contrast, pragmatic rationality holds that a belief is a guide for action, and this means that one must not only reflect upon existing commitments but also allow these existing commitments to be a factor in measuring the worth of any given reflective act. To return to Nussbaum for a moment and the Socratic task that she asks us to use as a model for education: in accepting his own fate—the death sentence dictated by the Athenian court—Socrates decided to reject the "rational" arguments of his friends, not because they were wrong but because to act on them would be to contradict his life's commitment as a citizen of Athens, a commitment developed from his dependence on Athens for his physical well-being and his moral development.

A commitment to pluralism is aided by a commitment at the educational level to pragmatic rationality where reasonable reflection connects to one's preformed and ongoing commitments. Given this commitment, Mr. S's concern is well justified, not because pragmatic rationality is superior to propositional rationality but because the rational thing to do now has something to do with who I am and what kinds of beliefs I have made as I have lived a life. And it does not mean, as perhaps he feared, that people committed to a certain set of religious beliefs must now refuse to hold those beliefs if impartial arguments cannot show definitively that they reflect the real state of affairs. Rather, to adopt pluralism as a desirable way of organizing society is to allow for an additional and more generous standard of rationality as a governor of the systems of educational and political life.

Pragmatic rationality allows that a belief is "warranted"[3] if it does not interfere with other beliefs that we hold and if those beliefs enable us to live productive, satisfying lives. Noninterference, as I am using the term, means that two beliefs may either cohere, and thus support one another, or function separately as long as they do not inhibit action. Pragmatic rationality allows that beliefs may live together in the same tent even if they are not entailed by one another or even if they do not support one another. There is here a live and let live attitude for many of our beliefs, and, indeed, people may hold contradictory beliefs. A parent believes in racial equality but also believes that children deserve an education free of racial tension. These beliefs may well exist side by side without tension as long as the person does not have to choose a school for her own child. If she does have to choose, then they will conflict if a choice *must* be made between a mixed, racially tense school in one neighborhood and a racially homogeneous but harmonious school in another.

If they do get in each other's way, then "inconsistency" becomes a problem leading to inconclusive action or paralysis. When this happens, then evidence and reasons are called for to resolve conflict between beliefs and to reenable action. For example, if we believe that water boils at 100 degrees centigrade, but we heat it to that temperature and it does not boil, then we need to alter belief, perhaps by holding that the boiling point can change, depending on atmospheric pressure and whether you heat it while above or below sea level.[4] This view of rationality is somewhat elastic given that inconsistent beliefs may, sometime in the future, handicap action; it can be prudent to conduct test runs on dormant beliefs to expunge the potential conflicts. Nevertheless, I could believe firmly that water boils at 100 degrees centigrade while also believing that the boiling point of fluids is related to atmospheric pressure, and I could hold these two beliefs simultaneously as long as they did not hamper my action. Critical reflection in this view need not just be a response to an immediate impasse, but it has a preventative function as well.

The contrast between these two modes of rationality is significant. The ideal for propositional rationality is purification. The procedure is to purge the mind of as many inconsistencies as possible and to hold on to only those beliefs that can be supported by sufficient evidence. The ideal for pragmatic rationality is reasonable peaceful coexistence of beliefs for the purpose of engagement, community, and action. Like two neighbors with different lifestyles, inconsistencies may live side by side quite peacefully as long as the noise level and messiness of one are inaudible, invisible, and harmless to the other, and as long as the other's compulsiveness to mow the lawn and trim the hedges does not involve trespassing on the neighbor's property line.

The conception of rationality that one adopts will determine how generous one will be in evaluating religious instruction because there is a core to most religions that extends beyond what those outside the religion will see as propositionally acceptable—a core that is, for the outsider, nonrational. Pluralism requires a conception of rationality that is generous, allowing many conceptions of the good and many systems of belief to gain support. However, it also requires a conception of rationality that is not permissive and that is able to maintain reasonable educational standards.

For the pragmatist, standards of evidence remain important, of course, but a school is judged not only in terms of the beliefs it transmits but also in terms of its developmental possibilities for children, where authenticity, autonomy, and critical reflection are valued as a part of the commitments that are fostered.

Critical Reflection in Religious and Nonreligious Traditions

For the most part children develop their initial conception of the good from their parents and other significant adults, but liberalism requires that they not be *destined* to live out this conception and that they have opportunities to reflect upon and revise it. The skills involved in critical reflection, viewed as the capacity for reflecting upon, choosing, and revising one's conception of the good, are viewed as an essential component of autonomy. Without this capacity a child is fated to live a life chosen by other people and by chance alone.

With the increasing importance of schooling in the formation of opportunities and life plans, many educators view critical reflection as an essential aim of education in modern, liberal societies.[5] Schools that fail to help children develop these skills do not meet the standard of adequacy that liberal institutions require. However, when it comes to religious education, there are significant differences within liberal society regarding what to count as autonomy and critical reflection.

As mentioned in the last chapter, in one view the specter of indoctrination looms over the very idea of religious education. Religious "education" and religious indoctrination are one and the same, and faith must always trump reason.[6] Because faith can never be inspected by reason, any form of critical reflective inquiry on religious beliefs is subversive and will be discouraged. While the cloak of reason may be displayed in harmless ways, anything that threatens to expose the weakness of the faith will be filtered out of consideration.[7] Given this view, religious education protects the basic tenets of the faith from evaluation and blunts critical reflective thinking.

In another, more friendly view of religious education, it is argued that critical reflective thinking can only take place within the context of a well-developed tradition, and religious traditions provide solid foundations for reflective critical appraisal.[8] Without a religious foundation children will likely become the victims of the dominant cultural tendencies and will develop few filters to appraise the egocentric commercialism that bombards them every day in this most materialistic of cultures. From this point of view, all moral reflection presupposes a certain standpoint, and the role of religious education is to provide that standpoint. We do not just ask how to be good in general. We ask how to be a good parent, a dutiful employer, and a loyal friend.[9] Here religious education provides the material for addressing these questions as well as for reflecting on different alternatives. Indeed, whether we agree or disagree about a particular answer, religion allows us to keep in mind what is at stake in moral deliberation—the well-being and spiritual health of a community that extends beyond ourselves. In learning to be religious, we also learn to be reflective and to ask, "What would a good person of my conviction do? How can I be a good Hindu, Muslim, Christian, or Jew?"[10]

Analysis

Those who advance an idea of propositional rationality, and the sense that truth claims must be sensible (subject to falsification by evidence)[11] and consistent, would argue that Mr. S's problem is that he is unwilling to take reason far enough so as to encourage his students to submit to its conclusions wherever it may lead them. In seeing argument as the means to an already established goal, he is denying his students their autonomy as rational beings. And, even though there may be some merit to his understanding of religion as a historical dialogue, it is still a dialogue in which the students are expected to come out nodding in agreement to those who have presumably found the one right answer in the official dogma of the Church. Thus Mr. S, according to this view, is caught in a trap of his own making. He wants the students to think critically, but ultimately he wants to decide for them just what the right answer should be. He does not want them to reject the Nicene Creed, just to think about it. And, when his exercise threatens to alienate them from their own religious beliefs, however irrational they may be, he loses his nerve and backs off.

I want to argue, against this critic, that Mr. S is right to be concerned and that the view of rationality presented by this imaginary critic is too narrow and constricting, failing to capture the rational character of the students' response to the assault on the Nicene Creed. And, because it fails to capture the way in which the response is rational, it fails to appreciate the dilemma that Mr. S is experiencing. In the cold logic of the critic, halfway to the truth is not enough, and Mr. S's loss of nerve is no justification for not moving all the way. Yet this view has its own absolutism and fails to understand the limits of its own conception of rationality.

Let me begin to defend Mr. S by suggesting that there are considerations that rest outside the "truths" of Catholicism that can help us to understand his hesitation. In other words, we need not be Catholics or religious believers to understand the strain that S feels. Putting aside the fact that S himself has a commitment to the beliefs expressed by the Nicene Creed and feels that it expresses a profound truth, his internal conflict is not between the rational and the irrational, but between two different conceptions of rationality—the propositional and the pragmatic.

From the outside (that is, for non-Christians), Mr. S's discomfort may be justified as pragmatically sound, arising from a fear of the danger that the propositional will replace the pragmatic and that his students, having accepted too constraining a view of truth, will lose an important guide to maturation, even if from the inside it is expressed in other terms—that they will fail to see the "truth" expressed through the Nicene Creed.

Narrowly speaking, a commitment to the "truth" of the Nicene Creed is not a commitment to either a rational or an irrational doctrine. By itself, the Nicene Creed is nonrational. It has to do with faith, commitment, and membership, and not the way in which premises follow conclusions. If it is taken as true in any propositional sense by believers, there is nothing that compels nonbelievers, by the power of the argument alone, to take it the same way. And the same holds in reverse.

Pragmatic rationality would take a lighter view of things. Human beings make investments, they build on capital that others have created, and they should not walk away from this investment lightly, even though walk away they might. Regarding religion, this investment begins at an early age, involves much work, and leads to an enfolding with and by others who have made the same investment and whose payoff depends partly on a shared participation in some of life's most significant experiences. While there may be times when it makes sense to move away from one's own religious commitment, to do so without due consideration of the special meaning a given tradition has in one's life would be pragmatically irrational. From the pragmatist's point of view, the mistake made by the advocates of propositional rationality is to focus exclusively on arguments and not to include in the calculation the work involved in the development of a religious identity and the benefits of the coparticipation that come from it.[12]

The Rationality of Religious Partiality

Prayer, faith, and devotion, not argument, are the foundation of religious communities. Both the words of the prayer and the comportment of those who are praying are expressions of human vulnerability, dependency, and humility. Whether we kneel, bow our heads, prostrate ourselves, or pyramid the fingers of both hands, we are signaling our weakness and frailty. But the way we pray, the words we say, the way we say them, the language in which we utter them, the posture we assume as the words are uttered, and the rules we abide by that tell us how old you can be before you utter them, and who is authorized to say them, are all signs of a person's membership in one particular religious community and not another. Once a person learns to pray, it seems like second nature; but it is also easy to forget the effort that goes into learning how to do so in the accepted and proper way and in thus constructing and reconstructing a religious community.

Learning to Pray

Prayer and the activities associated with it are complicated matters. We saw in an earlier chapter that the Jewish school hired a prayer master primarily to teach children the correct words and method of prayer. This is understandable, given that the children in the Moses Day School were expected to pray in Hebrew and that biblical Hebrew has its own peculiar features, quite distinct from Modern Hebrew, which is spoken on the streets of Israel. Indeed, when a Jewish child is bar or bat mitzvahed, depending on the portion of the Torah required for that week he or she may be reading for close to an hour.[13] While it is perhaps unusual, even for Jewish schools, to hire one specialist to teach the techniques of prayer, prayer frames the activity of religious schools.[14] It usually begins and ends the day, and frequently each class begins the period with a prayer.

Young children undergoing religious education are expected to learn how to pray, and this continues throughout their schooling. Often, as they grow older, the students might take over some of the prayer work and lead the class or the school in a devotional moment. Thus, learning to pray is not at all a simple matter. It is real work and serves not only to worship God but also to continually reconstitute a religious community. To pray "like *this!*" is to reconstruct *this* community.

In learning how to do prayer work, students are internalizing communal rhythmic patterns, postures, and practices, thereby establishing a bond with similar prayer workers across space and generations. And in this work, teacher and student reconstruct the community. Even when there is no specialized prayer master to supervise this activity and when a special language is not a requirement, considerable effort is spent on both the teacher and the students' part, and sometimes, as in the episode below, prayer work is an explicit instrument to connect children of different ages and races within a school.

Building a Faith Community

As we walk into the second grade classroom, the teacher explains to the students that "the eighth graders are going to help you with prayer so that when they go to church, you will know what they are doing." Each second grader is paired with an eighth grader, and the eighth grade teachers explain that if they can get one prayer down today, that would be nice. The students start, and out of the general mumble I can discern phrases from different students. "All mighty God," one second grader says, "forgive me for I have sinned." Another says, "I confessed to almighty God I have sinned." An African American eighth grade girl is working with two white second graders, having them say hosannas. One boy says the prayer in front of the teacher with his eighth grade tutor standing proudly at his side. When the boy successfully completes the prayer, the teacher gives him a high-five.

The eighth grade teacher says to her students, "You might also teach them the symbols we use before prayer and what it means." And then, crossing herself, she says, "The Lord is on my mind, on my lips, and in my heart." A second grade girl says her prayer successfully with her eighth grade tutor by her side, and the eighth grade teacher applauds when she is finished. When the class is about over, the second grade teacher says, "Second graders, what do you say to the eighth graders?" And they respond, "Thank you." Walking away with the eighth graders down the hall, I hear an "I confess . . ." and "The Lord is on. . ." coming from the second grade classroom.

Learning to pray illustrates something important about becoming a Catholic, for both the second graders and the eighth graders. The second graders are learning the mechanics of the faith, how to join in and say their prayers. The eighth graders are learning what it is like to be a senior member of a community responsible for initiating new members into the mechanics of attachment. They express the frustration of adults who have had a hard time instructing the young. When the class is over, for example, one of the eighth graders complains to the teacher that "the kids don't listen to me," a complaint that caring parents and teachers make often. Here in this classroom, then, a group of children (eighth graders) have become, momentarily, a group of responsible adults, and individual second graders are on their way to becoming members of an embracing community.

From the standpoint of propositional rationality, the words said have no significance. From the point of view of pragmatic rationality, they allow us to see beneath the surface to the work involved in becoming a Catholic and the benefits that belonging to an embracing and enduring community provides. From the stumbling of the apprentice to the frustration of their tutors, there is no doubt that hard work is being done here. The pride that apprentice, tutor, and teacher take in the successful performance is an expression of the "we" that is forming and of the intergenerational project that is entailed by the notion of a faith community.

Reflection: Discomfort and Commitment

Reflection is an engagement that brings out familiar but taken-for-granted features of a situation, and thus it is always in some sense self-referential and partial. While I may reflect on the meaning of a passage in a book or a remark of a friend, the object of that reflection is an assumed meaning that

I once held but that now appears problematic to me. The passage may seem inconsistent with the meaning I gave to the rest of the book, and I need to now see how it might fit. Do I need to change my understanding of the book, or might I have misread the passage? My friend's warm words seemed inconsistent with her cold stare. Have I done anything to annoy her? Might I have just misread her look?

Reflection has as its object *some* (not all) feature(s) of a self, and as such it is inherently tied to commitment. The root of the term is physical—a glance in a mirror. The noodle on my chin, the smudge on my nose are hidden until I see them reflected. But when I see the smudge, I am not seeing it from my exclusive vantage point. Rather, I *see* the face with the noodle peering back at me, as another would see it, and with some mild discomfort but not the full disgust that another might feel. I just feel a need to wipe my chin. Nevertheless, even though I do not have exactly the same feelings as my audience, I contain its gaze within my own. I see the noodle on the chin as they would view it—as out of place and in need of removal.

There are some experiences where we may be more content with an imaged audience rather than a real one and where reflection matters little. Since I expect never to sing in public, I perform only for my own pleasure. Yet part of that pleasure comes as I hear myself in a way that I would want an audience to hear me. Not in how they would, in fact, hear me—which is, in fact, the reason I do not plan to sing in public—but in the way I imagine they would hear me if only they could hear me the way I hear myself. For me, the performance and my "hearing" the performance as my imaginary audience would "hear" it provide the pleasure of the experience. I am pleased because I create my own audience and then hear my voice through my image of the way they should hear it. On good days, I am tempted to take a bow. On those rare moments when I actually do *hear* my voice crack, I am disappointed in myself because I understand just how much I have let down my (imagined) audience. At that moment, I can no longer keep the performance in my imagination, and I cannot fully control the way my projected audience hears the performance. A bit of reality has crept into the activity and intruded on my imaginary triumph. *My* letdown comes from having let down that audience, imaginary though it may be, that serves as the condition of my pleasure. In reality, I know little about public singing, and those few occasions when I have had enough courage to tape my own voice have been occasions to forget. Reflection, in this case, is difficult precisely because it allows me to hear as that audience would truly hear, not as I imagine that they might.

Reflection kills undisciplined imagination and can be risky and painful. It can lead to resignation and defeat. If it were a real audience standing out there, challenging the glory of my creation, I would never again attempt another serenade. It can also lead to paralysis, as when a person tries to second-guess herself all the time, as might have been the situation of Mr. S, when the very foundation of commitment is under inspection in a classroom.

Yet, as Mr. S is so courageously aware, reflection is also a necessary condition for development. Teachers, coaches, directors, and conductors serve as mirrors, refining the image we have of ourselves and reflecting back to us the way they experience our behavior. A youngster keeps swinging and missing the ball. The coach pushes him three inches closer to the plate, and his batting average improves. With a mere push, he now sees the invisible line that separated the end of his bat from the ball. The push opens his eyes to a new way of being in that space that defines the batter's box. Nevertheless the push is not without its discomfort, especially if it seems to come out of nowhere. It feels like an insult, almost an assault, and if done by, say, the catcher on an opposing team, it would be cause for protest.

There are two kinds of pain associated with critical reflection. The first is illustrated by the push and involves a shared understanding of success and failure and a clear-cut consensus about a performance. It is a momentary jolt that leads from failure to success. Another, more difficult example comes when there is no clear-cut consensus about the value of a given performance but where there is a possibility, unperceived by the performer, of a better performance. The youngster has a good batting average but tends to hit mischievous bloopers between second base and center field. In practice, the coach walks up to him, takes hold of the batter's legs, and gently pushes them into a wider stance. Singles turn into doubles, triples, and home runs.

Reflection often requires exaggeration and even distortion. The director deliberately exaggerates the actor's body language, showing her that she is unintentionally communicating fright, not fight. The conductor consciously embellishes the singsong phrasing of the choir, allowing them to hear how miserably banal they sound.

In another context any one of these acts could be taken as a cruel satire of an incompetent performance, but in the teaching context such mimicry should provoke a critical eye within the actor herself and, if successful, should initiate a change in her performance. Unlike perhaps the role of the director or the conductor, the role of the teacher or the coach is to limit the occasions on which they need to be called and to allow the student to internalize the standard required to evaluate and readjust her own performance. In the teaching act, then, reflection is paired with criticism, performance, and growing autonomy. In this context, critical reflection is an act that often requires another but that is also undertaken to achieve a greater level of autonomy and independence from the other.

Critical reflection is the opposite of both narcissistic admiration or self-loathing and the paralysis that comes with both of them. It is undertaken as a way to improve practice by making adjustments while keeping the standpoint of another in mind. The conductor listens to her symphony as the audience would hear it and adjusts the volume and tone accordingly. Yet just as autonomy requires that we free ourselves from the paralyzing effect of self-love, it also requires that we free ourselves from the gaze of the other and develop the standpoint of an independent person. In the final analysis the batter must determine exactly how wide a stance he should have, the actor just how best to express fight, and the conductor how to modulate the string section.

The aim, then, of critical reflection is not just to improve this or that performance but also to open new ways of seeing and engaging a world. Reflective teaching asks for a certain amount of empathy from a student—the student must see or hear as the teacher does—but it is empathy that reaches for a different standpoint in order to better see something about ourselves. When we look into a mirror, we are seeing ourselves in a way that, while not usually available to us, is nevertheless quite a common view from the standpoint of others. I might have trouble seeing the noodle on my beard, but you do not.

Self-reflection has to do with who we are and, within limits, the way in which we choose to engage with the world, allowing us to see who we are at this moment (a knock-kneed batter, a befuddled actor, a scratchy singer, or a careless eater) so that we may also see the potential that remains yet unrealized. The critical element is required not just to see this momentary self but also to understand the way it is situated in a nexus of openings and possibilities. And it takes place as a commentary on our ongoing commitments—to become a better batter, a more consistent actor, a pleasant singer, or a neater eater.

Extended Identities and Critical Reflection

Our identities extend beyond our own skin. Devotion to *our* religion, like loyalty to *our* nation or affirmation of *our* ethnicity, is an aspect of an extended identity and could, in some sense,[15] have been otherwise. As noted in the sections above, it takes work to become Lutheran, Jewish, or Catholic. To take on a religious identity entails learning to perform certain practices, coming to understand their meaning, and learning to accept certain beliefs as one's own. Yet to engage in critical reflection entails distancing one's self from certain practices and meanings, entertaining doubt about certain beliefs, and being willing to consider evidence and arguments that might counter those beliefs.

Both those who are skeptical that religious education can foster critical reflective thinking and those who believe that it is a condition of such thinking are aware of this dichotomy. The difference is that the first one holds that the test of critical reflection is the capacity to distance oneself from one's own religious commitments, whereas the second assumes that there must be a reasonably fixed platform from which the light of critical reflection can be extended, and that religion must be that platform. Thus, the skeptic will fail to see any critical reflection short of a total examination of the premises of one's own faith community, while those who speak for the faith community will see such "reflection" as destructive nihilism on the route to annihilating the very standards that any meaningful criticism must employ.

The question of the relation between religious instruction and critical reflection is really two questions. First, what are the limits of critical reflection within religious education? And second, given these limits, what possibilities might religious education provide for critical reflection? The answers to these questions vary from one religious school to another, and resistance builds as the inquiry gets closer to what believers take to be the foundation of their faith. Given the work that goes into becoming a believer of a certain kind (a Lutheran, a Jew, a Muslim, or a Catholic), this is perfectly reasonable, and the critic who assumes that the only kind of critical inquiry acceptable is the one that pits my present beliefs against all comers is proposing, at least from the pragmatic point of view, a largely problematic standard. If I am searching for something new, finding my "investment" wanting, I still give the benefit of the doubt to the faith I was raised in. As a Catholic, I might look at Hinduism, Buddhism, Islam, and so on, but my pivotal point will most likely be the religion I know best, Catholicism. Are the rituals of Buddhism as rich as those of Catholicism? Are those of Islam? And is the moral guidance, first of Buddhism, then of Judaism, and then of Islam, as sound as that of Catholicism? When we are born into a religion (or an antireligion), we are born to a point of view, and that becomes our initial guide for making comparisons. The process is rational in the sense that it provides a familiar standpoint from which to make a comparison.

Critical reflection is considerably different from the kind of resistance that some recent educational theorists, following Paul Willis, seem to valorize.[16] Critical reflection may result in resistance, and resistance may result in critical reflection. However, resistance may be blind, and critical reflection may result in a greater rather than a reduced accommodation to the rules and regulations that authority lays down. Yet to encourage critical reflection, even if the object of such reflection is not as deep-seated as the Nicene Creed is with Catholicism, is to court risks because the conclusions that any student may arrive at cannot be guaranteed.

Conclusion

I have argued that a pragmatic conception of rationality is appropriate to evaluate the partiality that people show to their own religious traditions and to the education that they receive in those traditions. Once this conception of reasonableness is acknowledged, a rational reconstruction of the religious core becomes possible in terms of the kind of investment people make in the co-construction of a religious identity. From the pragmatic point of view, allowing this nonrational core the benefit of the doubt may be the right and rational thing to do, even though from a propositional point of view gaps in the logic may be apparent.

In providing a generous reading of different and even conflicting religious educational traditions, pragmatic rationality is consistent with the requirements of liberal pluralism. Yet a generous reading is not the same as a permissive reading or one that holds that liberal pluralism must value all religious education equally. Liberal pluralism also requires that schools promote the frame of mind and understandings needed to sustain and reproduce the basic principles of liberal pluralism. These include the basic requirements of all societies (reasonable security and safety), the basic requirement of liberalism (autonomy and intellectual growth), the basic requirement of pluralism (reasonable respect for difference), and the requirement of democracy (public accountability). Because these are the conditions for the reproduction of liberal pluralism, they must also be the conditions of any state-approved education. In the next chapters I examine these conditions.

PART II

The Nature of the Public Interest in Religious Education: A Critical Analysis

CHAPTER 5

Safety and the Question of Educational Negligence

School Safety versus Educational Safety

On the surface, safety seems like a simple affair. If schools are unsafe, they are unacceptable, pure and simple. While children are always at some risk wherever they are, it is especially shocking when a child is hurt or abused at school. An unsafe building, or an assault on a child or teacher in a classroom or on the playground, harms both the child and the fabric of social trust on which we all depend. This is why the horror of an attack at a school in Belsen, Russia, or Littleton, Colorado, seems even worse than had the same number died in an earthquake or a hurricane. We want to believe that we can depend on each other, and we would like to think that even terrorists do not go out of their way to target children—that there is a basic humanity that we can all acknowledge.

Nevertheless we live in a world where, despite their overall safety, bad things do occur in schools. Students and teachers have been assaulted, harassed, raped, and even killed. Deranged students have stalked and hunted down their classmates, marksmen have made sport of shooting students and teachers on the playground, and terrorists have spent months (in Russia) meticulously planting explosives in a school under repair. These tragedies notwithstanding, schools are still among the most secure environments for children. Today, however, this security comes with a price. Many schools lock their doors, some require students to pass through metal detectors, and others have police patrolling the corridors—hardly the ideal situation for sustained inquiry. Even most of the faith-based schools in our study locked their doors, although they did not have metal detectors or police inside the building. Only two schools maintained an unlocked-door policy, and both were located in suburban communities that had little violence.[1]

During this study, American newspapers were filled with headlines about Catholic priests abusing their authority and sexually harassing young boys while the Church hierarchy covered up the crimes. These episodes involved a relatively small minority of priests but did considerable damage to the reputation of Catholic institutions and the trust that people put in them. Unlike an exposé of criminal clergy in other religions, the problem for the Catholic Church is exacerbated because of its hierarchical structure. Headlines of abuse notwithstanding, religious schools are generally safe places for children and may have a slight advantage over public schools (which are also generally safe places) if only because they can decide to accept or reject a student, can expel an unruly youngster, and can set their own discipline codes.

School safety, however, needs to be distinguished from educational safety. The first speaks to the level of risk in the physical environment of the school. The second speaks to the information and skills that students will need to reduce the risk to themselves and others outside of the school environment. Schools that do not have lead paint on their walls are generally safer, everything else being equal, than schools that do, but schools that have good driver's education programs are *educationally* safer than schools that do not. In both cases the risk of harm is minimized. In the first, it is minimized while the student is in school; in the second, the reduction of risk continues beyond graduation.

Security is more than the prevention of immediate harm. Besides risk reduction and prevention, it entails a reasonable trust that people can count on those around them to come to their aid in times of need and to promote their interests. A community arises when this trust is mutual and when it includes a commitment to building the intersubjective attitudes (for example, compassion and cooperation), the common symbols, and the collective awareness that trust requires. One of the tragedies of the priest scandal for Catholics is that it raised serious questions about the reliability of this community and its leadership.

Yet this should not discount the importance that the development of a reliable, trusting community holds for Catholic educators. Their efforts often go much deeper than the minimum level of security presented by the idea of safety as freedom from bodily risk or assault. Many Catholic schools go out of their way to promote a strong sense of community by establishing personal bonds of care and compassion across the student body and through this to the larger community. The Catholic bishops have stressed community building as an essential component of Catholic education.

> The educational mission of the Church is an integrating Ministry embracing three interlocking dimensions: The message revealed by God . . . which the church proclaims; fellowship in the life of the Holy Spirit . . . ; service to the Christian community and the entire human community.[2]

The religious component of the curriculum is especially designed to serve the community, first within the classroom—prayer is used by some teachers to acknowledge students or other teachers with a special need, such as a death in the family, a prolonged illness, or a special challenge, thereby adding content to the prayer and perhaps helping to cement a communal bond that extends beyond the school experience—and then in the school and beyond to the wider community.

Community and Trust

In many Catholic schools a major weekend retreat, usually attended in the junior or senior year of high school, helps crystallize the idea of the school as a religious and academic community that reaches beyond the individual student. Prior to the retreat a school may ask parents, without their child's knowledge, to write letters that will be waiting for the students when they arrive at the gathering. The parents' letters speak to the special qualities of their child and to challenges that he or she has overcome, and they offer words of love and encouragement that are to be reinforced by the classmates and teachers. Each student is asked to share significant personal experiences, and many of those we interviewed came away with vivid memories of their own or other students' presentations. Students we interviewed spoke to their classmates about overcoming cancer, emerging out of a deep depression, struggling with obesity, and discovering that they are gay.[3] Other students and staff provide the emotional support to validate the person and acknowledge the courage it takes to share their lives in this intimate way. These retreats are intended to create a bond of compassion between students and strengthen bonds between students, teachers, and parents. Students are seen in more than one dimension, such as a "good student," an "excellent swimmer," or a "talented musician." Each is identified through his or her own special quality of character, by the struggles endured, the challenges met, and the kindnesses offered, and then is encouraged to appreciate the special light of others.

The required course Catholic Moral Theory extends this bond to the larger society through a community service requirement. Students work with the poor, the sick, or the young in shelters, nursing homes, hospitals, and child care centers. They may spend a night in a homeless shelter serving food and talking to the lonely, or care for an older neighbor who needs someone to talk to. Liberation High held community health fairs and vaccination programs to bring the school into the community and the community into the school.

A school's responsibility for its students does not end when the bell rings. At Dillon, for example, if the police catch students drinking, the school will often hear about it and the offender will be punished under a system aptly labeled JUG, or justice under God. Even though students from rival gangs may sit in the same classroom at Liberation High, located in an area of gang activity, there are no sign of gangs in the school. The absence of graffiti in the bathroom, the polite and friendly demeanor of the students, the absence of litter in the hallways, and the generally immaculate appearance of the school are clear signs that the students see this school as a place worthy of their care and loyalty.

In general, every school in this study would rank well on indicators of school safety. Through the retreat and the emphasis on community service, Catholic schools, often located in poorer areas of a city, may work especially hard to create a communal, safe environment of trust and security. However, while these schools would rank high on most scales of school safety, educational safety is a different matter; and when it comes to issues of sexuality, the needs of homosexual, bisexual, and lesbian students are often neglected along with those of the significant number of students who are sexually active. Many teachers worry about this neglect, but their hands are often tied because of the official policy of the Church toward these issues. Hence, for example, counselors do not as a rule send sexually active students to Planned Parenthood for advice because of its approval of abortion, and in many schools they are forbidden to do so. While some teachers in this study dismissed the issue by, for example, asserting that the students know more about sex than they do, others seemed to try to provide critical information about such areas as contraception while remaining within the constraint imposed by the Church to take an abstinence-only stance on contraception and birth control.

Working the Margins

The Catholic Church views what it calls *artificial* means of birth control to be sinful and condones only *natural* birth control methods (and only, of course, for married couples) that depend on calculating the woman's reproductive cycle and the days she cannot conceive.[4] The nurse at Liberation High tells me that a high percentage of their students are sexually active. These two facts pose a dilemma for Father J—how can he provide these students with the information they need to protect themselves while remaining faithful to the Church's teachings on the sinfulness of both premarital sex and birth control? Below he attempts to meet this challenge.

Father J: Let's talk about birth control [devices]. What kind are there?

Student: A condom.

J: What is a condom? A piece of rubber or latex that you put on your penis to prevent conception. Are condoms effective?

[Student responds that they are about eighty or eighty-eight percent effective.]

J: Well let's assume they're about ninety percent effective. That means that one out of ten times, they might fail. They might leak. They might rip. The guy puts the condom on. He's hard as a rock. Bang, bang. What happens to that condom as it gets soft? So that's seepage. The other issue is what? Breakage.

J: OK, what's another form of birth control?

J: Withdrawal doesn't work because there's fluid before ejaculation that might have semen in it. This kind of birth control is called stupidity. Another method is the pill. The pill prevents ovulation. It does not allow for the egg to be fertilized.

J: Girls, what are possible side effects of the pill? Some women might find it hard to begin ovulation after they are off the pill.

Student: Birth defects?

J: I have not heard of that, but depression is a possibility, and weight gain as well. What else is used for contraception?

Student (male): Diaphragm.

J (jokingly): Are you a sexologist?

J (drawing a picture of a woman's reproductive system on the board):
                If you use a diaphragm, you need to be properly fitted or it won't work. This prevents conception.

He doesn't say much about the problems with diaphragms except the need for proper fitting. And then he says, "Spermicide. I don't like to talk about spermicide because they are not effective, except if it's used with another method."

The lesson may well meet the minimum standards of the Church. It discusses the limits of different methods of birth controls, and one could easily draw the conclusion that abstinence is the only safe alternative. Yet by going into the mechanisms of birth control methods and by discussing their relative efficiency, he is providing useful information for students who may be considering engaging in sex. Clearly the discussion is biased toward abstinence, the Church's only authorized method for single people, but he is introducing the uninitiated to instruments of birth control without a heavy guilt trip. When J later speaks about the use of the RU 486 (morning after) pill and abortion, he is considerably less compromising, and his language becomes so graphic that it would be difficult to find much room for openly challenging the Church's position. However, in the segment above he is providing some of the technical information that sexually active students will need to avoid pregnancy. The fact that there is no discussion of the use of condoms in the prevention of sexually transmitted disease limits the effectiveness of the lesson, however.

Father J managed to provide students with technical instruction about birth control without disavowing the Church's objections, and both Mr. P and Father J in different ways used examples of homophobia as illustrations of intolerance. They have become adept at working the margins and improving the educational safety of their school curriculum. Yet these are likely exceptions, and Father D with his strong condemnation of birth control and homosexuality represents the official norm. The spiritual leaders of the Catholic Church believe that it is sinful to have sexual intercourse outside of marriage. They also believe that it is sinful to engage in homosexual acts, although the Church allows that some people are inclined toward homosexuality, and it advises compassion and understanding, but in no way is the homosexual act to be justified or condoned. And, where love and kindness fail, those who engage in homosexual acts may need "medical-psychological assistance from persons attentive to and respectful of the teaching of the Church."[5]

The Church's official, uncompromising stance is difficult for many to accept, and it tries the moral sensitivities of many, Catholic and non-Catholic alike. A fetus will be born without the capacity for cognitive function, and if the mother does not abort, she will likely never be able to conceive again. A father has sexually abused all of his children, and, out of desperation, his wife seeks an abortion. A poor family cannot feed its present children and wants to abort a week-old fetus. It is not difficult to think of examples that strain the Church's prohibition against abortion, a prohibition that sometimes seems to place aborting a week-old fetus on the same moral plane as murdering a child.

The Church will argue its case against abortion on the grounds of the Bible and the commandment against killing, but since it allows some killing, even of innocent people (say, in the case of war), additional justifications are needed to show that abortion under every circumstance is an unjustified killing. One argument that appeals to secular as well as religious temperaments holds that high standards are required if we are to maintain our fundamental commitment to the value of life and that Church doctrine on sexuality constitutes one seamless web affirming the sacredness of human life.

An analogy might be the absolute ban on torture advanced by international law as an example of the same way of thinking. There are those who object to the absolute character of the ban against torture, arguing that it is unrealistic and that torture can sometimes save lives. Yet from the point of view of those who support the ban, the argument is problematic because it allows the standard to be held hostage to the good results that might arise from breaking it and thereby allows that norm against torture to be adjusted in terms of its likely consequences in any given instance. The result is that there would then be no meaningful norm at all. Granted, there may be some cases in which the torturer may be forgiven, just as in light of sorrow and contrition, the person who has an abortion may be forgiven, but the act of forgiveness is itself a way to reaffirm the standard. The Church's stand on abortion follows a similar logic. To make exceptions is to reduce the strength of the standard.[6] It is a slippery slope with no sand.

In asserting the absolute value of life, the Church is affirming a standard that it hopes people will strive to live up to and is affirming as well that abortion can never be an everyday, taken-for-granted occurrence. This is why, even if performed under the most difficult of circumstances, it still requires an act of forgiveness. To the Church, life constitutes "one seamless garment": unravel one thread and, it believes, the entire cloth will come apart. To put this in somewhat less religious terms: the Church believes that human beings have an instinct for the value of life and that one of its most important functions is to preserve that instinct. It also believes that this instinct is in danger of being overwhelmed by the expediencies of everyday life and that the Church has a primary responsibility to protect those forms of life that are the most vulnerable, including expressions of life that have not yet come into full being. If it fails to uphold the standard of life in one situation, it is threatened in all. And hence the Church must support those practices and institutions—the family is the primary one—that it believes stand in support of life. And, as such, it also takes strong stands against war, capital punishment, masturbation, and birth control.

The argument rests on some contestable empirical assumptions. Whether children who masturbate, for example, will value life any less than those who do not is an empirical question, as is the view that those who practice birth control value life less than those who do not. These issues could be settled by studies about the correlation between masturbators and pacifists or between those who practice birth control and those who murder. The findings might possibly come out in the Church's favor, but they might not. It is certainly not clear unless one accepts the view that the life of, say, a two-day-old fetus is equivalent to the life of a fully born child—an equivalence that would require the same penalty for abortion as for murder—and that anyone who has an abortion, regardless of the circumstances, will value their children's or their neighbor's children's lives any less than a person who has not had an abortion.

While this objection may sound crass to believers, placing these issues in an empirical and legal frame encourages additional questions to be raised—what are the conditions that are likely to inhibit or to promote abortions? And here among the most important factors are poverty, the availability of good child care, and a reasonable social safety net for families.[7] The official position of the Church that abortion is a sin might also be judged on empirical grounds in terms of whether it encourages or discourages teachers from discussing the social and economic causes of abortion. Will teachers hesitate to discuss the conditions that contribute to abortions, fearing that students will seize on them as an excuse for promiscuity, or will it encourage such discussions on the grounds that they will promote a larger commitment to social justice?

The Church's absolute stance comes at a price for educational safety. The Church can forgive an abortion, acknowledging that we are all human—all too human—while maintaining the standard unadulterated by the reality of human frailty. However, it cannot allow neutral information about safe sex to be presented to students in Catholic schools; and without such information, the educational safety of sexually active students is compromised.

Moreover, the distinction between school and educational safety often breaks down in both Catholic and public schools for homosexual students when gay students are harassed and physically abused by fellow students, and it is not unusual for these students to contemplate or attempt suicide.[8] While the Church disapproves of homophobia and condemns "violence and malice in speech and action" directed against homosexuals, there is institutional reluctance to establish support groups for homosexual students. A few schools have begun to take steps in this direction,[9] but the majority do not, either on conservative grounds that to do so would be to aid and abet sin or on more "liberal" ones that hold that the parish rather than the school is the best place for such groups, thus contextualizing homosexuality in a religious rather than an educational context. As one writer put it,

> Schools and parish programs can create appropriate support groups for gay and lesbian students, groups geared toward information and honest sharing of ideas and feelings.

> In primary and secondary levels of education, it is not wise to promote the kind of support group which presupposes that a student is a homosexual since . . . a true understanding of one's sexual identity probably does not occur until the late 20s.

> The same viewpoint should contextualize all questions about support for same-sex couples admitted to school dances. It is not wise to uncritically support sexual orientation and thus unwittingly promote homogenital behavior before authentic maturity in this area takes place.

> Support groups for young people are better designed to facilitate an honest exchange of accurate knowledge of the Church's teachings about homosexuality. . . . The group might investigate . . . what the Bible does and does not teach about this subject.[10]

The proposal contains some questionable assumptions about the onset of sexual identity and whether the parish is a likely place for the sharing of honest feelings, given the Church's condemnation of homosexual acts. More importantly, it fails to say what a parish group could do that a school group could not or what should be done with the many students in Catholic schools who do not attend church on a regular basis and do not belong to a parish.

Knowledge and Negligence

Educational negligence involves the failure to teach students the knowledge and skills they will need to function productively and safely in the world, or involves teaching them in such a way that they will be unable to exercise choice in a safe or healthy way. If parents fail to teach their children to look both ways before crossing a busy street, they are negligent. If a school fails to teach students to read, it is negligent.

Responsible teachers in Catholic schools are in a bind. Strict adherence to Church doctrine limits the information they could provide to their students about basic issues of sexuality, and while they may not express it as negligence, something tells them that they are not meeting their students' needs. If Father J were to directly teach his students about safe sex and the various techniques available to prevent disease and pregnancy, he would be seen as rejecting abstinence. Yet not to teach their students about the availability of such protection is to neglect a very basic educational requirement.

When Catholic teachers like Mr. P and Father J work the margins, they are implicitly acknowledging the tension between their two responsibilities—to teach Catholic moral doctrine and to provide students with the knowledge and understanding they need to function as secure adults (and, in the case of homosexuals, within the context of a supportive community).

Institutional Issues

While the overt philosophy of the Church presents issues of life and procreation as a seamless garment, suggesting that value distinctions are to be avoided, nevertheless distinctions are made. For example, a number of schools encourage pregnant girls to complete their education and do not view pregnancy as a cause for expulsion. Here, in their belief that a stricter policy would simply encourage pregnant girls to have abortions—which is grounds for expulsion—they do embrace a consequentialist standard and go for the lesser of two "evils." Abortion, itself, is most often a cause for expulsion (assuming the school authorities find out).

The level of sexually active students in Catholic schools is thought to be similar to that of students in the nation at large, and the fact that there were few pregnancies in the schools in this study was attributed by teachers and students alike not to abstinence alone but also to the use of birth control devices and unreported abortions. Indeed, the abstinence-only curriculum has serious problems in terms of its main aims—reducing pregnancy.

> The abstinence only approach to sex education is not supported by the extensive body of scientific research on what works to protect young people from HIV/AIDS, sexually transmitted infections (STIs), and unplanned pregnancy. An assessment of the peer reviewed, published research reveals no evidence that abstinence only programs delay sexual initiation or reduce STIs or pregnancy.[11]

Those who break an abstinence-only pledge are more likely to have unprotected sex than those who never took the pledge in the first place.[12]

Homosexuality provides a somewhat different risk. In many schools, public and private, homosexual students are at risk from two sources—the assaults, verbal or physical, of other students, and a lowered self-esteem that can result in self-inflicted physical harm. In those all-too-few public schools where students can receive recognition and where student support groups with both gay and nongay students are formed, homophobic activities can be confronted collectively.[13]

The potential advantages and disadvantages of Catholic and public schools for homosexual students are mixed. While too few public schools aid gay and lesbian students,[14] there is nothing in the public school philosophy that prohibits them from establishing support groups that would allow official recognition and mutual aid, and, given certain other considerations, it may be unconstitutional to do so.[15] Barring a constitutional challenge, public schools are limited by what the community and its school board will allow, and many conservative boards resist the policy.

Catholic schools have a different set of advantages and disadvantages. As we have seen, classes on religious education can become opportunities to establish a moral tone in favor of tolerance, and the high school retreat can serve as a source of support. Even though the Church rejects homosexual activity as deviant and abnormal, some teachers are able to appropriate the doctrine of original sin in creative ways, reminding the students of the biblical warning that only those without sin should cast the first stone. Nevertheless, the idea that gay and lesbian people in their loving relationships have done something that needs forgiving must be a painful and bewildering idea, hardly likely to build self-esteem in a youngster coming to terms with an emerging sexual identity.

In principle, public schools can authorize gay and lesbian support groups, although for strategic and political reasons few take advantage of this opportunity. Yet in Catholic schools, the institutional pressures against such groups are not just strategic. They are often taken as part of the meaning of a "Catholic" education. Teachers and counselors in this study who expressed personal sympathy for the situation of gay students fear that parents and other Catholics would vocally reject a school that established a gay support group as "un-Catholic."

Individual counselors may address the concerns of gay and lesbian students as they become aware of them, but most wait until an individual student informs them of a problem and do not initiate needed support. It is not quite a "Don't ask, don't tell policy," but the antihomosexual message of the Church is unlikely to create a setting where asking or telling is easy. While students may be moved by the influence of an individual teacher or by a story told by a gay student at a retreat, these are individual cases, and the institutional climate of silence is very difficult for students or their sympathetic teachers to challenge. Thus, although both public and Catholic schools may be guilty of neglect, the motivation is very different in each. For the public school, neglect is a matter of political will; for the Catholic school, it is a matter of basic philosophy.

The absence of *public* recognition for homosexual students, together with the Church's official condemnation for homosexual acts, creates a dilemma. The need for religious freedom suggests that Catholic schools should be able to advance their own views on sexuality as a condition of liberal pluralism. However, the safety of sexually active students highlights the risks that accompany silence, distortion, and neglect. The only alternative to condemnation is official silence, or working the margins.

Yet even the most creative teacher is limited in the kind of aid that can be given. Counselors are discouraged from recommending Planned Parenthood because of the stand it takes on abortion. Openly gay teachers who could serve as role models are not officially visible, and, as mentioned, officially sanctioned support groups for homosexual students are generally off-limits. This means that accurate information needs to be obtained but that Catholic schools can risk their Catholic identity if they provide it in a systematic way.

Searching for a Resolution: Resources within the Church

Catholic teachers can be caught between two conflicting responsibilities. There is the responsibility to meet the requirement of Catholic schools to maintain and promote a Catholic identity, and there is the responsibility to ensure the long-term as well as the short-term safety of all students. Some of the intellectual resources for addressing this tension are available within the tradition of Catholicism (Mr. P's stress on the informed conscience may be one of them), but it would require that the process of tradition making become more transparent to high school students in their classes on moral theology.

Under the surface of perennial stability, much of Catholic doctrine is an evolving set of rules, practices, beliefs, and interpretations forged by rich discussion and debate. As with many other intellectual fields, students in classes on moral theology are often taught only the consensus that prevails at the time as expressed by official organs and textbook writers. To the extent that the historical tensions and sociological conditions leading to the present consensus are not emphasized, the way in which courses in religion are taught is similar to the way in which Thomas Kuhn describes the teaching of science. Chemistry and physics students are not usually taught the history of the discipline and how it evolved, but only the basic formulation as it is presently understood. In science this gives a distorted impression of the nature of scientific progress and delivers the message that the only thing worth knowing is the present consensus.[16] What is gained is a certain amount of efficiency in inducting new initiates into the scientific community. What may be lost is a deeper understanding of the process whereby scientific consensus is formed. Something similar may happen in religion. Students are inducted into the moral framework of a religious community without a sense of the tensions and debates that led to the current consensus. As we saw in the case of the Nicene Creed, too much transparency too early may disrupt this induction and shatter the faith that the child needs to become a member of this community and to profit from its spiritual tradition. However, this justification resides outside of the principles of the community itself and makes its appeal on pragmatic and psychological ground, allowing that the mystery of the faith may well serve the growth and communal integration of the child.

The burden shifts considerably, however, if doctrine serves to neglect the physical or psychological well-being of certain classes of students, as it does in the case of sexually active and gay and lesbian students. In these cases the doctrine of the Church may well serve to lower self-esteem and contribute to self-loathing and alienation. The requirements for the intellectual, psychological, and social development of gay and lesbian students speak against keeping the source of the doctrine opaque and for opening it up to critical discussion.

This approach might be developed in courses on Church history that highlight the social and political factors as well as the theological debates involved in the development of moral doctrine. Specifically, courses in Church history could follow the changing ideas on sexuality from Saint Augustine's view that "the prime purpose of sex . . . is to have children within marriage"[17] to the present view that sexual pleasure is a part of the conjugal act and that it should be always open to the possibility of conception. It could include the influence that this change has had over time on the definition of perversion and the dropping from the list of perverse acts behavior such as sex between sterile partners, postmenopausal sex, and sex during the time of the month when contraception is unlikely.[18]

Students who study the evolution of Church doctrine on sexuality would also learn that there are limitations to natural law argument and that when these limitations are acknowledged, the Church will draw on other sources. For example, when Pope Paul VI decided to rule against his own appointed commission and to reinforce the Church's ban on most forms of contraception, he did so not because there was unambiguous agreement about what conclusion to draw from natural law philosophy. It was decided on other grounds such as the need to preserve the credibility of the Church and to avoid "disastrous consequences for moral theology."[19] These are matters that can be debated in light of the changes that have occurred in the Church since the ban on contraception was upheld and in light of respected opinions to the contrary, which state that the ban has confused Catholics and motivated many to leave the Church.[20] A religious education consistent with the ideal of the liberal arts would require not just that the students learn *what* the Church's position is now but also that they would learn *how* it came to hold the position that it presently does.[21] This would help students formulate their own views in light of a much deeper understanding of Church doctrine than they get by a superficial treatment of sin and sexuality.

This kind of open discussion would help high school students see how the justification has altered over the years and would enable them to consider the extent to which conceptions of sin have changed. For example, whereas once the Church was very suspicious of sexual pleasure[22] and held that the only legitimate reason for intercourse was procreation, now openness to the possibility of procreation, allowing for all of the pleasure that intercourse can bring, has become the sign of a complete and full union. To understand the process by which these doctrines change frees students to accept the tradition while promoting a full understanding of its complexity and richness. The question may even be asked whether the Church's conception of sin has remained the same over the centuries when it comes to issues like birth control. Or whether it is a different order of sin to *not* enjoy a full and complete union than it is to "destroy" a possible, even though never conceived, life that God, with but a bit of cooperation, would have destined to be born. A better understanding, then, of the history and philosophy of the Church for students in high school would help to open up this most difficult of issues and need not weaken the Church's view of the sanctity of marriage and its central role in nurturing children.

Granted, there are limits to what could be officially sanctioned by the Church without raising concern about the Catholic mission of the school. It would be difficult for the school to sanction direct technical instruction on the use of contraception, for example, or to sponsor a gay support group that explicitly contradicted Church doctrine or appeared to approve of homosexual behavior. Even the most permissive junior year retreats, caring as they are, would find it very difficult for students who have had abortions to discuss their experience, knowing that it would be grounds for expulsion.

Yet in today's world these issues may involve life-and-death considerations. It is important that educators find ways to provide this information and to engage students who may be suffering profound emotional stress and humiliation for lack of information and support. A commitment to pluralism may require creative ways to satisfy these educational needs, hopefully without violating the religious integrity of the school. Certainly all students need to understand the potential emotional, medical, and material costs of early sexual activity, but they also need to know how to minimize the risk of incurring these costs should they choose to be sexually active. Church schools may not be the right venue for such teachings, but if they are not, then other venues may need to be developed to provide instruction for students who attend religious schools. These might be thought of as the equivalent of driver's training programs for students whose own high schools do not offer them.

The State: Constraints and Responsibilities

Sex education is about life and love, care and responsibility, but it is also about safety. While some people will argue that sexuality is a private matter and should not be interfered with by the state, this view is unrealistic given the transferability of many sexual diseases and the fate of unplanned and sometimes unwanted children. The state has an interest in the education of all children, and it should not matter if that education takes place in a religious school. Safety in the modern world requires full, complete, and informed sex education.

I do not believe that it is usually wise for a state to insist that a religious school treat other opinions on the matter as equal to their own, as a public school might. However, the state does have an obligation to see to it that students in religious schools are provided the information they need to ensure their own safety and that they are aware of an obligation to ensure the safety of their partners should they choose a different path than that of abstinence. This interest holds regardless of the views of the religion on sexual morality, and it holds for all levels of religious orientations, from the very liberal to the very traditional and orthodox.

Some will argue that this is not sufficient and that simply informing students about the technical means for safe sex is not sufficient to erase the guilt and psychological damage that a demand for abstinence can create. I am sympathetic to this argument, but if we are serious about pluralism, the state cannot micromanage a religious school curriculum, and we simply do not know enough to even weigh the psychological costs of a strong abstinence-only stand against the benefits of acceptance into a strong, religiously oriented community. At the very least, policy should not be based on the assumption that most religious teachers promote an "abstinence or damnation" message. Most of those I observed did not. Forgiveness was a more likely message than "damnation," although in the very idea of forgiveness, there is a presumption of guilt that some would find problematic.

While the state cannot be indifferent to the psychological health of children in religious schools, in the absence of compelling evidence to the contrary states should be cautious in advancing a thick set of requirements on religious schools in discussions of sexuality. The more immediate problem is the extent to which states themselves and the government have followed the lead of religious educators and are promoting an abstinence-only curriculum in public schools. When public schools adopt such a curriculum, it leaves sexually active students in both religious and public schools vulnerable to risks of unprotected sex.

Public schools that have moved in this direction need to reconsider how to approach the issue of sexuality realistically in ways that will both help students avoid the emotional consequences that often come with immature sexual relations and shield students who are sexually active from the most damaging physical and material consequences that arise from unprotected sex. Yet if the state has the obligation to inform public school students of safety risks and ways to reduce them, it may have a similar obligation for students whose schools, for religious reasons, are unwilling to provide this information. This obligation need not be carried out within the religious school or by those who teach there, but it is still a public obligation.

Summary

The state has two competing obligations when it comes to religious schools and sex education. Pluralism requires that the state exercise restraint in directing sex education in religious schools. However, the state has an even greater responsibility to protect future citizens from hazards brought about through ignorance and neglect. This responsibility is not waived just because parents choose a religious education for their children. Students must be provided with technical information that will protect the emotional and physical health of those who are sexually active.

True, the interest of pluralism requires a reasonable degree of separation between religious schools and public authority. However, this separation is never absolute, and there are numerous ways in which the two intersect, especially at the level of accreditation. Yet states have tended to take a hands-off approach, especially when it comes to the continuing education of those teachers who teach the core religious subjects, and they do very little to see to it that teachers of religious subjects are informed of the emotional and medical considerations that every sexually active person should be aware of. States need to find ways to encourage religion instructors to understand how religious teachings intersect with more general knowledge of the emotional and psychological development of students, and they need to ensure that a strong and viable public education system is available for those families who find the absoluteness of the religious message troubling or inappropriate for them. In addition, states need to ensure that all students receive the information they need to reduce risk, whether in their own school or elsewhere.

CHAPTER 6

Intellectual Growth, Autonomy, and Religious Education

Autonomy and Moral Novelty

One of the principal concerns of educators in a democracy is the development of autonomy. Autonomy means that people have developed the capacity to conceive and reevaluate their own conceptions of the good and that they not be destined to live out the plans and ideals of others. Autonomy requires intellectual growth and a capacity to evaluate different ways of life and competing moral claims. Autonomy also requires the capacity to acknowledge the complexity of moral issues and to allow moral intuitions to interrogate dominant religious moral theories.

Skeptics are critical of religious education because they believe that it promotes premature commitment, leaving little room for the consideration of moral issues on their own terms. Jean-Jacques Rousseau, who advised that children be allowed to grow up free of religious instruction until they were able to decide moral issues on their own terms,[1] expressed this view in its most extreme form. Today it is one reason why some people believe that education should be a religion-free zone.

This criticism is based on two notions. The first is the importance of authenticity, or the idea that we all have a certain unique way of being and that this uniqueness should be acknowledged and recognized. The second is a belief in moral novelty, or the idea that new conditions often require new and innovative moral ideas or inventions. The critic believes that religious education must reject both of these. Authenticity, at least as expressed in much of modern philosophy, entails the idea that people need to be able to choose their own good, relatively free from "the heavy hand of tradition."[2] The idea is that there is an inner, "authentic" self that stands outside of traditions; that the goal of education is the development of an autonomous self; and that the sign of such a self is its ability to engage critically with traditions and formative institutions. In this view, a moral choice must be an expression of an authentic self—one that is made by and for my self, and that expresses the deepest part of me. Those who voice this concern are skeptical of religious education because it advances the idea that a moral choice is one that must conform to God's will as interpreted through a religious tradition, and that there is thus a known source beyond the self that the will of the moral person must conform to. To the critic of religious education, since God's will is always being interpreted by a human source, this standpoint is equivalent to moral slavery, and, ironically, slavery aborts the condition of moral action—a will of one's own.[3] Religious chatter, according to extreme expressions of this view, is the noise that makes it difficult for me to hear that inner voice. A more moderate voice allows that religious conviction can certainly be an expression of an authentic self but that the convictions need to be formed reasonably free of coercive influences.

The second source of the skepticism about religious education rests on the belief that religions cannot address moral novelty and will dogmatically define every new moral issue in terms of established and traditional norms. The concern here is not that religion interferes with an innate moral sense but that it provides limited resources for addressing moral problems, especially in an age of unprecedented technological change. It is granted that religious sentiments have a practical moral function. They codify effective responses to past moral problems in ways that facilitated coordinated action and social cohesion. However, the argument continues, modern science and technology present completely new problems, many of which are beyond the realm of religious tradition to resolve. In fact a rigid reliance on religious formulas can be harmful, leading to dogmatic fanaticism. This is the concern that Mr. P expressed earlier when he described his problem with the Church's position on *in vitro* fertilization:

> An issue we'll talk about is *in vitro* fertilization, and the church is opposed to this. And a couple of years back, we were talking about it, and one kid put up their hand. A real nice girl. And she was talking about how her younger sibling had been conceived that way. And I'm like, "Whoa, okay." And again, I realize that in a few years, I'll probably have somebody sitting in front of me who was conceived that way. And so again, a tension that exists in the church is between faithfulness to the church's teaching and freedom of conscience.

Religious education is thus seen as morally problematic in two possible ways. It is problematic when conformity to existing norms blocks consideration of morally novel experiences. It is also problematic if the inward journey is discouraged, and the inner voice of authenticity muffled. Moral autonomy, one of the critical aims of liberal education, must engage the possibility of moral novelty. It must allow that the individual's moral intuitions may not be contained within a single religious system and that education must permit moral anomalies to be acknowledged.

Moral Education

Ideally, moral education involves enabling students to tack between three moments—standard moral theories of the good, their own moral intuitions regarding the right course of action,[4] and moral innovation or ideas and concepts desired to resolve the moral dilemmas arising out of new technologies and new information. The most serious concern about dogmatic moral education in a religious context is that it can overwhelm individual moral intuition and moral novelty with premature commitments to established moral theories. The concern is less that students will come to adopt an inadequate moral doctrine than that they will come to think that moral agency consists only in conforming to the teachings of authority and, as a result, that their capacity for independent intellectual thought and moral growth will be aborted. We have seen an example of this in the attempt by Saint Martin to inoculate its students against the teaching of evolution. The fact that students are taught a scientifically questionable doctrine is less important than the fact that they are being taught that religion has a veto on science. This lesson closes the door on novelty and delivers the message that permission needs to be granted before certain kinds of beliefs can be held.

The Pragmatic Response

One way to begin to reconcile the skeptic's concerns with the strong commitment of the religious believer is to adopt a pragmatic standpoint. The pragmatist takes the skeptic's concern seriously but allows that an accurate understanding of religious education must also consider the guidance that religion provides for addressing complicated moral issues with its ability to account for moral novelty and growth.

The pragmatist is concerned if the skeptic renders an a priori judgment about religious education without acknowledging the role that religious schools can play in promoting self-respect, or without exploring how far religious education might go in allowing for moral novelty and the growth of moral knowledge. Religions provide important guidelines on how we should treat each other, how we should respond to strangers, and what we owe to the sick and the poor. Religions also call on us to enact our humanness through channeling our appetites toward communal benefits. Fasting, a common religious practice, can serve as an example. To willfully deny ourselves food for no special personal reason, such as losing weight, both connects us to the suffering of others and serves to remind us of the control we can exert over our own appetites and desires. No doubt sublimation can have negative effects and result in desire "spilling over" in harmful ways. It may be, as some critics allege, that the abuse of young children by Catholic clergy is a result of the "abnormal" requirement of celibacy. Yet the skeptic's critique of religion needs to be balanced by an inventory of the moral assets that religions lend to human existence.

For the pragmatist, few long-term historical traditions are quite as monolithic as they seem from the outside. They are layered in ways that advance some forms of discourse as dominant for a time—favored frames through which events are viewed—but there are subordinate discourses that may be available should the dominant one prove inadequate. Where the sublimation of desire gets out of hand, moral intuition may direct our appreciation to a long-submerged aspect of the discourse, one where moral intuitions and practical concerns begin to challenge narrow interpretations of standard dogma. For example, in the situation of celibacy and the sexual abuse of children, a number of scholars have begun to point to an earlier time when priests were allowed to marry and have children as well as to those few modern instances where married members of other religions have converted and become priests.[5]

For the pragmatist, autonomy is never achieved outside of any and all traditions whatsoever. From the very beginning our lives are embedded in traditions, starting with what we count as food and what we reject as food (pork, for example). And, as mentioned in the last chapter, even when we become dissatisfied with our own traditions, they are the standpoint from which we evaluate a possible future with a different tradition. A Catholic does not stand outside of Catholicism, place it on an equal par with every other religion, and then make a judgment. If there is any deliberation, it is from the standpoint of her Catholicism. She places her tradition first alongside another, and if that does not measure, she may place it alongside yet another as she considers the match between her own beliefs and inclinations and the teachings of various religions.

Within a religion there are often subordinate discourses that provide resources for addressing moral novelty and that serve as sources for intellectual growth. While there may be considerable resistance against shifting to a subordinate discourse, there may be times when it becomes the least undesirable course to take. It is this tacking back and forth across and between traditions and within strands of a single tradition that provides the tensions and the material required for intellectual growth and realistic levels of autonomy within traditions. Pragmatism contextualizes autonomy and brings it down to earth around specific projects. The autonomous person operates from within a tradition, using part of it to gain critical distance on other parts of it.

Tradition and Inquiry

Pragmatism allows priority to be given to the resources provided by one's native tradition but also allows the possibility that the resources of any single tradition will not be adequate to all moral concerns. The best analogy would be the way in which one's native language provides a remarkable tool for engaging with the world as a foundation for complex cooperative activity. There are, however, limits to what can be expressed through one's own natural language, and some experiences may be better expressed through alternative natural or artificial languages. Thus, almost as important as mastering the resources provided by "one" tradition is the suppleness needed to recognize the limits of that tradition and to draw on nontraditional resources. One of the tests of a sound moral education is how well it transmits the resources of a given tradition and the suppleness required to augment it when needed.

Catholic Tradition and Moral Growth

Catholic moral pedagogy can be categorized into five stages of intellectual and religious development. The first stage is obedience and rule following. This stage requires that the language of the religion be understood and appropriated in the approved way. To say, for example, "Jesus wants you to attend Mass," provokes an act, not a question. You listen, and you then attend Mass. In this stage rituals are practiced and rules are followed without the need to give reasons or provide alternatives.

The second stage is apology. In this stage there is an awareness of the possibility of challenge and disagreement. Students learn the standard justifications and reasons for certain rituals and rules, and learn to repeat them on appropriate occasions. Here they are trained to be "lawyers" for the faith. They learn the official position; they are taught to anticipate standard objections and then may rehearse the "proper" responses to them.

The third stage is casuistry, where the rules are taken and applied to new and difficult cases. Casuistry allows for the application of religious principles to new cases but within the constraints of established tradition. To engage in casuist reasoning is at one and the same time to acknowledge the possibility of unanticipated moral issues and to affirm that their resolution will be found in the proper application of established religious principles.

The fourth stage is theology, where conflicts in principles and justification are systematized and where tensions within doctrine are addressed. The aim of theology is not to question the faith but to strengthen it by, among other things, addressing varying interpretations of doctrine and evaluating their merits.

A fifth stage is philosophy, where commitments are temporarily bracketed in order to evaluate competing claims and justifications in terms that do not necessarily require a prior commitment to the faith. In this stage there is an attempt to bind moral decision making to assumptions that are shared by a wide number of people who hold a variety of religious and nonreligious beliefs.[6] Philosophy is at some levels a highly abstract, technical activity, but at another level anyone who has ever stepped back, acknowledged his or her own framework, and considered the merits of alternative ones is engaged in a philosophical enterprise. This might occur in a classroom, in a therapy session, or in a meaningful encounter with a friend. It may occur to a newly married couple when a strain in their relationship causes them to rethink their basic relationship with their parents and decide how marriage provides new and different obligations and duties. This may not be laid out in the disciplined discursive way in which a philosopher might discuss the moral responsibilities of a child to a parent and a husband to a wife, but the impulse is similar—to make the familiar strange in order to reevaluate its merits.

A *framework* identifies the operational assumptions that we normally appropriate in everyday life to guide moral action, moral deliberation, and moral justification. *Moral novelty* is any experience that serves to stress those assumptions or to draw out a different set of moral sensitivities and intuitions, and to require a critical examination of accepted moral principles.[7] Moral novelty consists of information and experience that do not easily fit inside the frame and are in fact disturbed by it. To acknowledge a morally novel situation requires that a dominant framework be dislodged or bracketed as alternative ones are tried out. This does not always result in a different conclusion, but it will result in a more complex, more nuanced understanding. A premature commitment is one that makes this difficult to do. A moral invention is a new practice introduced to resolve a moral conflict or to address a morally new situation. A successful moral invention resolves older conflicts and opens up new experiential opportunities. It may also modify an existing frame. The change in the Church's position on the practice of usury, which I examine in a later chapter, is an example of a moral invention that modifies, without overthrowing, an existing frame. Moral inventions that overthrow existing frames, such as the change of people's status in France in the late 1700s from subject to citizen and the presumption of equality that accompanied it, comprise a moral revolution.

One important element of a frame is the presumed object of a moral decision—is it the individual, the race, the nation, the human species, all sentient beings, or the planet as a whole. In the abortion debate, which I address below, the assumed object of moral decision is the individual—either the individual woman or the individual fetus. Part of the test of the adequacy of moral education is whether it encourages the recognition of moral novelty and consideration of the inventions that might be required to address it. Below, I look at students' responses to a situation in which the assumption that the individual alone is the object of moral discourse about abortion is strained by a novel situation that is intended to introduce a social cost as well. I then use this situation to analyze the ways in which students use the moral teachings of their religion to respond to it, and to see the extent to which the social cost is acknowledged in their response.

Abortion: Theological and Philosophical Background

When a series of individual acts has ramifications for a large number of other people, they take on a social dimension. When this dimension cannot adequately be addressed through decisions of individuals alone, it calls for a new frame, one that can recognize the collectively unacceptable consequences of the morally "laudatory" acts of individual agents. For example, the way I get to work, whether by bicycle, automobile, bus, or streetcar, is my problem alone until so many of us decide to travel by high-polluting cars that it becomes a social issue. One of the marks of intellectual growth is the ability to recognize just when a shift in a frame is called for and to address issues in terms of more than one dimension. To see things through an "individual" frame, as we often do, means that the problem is seen as located in a "person"—a fetus/child or a woman—rather that an institution, a group, an association, or a community.

The abortion issue comes down to two questions: (1) is abortion moral? and (2) should abortion be made illegal? The Church's answer to the first is that abortion is not moral under any circumstances. It is a grave sin. Most Church officials also believe that abortion should be illegal.[8] However, some believers, many of whom hold that it is immoral, also believe that a person should have a legal right to an abortion, just as they might believe that divorce is immoral but also hold that a person should have a legal right to divorce. They may believe this for different reasons. Some might accept Judith Thompson's[9] argument that we have no obligation to save the life of another in certain circumstances of voluntary dependency. While we may deserve moral disapproval for allowing someone to die simply because saving them is an inconvenience, they may have no *right* to being saved by us. Thus, if your life depends on you being hooked up to my circulatory system for nine months, you could not claim a *right* to be hooked up. And if I choose to allow you to do so, but then change my mind, I may not be a nice person, but I should not be criminally culpable. Similarly, a fetus that is not viable outside of the womb has no *right* to life under this view.

Some others may allow that inconvenience should not be a legal justification for not saving another, but they may still reject the right of a fetus to life on the grounds that a fetus does not yet consciously own the value of its own life, and thus that it does not have the status of a rights-bearing person. And there are still others who would allow a general right to life but hold that there are just too many contingencies for any one rule to bind all pregnant women to the same moral norm. Those who hold this view could allow that in some circumstances taking the life of the fetus, while always regrettable, need not in every case violate a moral norm. People who take this position want to remain open to the possibility of new situations giving rise to new moral intuitions. And there are those who hold with the Catholic theologian Charles Courtney Murray that a good law must be enforceable,[10] or who take a stand similar to the one Aquinas took on prostitution: it is immoral but cannot be stopped, and to do so would create greater evil, so don't ban it—regulate it![11]

While the Church hierarchy often tends to conflate the moral with the legal aspects of the issue, for example by threatening to deny communion to politicians who support abortion rights, many Catholics accept the distinction between the moral and the legal statuses of abortion and then try, through adoption and other means, to reduce the number of abortions. And, as McBrien notes in his exhaustive treatise on Catholicism, "In a pluralist society, where consensus on such issues does not exist, only the path of political compromise is possible, St. Thomas Aquinas said as much over seven hundred years ago."[12]

Tensions in the Church's Stance   The Church's stance against abortion is closely linked to its stance on other matters, including its rejection of capital punishment and "artificial" forms of birth control. The Church holds that there is but one seamless garment of life, and that it has a sacred responsibility to affirm life in all of its manifestations. It thus works against capital punishment and war. It advances positions on social justice and workers' rights, and, of course, its teachings include strong positions against most forms of birth control and all intentional abortions. In its attempt to hold all of these expressions of life together, there are tensions. Consider, for example, the relation between the ban on birth control and the ban on abortion.

The official position on abortion is closely related to, but distinguishable from, the Church's position on birth control.[13] Both are prohibited as a violation of the "seamless garment of life."[14] However, there are important doctrinal differences in the justifications that are given for the different practices. In the case of contraception, it is the attempt on the part of a conjugal couple to prevent the formation of life that is objectionable.[15] Prohibitions against contraception are based on the view that God intended sexual intercourse to occur only in marriage and that sexual intercourse within marriage should always be open to the possibility of procreation.

Abortion, however, is seen in the same light as killing and is more directly related to the biblical command "Thou shalt not kill." Some Catholic theorists believe that the Church made a major tactical mistake when, in 1968, Pope Paul VI rejected the advice of his own commission to liberalize birth control policy.[16] They believe that this decision precipitated many Catholics leaving the Church and left many others little practical option but to disobey the Church's teachings. It is also likely that linking birth control and abortion in this way may have had the effect of loosening the attitude of many Catholics toward abortion. The Church's response is that both are wrong and that it has an obligation to protect life, regardless of the consequences to itself.[17] However, it would seem that the Church's prohibition against abortion is arguably stronger on religious grounds than its prohibition against birth control. Whereas the latter results from an *intent* not to allow a life to form and therefore is an interference with that which God *may* want, the latter is an interference with that which "we know" God *does want*—an already formed life. "Do not kill" would seem to be a stronger injunction than "Do not prevent conception."

The official Church position holds that the fetus is a living person and that it is covered by the prohibition against killing established by the Ten Commandments. Although the catechism still allows for "mercy," "willed" abortion and cooperation in aiding abortion are excommunicable offences.[18] Here the Church makes an important and nuanced distinction. While there are times when it may be permissible to do something that knowingly (but indirectly and without intending it) causes the fetus to die, it is not permissible to aim at the death of the fetus.

As mentioned above, the question of the legality of abortion is somewhat separable conceptually from the issue of its morality. While conservative Catholics will argue that all Catholics must work for making abortions illegal, more liberal ones, following the thought of the American theologian

Murray, allow that a "good law must be enforceable" and that "no group can impose its moral views on others through force or coercion."[19]

The stand against birth control, and to a lesser extent abortion, has not been a popular one,[20] and many practicing Catholics ignore it. Yet devout Catholics do take it seriously and will try to follow it. For those who fail, contrition, confession, and repentance may allow them to reenter the community, but these are not easy tests, and deep sincerity and regret are required—attitudes that ultimately only God can fully appreciate.

The stance of the Church, then, gives a discursive advantage to certain ways of viewing the problem, while other standpoints will have difficulty gaining legitimacy. For example, the Church addresses abortion as a matter of individual (as opposed to social) morality where the right decision is to choose as God would want us to choose. And God always wants us to choose life. Moreover, in so choosing, life always trumps other goals such as career advancement, equality, and even longevity and economic well-being. And God does not want us to measure the value of one life against that of another. An old person's life is no less valuable than a young person's, and a fetus's life is equal to the life of an already born child.

These rules set the stage for the discursive priorities that are promoted in discussions about abortion. There are interesting gray areas that arise. For example, at least one officially approved textbook provides that in cases of rape, medical personnel are allowed to do everything possible to prevent conception.[21] This position seems, at least on the surface, at odds with the Church's prohibition on contraception, but its approval suggest that in a pinch, the "Do not kill" rule takes priority over the "Do not prohibit conception" rule.

Abortion and Autonomy   Choice and autonomy are related,[22] but speaking from an official Catholic standpoint, to be against a right to choose abortion need not be seen as a blow to a woman's autonomy, properly understood. Rather, it is a conflict of rights—that of a woman to live *as she wants* and that of a fetus to live. However, there is a hierarchy of rights, and a right to live *as one wants*, according to the Church, is less defensible than a right not to be deliberately killed. Yet just how people think about the abortion issue—whether they simply allow the official Church councils to decide the matter for them, whether they understand the reasons employed, or whether they can apply the reasons to difficult cases and take into account reasoned objections—is a sign of their level of critical reflection and hence of autonomy. The Church wants people to follow its lead on abortion regardless of how well they understand its reasons, but it prizes those who do so after having considered the matter carefully and whose rationally *informed* conscience lines up with the Church's point of view.

The Church values autonomy, and this is expressed in the importance that it places on conscience. However, it is not free-floating autonomy that it values but rather autonomy formed through its relation to the religious tradition. This is expressed in its view that a well-formed conscience is one that is informed by Church doctrine. Indeed, from the Church's point of view, people can be as much enslaved by blindly following their passions as they can by following mindless routine. Religious traditions serve to preserve avenues of stable decision in situations where reason "threatens" to be overrun by passion. They provide young people with a codification of centuries of moral reasoning, together with a communal, rational, and aesthetic structure that helps motivate students in ways that abstract argument alone rarely can.[23]

Moral Novelty Modernity often calls for new responses and different understandings, and in the process of thinking through those responses, our collective moral understanding grows.[24] Moral knowledge is like scientific knowledge in at least one important respect—our collective moral understanding must accommodate new data and develop new understandings and modes of perceiving. Consider the following:

1. Discoveries in technology test our ideas about what is right and wrong. Now that doctors can keep the heart beating and the lungs breathing, even when a person is otherwise brain-dead, we are called upon to reexamine our understanding of killing.
2. New discoveries about human biology, and the possibility that sexual orientation is hard-wired, sorely test certain religious ideas about heterosexuality as natural and homosexuality as abnormal.
3. New trends in the workplace have contributed to the invention of new moral concepts. For example, sexual harassment, a concept that did not exist prior to the 1970s, was developed in response to women entering the workforce, but with it a new moral and legal discourse has been applied to gender relations in the home as well.[25]
4. New technologies test the limits of well-worn moral concepts. The ethical issues involved in the allocation of scarce organs require that we rethink the value of life and the meaning of human equality.

Students and the Abortion Issue This part of the study took place in the Catholic Center of a large public university. The center served both as a source for spiritual learning and renewal for Catholic students throughout the university, and as a dormitory for many who wanted to incorporate Catholic worship and values into their everyday lives. All of the students we interviewed who lived in this dorm mentioned the importance of religion as one of the reasons for doing so, and all supported the Church's stance on abortion.

We interviewed students who were recommended to us either by the priest[26] who directed the spiritual activities of the dorm or by the students he recommended. In addition, we interviewed other students who did not live in the Catholic dorm but who had graduated from Dillon. The report on the interviews is intended to be illustrative of different modes of moral reasoning among students educated in the Catholic tradition and is not intended as representative of how students educated within the Catholic tradition in general think about moral issues.

In our interviews with the dormitory students, we presented an example that complicated the framework on abortion that takes the individual fetus as the object of moral choice, and we pushed very hard on the social costs. We use the responses to help draw out some of the factors that distinguish levels of reflective growth within a tradition. The example was drawn about the effects of the disease thalassemia on the population of Cyprus. It was presented as follows:

a. Your spouse has a genetic condition, which involves living with a severe form of anemia called thalassemia. This means that your spouse's body does not make enough hemoglobin. Because of this, the bone marrow cannot produce enough red blood cells. The red blood cells that are produced are nearly empty. The bones are slightly deformed, the spleen is larger than normal, and people with this disease have many kidney problems. They have had to have blood transfusions every three weeks to survive as long as they have. Any children you and your spouse would have are likely to either suffer from the same problems or have a minor case of anemia and pass the gene for thalassemia onto their offspring.

b. You have the same version of thalassemia.

c. Your spouse and yourself recently became pregnant.

d. Given your spouse's and your own genetic makeup, there is a one hundred percent chance your baby will have the same severe sort of thalassemia that you and your spouse suffer from.

e. You are a citizen of Cyprus living in the capital of Nicosia.

f. You and your spouse are unable to seek treatment outside of Cyprus or from private treatment centers on Cyprus.

g. Cyprus does not have enough funds in their medical budget to treat patients with thalassemia. In fact, in five years, Cyprus will not be able to continue to provide blood transfusions for more than the 620 people on Cyprus who currently suffer from the severe form of thalassemia, As a result, Cyprus' government has started screening pregnancies and requiring prenatal blood tests.

h. Doctors are recommending that pregnant women whose fetuses have the severe sort of thalassemia that you and your spouse have obtain an abortion.

i. The Greek Orthodox Church has approved such abortions.[27]

j. You are a Roman Catholic.

1. Will you bear the child, given the great probability that he or she will die by the age of five because she or he will be unable to obtain a blood transfusion?

2. What do you think other Cypriots who are in the same situation but are not Roman Catholics should do?

In a-f we establish the problem and the constraints for the couple. In g the social costs are presented—that Cyprus will not be able to afford transfusions—with the implication that present sufferers will bear the cost in increased pain and shortened life if the present rate of births continues. In h and i we allow expert authority to enter in as a way to see the extent to which it will be acknowledged. In h expert opinion advises the couples to have an abortion, and i provides a religious opinion allowing it. The decision we ask the student to make is formulated in j. What will you do, and what do you believe others should do? This second part of j is important because it could prompt the distinction to be made between what is moral and what should be legal.

I have divided the responses to this question in terms of the complexity of considerations that are acknowledged by the students. The responses allow us to model the levels of discourse apology, casuistry, and theology/philosophy, and to see how they function to open up a dominant mode of discourse to greater complexity. We will also see in these students that there is difficulty in broadening the frame from the individual triadic of child/fetus, wife, and husband to one that can appropriate the social consequences of individually motivated decisions.

Apology Tracy comes from an upper-middle-class suburb where she, like the others in the study, attended a coeducational Catholic high school. She is now a senior at the university majoring in art. She expresses strong emotional attachment to the Church, although in fact her understanding of Catholic doctrine is limited. In her responses to the thalassemia example, her answers were simple and largely reiterated the rules. She restated the thalassemia case as if it were simply a routine question of contraception or abortion, and she then recites the rule and the Church's alternative form of "birth control."

When you're in Catholicism, you don't practice any kind of birth control or contraception because it's a barrier between your body and your spouse's body. You're not fully open to life so what they practice is called *NFP*, natural family planning. . . . With this thing that is happening in Cyprus . . . if you give birth to a child who has these deformities and people say, "What if you know they are not going to live past three years old?"—well, I would say, "Who are you to say that they should not give someone love for three years of their life?" . . . They are still a child of God. Now because these children might still have these problems—they can still know love. I mean, they can still know the feeling of being loved, and other people can know the feeling of love by sacrificing their time to help these children.

Tracy did not mention the well-being of yet-to-be conceived children or the fate of those who already suffer from thalassemia and who could be denied treatment as the population grows. Instead, she fits the problem into a familiar framework where two people are making a decision about their own future and the future of a yet-to-be-born child. In doing so, she fails to recognize the novelty of the situation and thereby to allow additional moral considerations to be expressed.

Apology has a role to play when circumstances are normal and religious principles are not strained by situations that could give rise to strong counterintuitions. "A fetus is a human life and killing such a life is forbidden; abortion is the killing of a human life; therefore, abortion, is forbidden." Yet circumstances are not always normal, and sometimes, as in the thalassemia case, moral intuitions are potentially strained—pulled in different directions. Tracy is only able to address the thalassemia case by denying its complexities and by placing it into a deductive framework where apology works. She does not consider the fact that by following the "Do not kill" rule, others who are equally innocent could die. Nor does she consider cases of killing that the Church allows, for example in war and, under certain circumstances, the killing of innocent civilians. Instead her own relation with a beloved retarded older sibling takes over the narrative, and she ponders the empty place that would have occupied her family had they chosen to abort her sister.

Technically, of course, she applies the rule correctly. The Church rejects the idea that one person should be sacrificed for the benefit of another, and the Church does see the fetus as a person. However, by failing to acknowledge the social dimension, she also blocks other possible remedies from consideration.

Casuistry Casuistry takes over where apology leaves off, allowing conflicting intuitions to surface while providing intellectual resources to resolve them. Although Tracy does not say why Church doctrine requires that the unborn be spared even when the result is to condemn others, her dorm mate, Larry, fixes the problem in a broader theoretical context bringing in the Church's principle of *double effect*. He tells us that the principle involves situations where "two effects follow, one good and one evil, from an essentially good or at least morally neutral act. If the evil effect is unintended and not a direct result of the act, and if the good effect is proportionate to the evil effect, the act itself is morally legitimate."[28] Given this principle, Larry is able to acknowledge that conflicting intuitions are at work here and to draw on a more complex algorithm for addressing them.

While Larry rejects abortion as a legitimate alternative, he acknowledges difficult cases such as rape, where he tells us that the proper response is not abortion but community aid and cites examples where a diocese has established homes for women who are too poor to care for their babies. To be pro-life is not just to be anti-abortion, in his eyes; it is to help create a situation where abortion is not a desired option. Unlike Tracy, who fails to acknowledge that thalassemia is not your-run-of-the-mill abortion case, and who thereby solves it through the application of the "Do not kill" rule, Larry is willing to tackle what he considers difficult cases and explain to us how the doctrine of double effect applies. Without any prodding from the interviewer, he develops his own example, ectopic pregnancy, to illustrate the principle.

He explains that in this kind of pregnancy, the zygote implants itself in the fallopian tube, and an operation is performed to save the life of the mother, but the operation inevitably must result in aborting the zygote. He tells us that such an operation is permissible since the aborting of the zygote is not the intended reason for the operation but only a necessary consequence of it. Yet when the thalassemia case is presented to him, he appropriates the same deductive strategy as Tracy where the moral alternative is clear and counterintuitions are blocked out.

He begins by rehearsing the acceptable options to abortion, saying, "You can abstain and try adoption if you are a married couple," and "There's always the option of appealing to others for charity." When he addresses the financial reasons, it is still in terms of the impact on the family. He tells us, "If you're not going to break the bank on it, I'd probably go with the natural family planning thing, but not with contraceptives. Marriage to be valid has to be open to sex" (he may mean procreation here). We push him a bit on the Greek Orthodox Church, expecting that he might see the gravity of the issue in social terms here; but he deflects the question, dismissing the response of the Orthodox Church as bending to political pressure.

> Interviewer: Can you see any reason why the Greek Orthodoxy . . .
> Larry: I think it might have been partially a political thing in that case. I don't know for sure.

The issue was pressed in order to prompt him to acknowledge the social cost:

> I: They didn't have the resources for the blood transfusions, and the babies would die.

He responds in a formulaic way that there is a difference between letting somebody die and killing somebody.

Then, when we explicitly point out the social consequences of his decision, he responds by "plead(ing) the Fifth" and telling us that he will need to consult his priest.

Larry's strength is also his weakness, and suggests the limits of casuistry. Taking the Church's stance against abortion as his major constraint, he is open to difficult cases, and together these lead him to seek out creative solutions. His more sophisticated understanding of Catholic principles allows him to initiate more complex examples. He has obviously thought about the Church's principles, and he tells us that he finds the Church's concern for consistency an important part of its appeal. He volunteers that he believes that the death penalty is as much a violation of the teachings of the Church as is abortion. Given the appeal of consistency, it is understandable that he places his own sympathies for the victims of rape under greater scrutiny and thus seeks alternatives that are consistent with both mercy and the Church's views on killing a fetus.

Moreover, he understands the limits of his own knowledge and is willing to seek the advice of people who spend their lives thinking about moral issues. Thus, when he says he is going to speak to a priest, he does not just mean any priest. The one he has in mind has studied in Rome and is a recognized authority on Catholic morality. Yet he never tells us exactly why he finds the problem so difficult, but it seems clear that he fears, perhaps instinctively, that were he to acknowledge that there is a social frame that is relevant here, his appeal to personal, Church-defined morality would be at risk.

Yet if Larry illustrates a strong grasp of Catholic principles, he has overgeneralized the situations in which they are normally applied in discussions of sexuality. Larry's response is incomplete because he has not yet removed the scaffolding that binds him to one set of circumstances and limits a more open and flexible response.

Philosophy While Larry displayed an ample knowledge of Catholic doctrine, his response did not suggest an awareness of other points of view or a sense of the arguments that might be brought on their behalf. Linda has taken philosophy with a professor who has offered strong arguments in favor of both abortion as well as euthanasia, a practice that the Church also opposes, and unlike the other students, she addresses opposing arguments that hold that it is not just life itself that is important, but also the pleasure that we can derive from life—the quality of life.

When the thalassemia case is presented, she responds, "I took a class, Introduction to Mental Retardation, and this is one of the questions we dealt with. Obviously not this exact question, but if you know your baby is going to be born severely retarded, should abortion be allowed, maybe even encouraged?"

Her way of framing the question and the distinction that she makes between allowing and encouraging abortion suggest a reasonable awareness of some of the arguments that are made by advocates of abortion and a willingness to address them. She then tells us,

> How can I know anyone else's quality or what their quality of life is going to be, and does that even matter? Does it matter whether I am going to have a good life or a bad life? It's my life, you know. . . . No one has a crystal ball and even if they did, you know even if they knew I was going to be born with a severe form of anemia and suffer my whole life, you know suffer physical pain. You just don't know what that means—that it won't serve a purpose, that doesn't mean that I won't contribute some good. Every life has value, such value that no one can take it away. . . . Who knows what cures are going to be out there? Who knows what the future holds? To deprive someone of being born, that's playing God.

Linda then talks about her class with Professor M and the argument that she used to support her position.

> I wrote a paper on the morality of abortion with Professor M. Awesome class. He's a great teacher. We completely disagree on just about everything, and I can honestly say that's one of the best classes I ever took here. I think he's a great teacher. For my final paper, what I basically said was "Okay. You've convinced me: I'm pro-choice now, but only, you know, up to the first two weeks because after that the baby's got a heartbeat," [but yes] it is still part of the woman [as you say.] "So, OK I will allow it up to the first three months." And it basically went on and so forth

> justifying it to the point where you could kill anyone you wanted. Because if I allow you to kill this fetus, you know it's in its most dependent stage: weak and helpless. So if I allow you to kill that, you know we are supposed to be protecting because it can't do anything for itself—like, why can't you just go and kill anyone? [Brackets mine for clarity]

Linda is aware of and able to address a strong counterargument that comes from a different and quite antagonistic tradition. She is able to counter a "quality of life argument" with the "sanctity of life argument" and to bolster that with an appeal to uncertainty and to arguments that appeal to the intrinsic value of life, its value as such, and its potential extrinsic value—the chance that we can all make a contribution. And finally, there is the logic of the slippery slope—start with the two-week-old fetus, and where do you end? Yet for all her sophistication, Linda too avoids putting the problem into a social frame. When she says the two problems are not exactly alike, she is quite right, but then she proceeds to treat them as if they were exactly the same. She is asked to solve for X *and* Y but she, without realizing it, only solves for X while ignoring Y.

There is considerable internal development from one student to the other as they move from Tracy's apologetic mode to Linda's philosophical response. Yet none of the three students acknowledges the social dimension of the problem, approaching it exclusively through an individual framework. Interestingly, none distinguished between the moral and the legal obligation, assuming perhaps that by responding to the one, they were also responding to the other.

The next interview was conducted with an advanced graduate student in law, a devout believer who had previously studied Catholic theology and philosophy. Interestingly, his initial response, while more complete than that of the other students, also initially missed the social dimension, acknowledging it only when it was explicitly pointed out. He was asked to specifically address the social consequences of his decision not to abort. He responded,[29]

> Even assuming that the decision not to abort fetuses with thalassemia would hasten the deaths of those currently suffering from the disease, abortion still would not be morally permissible. For one thing, Catholic moral theology teaches that one may never do evil to bring about something good (or, by extension, to prevent some further evil). Because abortion is categorically wrong, it is not a morally acceptable option, even if performing more abortions would save the lives of others.

Like Linda, he too indicates an awareness of more consequentialist positions and actually appropriates them to support his case while at the same time marking them with statements like "this is only a peripheral consideration" to indicate that they are not the telling considerations for Catholics like him.

> In addition—though this is only a peripheral consideration—it would appear that, given the scarcity of the resources in question, the benefit of aborting fetuses to those currently living with thalassemia may well be marginal at best. That is, the facts of the hypothetical seem to indicate that it is only a matter of time before the blood necessary for transfusions disappears. Although the blood supply may last somewhat longer if fetuses with the condition are aborted, it is not clear how much longer the lives of those currently living with thalassemia would be extended. To be sure, utilitarian considerations of this sort are alien to Catholic moral theology. Still, given the moral difficulty of the situation, a believer might find such a factor to be reassuring (if indeed it is true that the benefit to be gained by aborting the fetuses is only marginal at best).

> Finally, aside from (and perhaps not entirely consistent with) the abstract moral and theological principles involved, a believer's position on the issue might be informed more generally by some of the basic intuitions embedded in the Christian worldview. Although these intuitions are difficult to articulate, they might be stated as follows: all life is precious. When a child is conceived, it is not an accident. Rather, it is as though God has called *this* particular creature into being. It simply cannot be God's will that this wondrous process once begun should now be abruptly stopped. It may be that the lives of other, currently living human beings will be shortened as a result of this child's life. But these people have already had an opportunity to live. And at some point, we all must die. Indeed, Christianity teaches that salvation requires loosening one's attachments to this world and this life. Although it would be a mistake to try to weigh the value of one life against another, it makes some sense to think that those already having enjoyed the benefit of life must yield to those who have yet to do so—even if the child will not live long enough to appreciate life in the fullest sense.

> As to the legal dimension of the issue, I would support legislation making abortion in Cyprus illegal. From the Church's perspective,

abortion is murder. Hence, a law banning abortion is essentially no different from a law banning murder. Of course, there is a much greater degree of moral disagreement in our society about abortion than there is about murder. But the current situation is not very different from that obtaining during the 19th century in connection with the moral/legal status of slavery. The fundamental issue in each case had to do with whether or not a certain class of beings were to be regarded as persons. Regardless of the deep social divisions around the issue and the political upheaval resulting from the abolition of slavery, abolitionists were correct in believing that African-Americans were persons in the full sense and thus that slavery should be outlawed. In the same way, current day opponents of abortion are justified in trying to overturn laws allowing abortion, notwithstanding the disagreement over the issue.

I then asked, "What do you think other Cypriots who are in the same situation, but are not Roman Catholics, should do?"

As a Catholic, I view the Church's teachings as universally as true. While there is some room for relativity with regard to minor issues of practice and doctrine (e.g., whether fasting is required on particular occasions, perhaps even priestly celibacy), the Church's moral teachings are categorically true: they apply to everyone, Catholic and non-Catholic, theist and atheist alike. As mentioned above, moreover, the Church has taken pains to consistently underscore the absoluteness of its teaching on abortion: under no circumstances is it allowed. Thus, while I sympathize with their plight, I do not believe Cypriots who face a significant likelihood (or even a certainty) of having a child with thalassemia may resort to abortion.

However, there is an element of theological flexibility that this respondent finds in the primacy of the individual conscience, a factor which the other student respondents did not appeal to and which allows some softening of the judgment but not its legal consequences.

At the same time, the Church teaches that all persons are bound to follow their consciences. Thus, if a person, after searching his or her heart, believes that abortion is a truly moral course of action, he or she must do so. Such a person's action is objectively still a grave sin. But the person's subjective level of culpability may be mitigated, or even removed entirely, under the circumstances.

The majority of Catholics in the United States might well reject the absolutism of this position, even without the dire situation facing Cyprus. As one graduate of Dillon told us without being presented with the thalassemia example, she changed her mind after realizing that women were not going to stop having abortions and so she wants to make them as safe as possible. She did not take on this position lightly and came to it only after an assignment in one of her college classes required her to find research in favor of a position that she does not agree with. Her research turned her mind, and while she still has moral reservations, she believes that a safe abortion is at times the best of the bad alternatives. Her reservations did not, however, spontaneously extend to some of the larger *social* issues regarding abortion, such as overpopulation.

For many people the official Church position blocks out too many of our strongest moral intuitions arbitrarily and does not allow the nuances required when a single tradition cannot satisfy our best judgment. Even the doctrine of double effect, while sounding quite sophisticated, clearly has problems. If it is allowable to let the fetus die while an attempt is made to save the mother, why is it not also allowable to let the fetus die as we work to save the population of Cyprus from the scourge of thalassemia? While we would know that the fetus would die, we would not intend it to do so, but it would be an unintended effect of attempts to save the larger population. Of course, this will not satisfy either side. It will satisfy neither the Church hierarchy who would seek to limit the application of the doctrine of double effect to the narrowest situation nor those who want a very liberal policy on abortion, where the decision need not depend on a life for a life but on the desire of a woman not to have a baby.

Yet this is a different issue and it depends in part on whether (as the Church would have it) all life is of equal worth at each and every stage of its development or whether there is a considerable difference in, say, the worth of a fetus that may be no larger than a thumbnail and does not have a developed nervous system and the worth of a born child. The point of this discussion is not to settle that question but rather to see how growth within a tradition can accommodate alternative frameworks that seem to stretch the tradition beyond its bounds. My own view is that the doctrine of double effect may be open and vague enough to provide the material that would be required to address the Cyprus problem, but that it is an extremely awkward tool and one that the Church would not likely employ for this purpose at this time. The doctrine of conscience that our last respondent employs could perhaps do some of the work that is required to acknowledge the social consequences in cases like thalassemia as well the severity of the individual hardships. However, to those not raised in this tradition, a clear conscience may be valued less than a record free of criminal conviction.

The difficulty that most of these respondents have in acknowledging the social dimension of the issue clearly handicaps them in responding to a morally novel situation. The Greek Orthodox Church, with similar prohibitions against abortion, was not in a position to take this as just an abstract academic exercise and did have to confront the social costs of its stance. By acknowledging the effects to Cyprus as a whole, it was able to come up with a resolution of sorts that involved strict genetic counseling for any couple married by the Church and strong counsel against the marriage of two carriers.[30] Whether or not this is the ideal solution is not the point. The point is that any adequate resolution cannot disregard the moral novelty and the need to appropriate unfamiliar frameworks in order to invent a morally acceptable remedy.

Moral Intuitions and Intellectual Growth Intellectual and moral development are the results of an interactive process, one that seeks, in philosopher John Rawls's terms, a "reflective equilibrium" between our moral theory and our moral intuitions. If moral growth is to occur, it is important to maintain a dialogical balance between the two. Moral intuitions provide the material that enables us to respond to each other and the subjective foundations for systems of aid, affection, and mutuality. Moral theory orders these intuitions, gives us reason to act on one rather than another should they conflict in certain situations, and provides the larger principles that allow us to understand and to justify action. To paraphrase the philosopher Immanuel Kant, moral intuition without theory is chaotic, and moral theory without intuition is bloodless and calculating. One speaks the case for mercy, and the other for justice; moral growth requires both.

The earlier student respondents relied on an appeal to the interviewer's moral intuitions, but in making this appeal they were unable to address the social fallout of their positions. One student asked us to step into the shoes of her retarded sister. Another likened it to killing the weakest and most vulnerable. The problem is that other intuitions, such as those that take account of the pain and suffering of the yet-to-be born as well as the reduction in the quality of life of thalassemia patients already born, do not surface easily for these students.

The law student did address the issue of suffering head on:

> It is important here, as in all things, to prayerfully consider the broader ways in which God's providence may be at work. One can always hope that a cure might be found during the child's lifetime. One must also remain open to the possibility of a miracle

(e.g., the child's condition spontaneously disappears, as some-times happens in the case of individuals who, though born blind or deaf, gain the ability to see or hear). More importantly—and more realistically—part of Christianity's central message is the salvific value of suffering. Although it is difficult to understand why or how, we often become "better" through suffering, and good things more generally often come from bad ones. I believe that this child is a gift from God. I will cherish it, even it if lasts but a short time. And I know that after its short life, the child will be with God, and that all of us will be united in the hereafter.

Suffering confronts our moral intuitions directly, and it is easy to think that his words about the salvific value of suffering might serve to comfort a parent who has just lost a child. Yet it seems almost to add to the pain of someone who has to decide whether to have a child who will suffer pain throughout her brief life, and whose very birth will add to the suffering and the pain of those already born. It seems that the natural law tradition where everything has an assigned Godly purpose, if judged strictly on psychological grounds, might work very nicely in the former case. If we know our suffering serves a purpose that we identify with—be it the worth of our group or even the life of a stranger—we endure. Purpose mitigates pain and allows us to go on.

And yet, in the case of thalassemia, it seems as if the comfort that flows from the idea of God's purpose that grounds natural law theory has gone amuck. We are not trying to endure a pain already present but to determine whether to bring into being a life that could know little but suffering and whose very existence would necessarily add to the suffering of others. The tradition that may serve us well in helping to endure the suffering does less well in helping us to decide whether to add to the suffering in the world.

It might be objected that this example of the limits of growth within a tradition assumes that utilitarian intuitions based on some summation of pleasure or happiness trump natural law tradition, one that takes conforming to the will of God as the essence of goodness. Putting aside the problem in deciphering just what it is that God wills in any given instance, one need not travel all the way down the road of utilitarianism to see that there is a certain everyday agreement to assigning more value to the life of a child than to the life of a fetus. The numbers of fetuses that are aborted unintentionally greatly exceeds the number of those that are intentionally aborted. And yet even the strongest opponent of abortion seems unwilling to suggest that we shift research and medical funds away from addressing the problems of the newly born in order to save the lives of the smallest zygote.

If the life of a born child and that of an unborn fetus were of equal value, we should want to spend as much time, research, and money attempting to save the life of every future fetus in danger of a natural abortion as we would to save the life of every child in danger from hunger, poverty, war, and disease. The fact that we do not spend equal funding to protect an unborn fetus from a natural abortion as we do to protect the born child suggests that we do not give equal weight to the born and the unborn. In ideal circumstances perhaps we should, but moral decisions are usually made in less-than-ideal circumstances where resources are scarce and where critical choices must be made. The moral intuitions that make the thalassemia issue such a potential problem for normal Catholic moral theory are the same ones that find reason to spend a great amount of resources on finding ways to save the life of a child but much less on research intended to find ways to prevent the natural abortion of a fetus.[31]

Pragmatism and Moral Growth   The pragmatist may be less concerned with finding *the* "right" answer to a problem that has so many sides, and is more concerned with finding a process that can allow a range of moral intuitions to be expressed. To the pragmatist the social costs of thalassemia cannot be ignored, but neither can the emotions and solidarity that have been vested in a religious tradition. While a pragmatic response would aim to reduce to zero the number of new cases of thalassemia, it would work also to reduce the number of abortions required to reach this goal, using genetic counseling and state aid for adoption just as the Greek Orthodox Church has done. The pragmatist would see the value that a belief in God's ultimate purpose could serve in helping someone with the disease cope. At the same time the pragmatist might well ask, engaging a religious discursive framework, that the Church should allow that we know very little of God's intent when it comes to the question of whether to bring a suffering child into this world. For the pragmatist the acknowledgment of ignorance about ultimate matters is a critical component of moral and intellectual development, and serves as a condition of autonomy for all of us. For those believers who would find abortion under any circumstances unacceptable, the pragmatist could ask that the Church reconsider its seamless garment argument. At the very least it might distinguish, as mentioned earlier, between contraception which from the Church's view is not allowing a life that God *may* want to come into being, on the one hand, from stopping the development of a life that has already started, on the other hand. While this would not satisfy those who believe that there should be a right to abortion, it would at least allow contraceptive devices to be used by devout believers.

Religion as More than Principles and Rational Arguments   In the last analysis, religion and religious education have to do as much with connections and relationships as they do with abstract principles and fine-grained moral arguments. Students often graduate from Catholic schools valuing their education and feeling great fidelity with their religion, yet they do not always agree with all of its basic teachings. Consistency is not as important to everyone as it is to Larry. We need to look at these cases as well—at people who have decided to grow outside of their religion but who still maintain strong attachments to the people and traditions that comprise it.

Joyce, a graduate of Dillon and the student mentioned earlier who came to accept the idea of abortion, explains the process by which she changed her mind, thus illustrating the tensions that growth outside of the tradition entail. She had once opposed abortion but not any longer. Her mind was changed when she was challenged in a college class to write a paper developing an argument against something she believed in strongly. In the course of researching the paper, her views changed. We begin where she is discussing her concerns at the time of the social cost of the change—a possible alienation from her parents.

J: My mom and dad have both been raised Catholic grade schools, high schools. They went to Catholic college. They go to church every Sunday, and confession. My mom basically, when we talked about abortion, she just completely agrees with the church, and she just thinks abortion should be outlawed completely.

   But I know that the laws are not going to change. Women will always have the right to abort their child in some form, whether it's just with the pill, just the surgical abortion, with both. I just feel like, this is not logically going to happen that abortion's going to be outlawed. I just agree with just the abortion pill.

I: Can I ask you this? When you were of a different mind, do you recall your reasoning? Can you reconstruct your reasoning?

J: It was like abortion was just this thing, like terrible people have abortions. I don't really know that, and I want to say we talked about it a little bit in moral theology. Because we'd watch videos . . . stereotyping abortion to irresponsible mothers and stuff; teenage pregnancies and stuff. It never really got into, for instance, you know, a media studies matter, that we, we kind of talked about that. Different representations of abortion in the media.

And I mean, now it's kind of, like, what they, they kind of like, I don't know. They wanted us to believe at Dillon just never, under any circumstances, to be OK with having an abortion. And now it's just kind of, like, it's not just irresponsible mothers. It's people that were raped or things like that. Now you, like, I've kind of learned, come to understand a little bit more.

At Dillon, it was just kind of "Don't ask questions. This is right; this is wrong." Abortion, you know, you're never to be accepting of abortion. And now it's kind of, like, I'm in the real world; I'm not just living in the Dillon community. Not that I am accepting of abortion at all, but I'm just, I don't know.

I: By not accepting, by saying you're not accepting at all, what is that?

J: Well, I, like, what I believe is, I'm very much pro-life. Like, and I, the only thing is, I am anti-abortion. However, I can understand in circumstances of rape and incest, those type of things, I can understand definitely, like, and I could, I can sympathize with people who are in positions like that. I think it should be OK for them to be able to have abortions. Because, what if they can't support a child? Some people say, then have the baby, give it up for adoption. Some people cannot afford to leave work, whatever. That type of thing, to have a child. And they shouldn't be punished because they were raped, that type of thing. I don't think, so I think it should be only accepted those circumstances.

However, like I said, I don't see an end to, I can't see the government banning abortion. And if they do, I think it'd be disastrous. Because women would be hurting themselves and trying to abort their children, you know, themselves. And it would just be, it would be absolutely disastrous. So I'm just saying I would agree with just RU-486 abortion pill.

The interview shows a great deal of hesitation and discord as Joyce now tries to bring together her conflicting beliefs about abortion. It is not the smooth easy growth that seemed to occur in our earlier respondents as they discussed with ease the reasons for their rejection. Anguish brings confusion, but it also allows for a different strategy for choosing. While still uneasy about abortion, her view that it will never end persuades her to adopt a strategy that minimizes the risks and increases the safety of the woman. She develops a pragmatic solution that allows her to both engage the issue on a practical level—women will always have abortions, so make them as safe as possible by promoting the RU-486 abortion pill and by implicitly establishing a sense of moral priorities in her own mind that places the well-being of the mother first and allows the fetus to have a moral status, as indicated by her continuing hesitation and reservations about abortion—and allow that status to be a graduated one. It is more permissible when it is no bigger than a "grain of rice" than it is later on when it is more developed.

In this process of complexity and change, she is unwilling to abandon her earlier views fully and accept abortion unconditionally. It is acceptable in extreme situations as a last resort, but because it is acceptable at all it should be safe and sure. Yet she and her parents continue their relationship. Her fear of alienation did not materialize. She shared her reasons with them, and she understands some of the factors that are involved in their continuing disagreement, but it remains only disagreement—never reaching the stage of alienation or separation.

Growth comes by reflecting on the way in which her earlier views were formed and on the distortions that, as she remembers them, were used to shape her views. Yet recognizing these distortions does not lead Joyce to reject the value of her Catholic education as a whole, which she reports on very favorably in other places, nor does it lead her to simply abandon a concern about the morality of abortion. Rather, she is willing to draw a distinction that many in the Church reject between what is morally right and what is politically acceptable, which Murray, and perhaps Aquinas before him, advanced many years before she was born. She is also willing to allow that under less-than-normal conditions, we need to recalibrate ideas about what to accept as morally permissible. Her ability to reflect on her formative socialization also allows her to maintain a continuity with her own past, especially through her continuing respect and closeness to her own parents, a respect that is maintained by understanding the depth of their commitment as well as the path that led them to it.

Joyce is forced to moderate her view on abortion because she understands the difficult situations that some women are faced with, and she addresses the issue on this level. She might have considered other dimensions of the problem, such as population growth and environmental depletion—factors that would have allowed for a more social analysis, one that could have addressed issues of overconsumption as well as overpopulation. This was not unusual; graduates had a strong tendency to view issues like birth control or abortion in individual rather than social terms.

Frameworks, Traditions, and Growth

Religious traditions are not uniform, and within them can be found elements (many submerged) that may, given certain concerns, resurface to challenge an officially preferred framework. In the presentation of our informed respondent, the suggestion that conscience may serve to override the subjective aspect of sin provides an example of the way in which a favored framework can be in tension with and even displaced by other elements within the larger historical tradition.

The Roman Catholic Church's stand on birth control, but not abortion, was almost overturned under Pope Paul VI, only to experience a last-minute reprieve engineered by conservative cardinals who convinced the pope that such a reversal would not serve the credibility of the Church very well. Abortion is a more complex matter, but even early Church figures such as Augustine and Aquinas held positions that are different from those that the Church holds today that were based on a different calculation about when the soul entered the fetus. Some modern progressive Catholics have translated these earlier calculations into scientific findings about the development of the fetal nervous system.[32] For students to understand that their own tradition is not closed, and that within it is contained both tensions and resources for engaging novelty, is to allow for the possibility for intellectual growth that continues to respect the authority of the tradition. The question of growth can be best accomplished for the pragmatist by teaching the religious traditions in all of their historical and philosophical richness and by allowing space for submerged voices, voices whose opinions fall outside of the present moral consensus, to be considered, not necessarily as authoritative but as a way to enhance the appreciation of the richness and the resources of the tradition, and to guide action in a more complete but more nuanced way.

CHAPTER 7

Religious Chauvinism and the Democratic Citizen

Much of religious education occurs under the radar of public scrutiny, and as such some religious schools are prone to more extremes than their public school counterparts. When concern is voiced from the outside, it is often over the extremes: the Amish schools that encourage separation, the Christian fundamentalist schools where children are taught that they have a monopoly on salvation, or the Islamic school mentioned in the introduction that prohibits boys and girls to speak to each other, describing it as "conduct that is serious or illegal and is potentially life or health threatening," and that discourages identification with American culture.[1] These schools test the limits of pluralism either because the overt curriculum advances an exclusivist lesson or because it infringes on otherwise reasonable forms of association. They are, thus, the subject of deep legal and political debate about parental and children's rights, state authority, and educational legitimacy. However, most religious schools have an agenda that is generally consistent with the larger social consensus, even while they promote a more palatable form of religious chauvinism.

In this chapter I want to explore the implications of religious chauvinism in more mainstream religious schools, that is, schools in which the overt curriculum teaches neither an exclusivist nor a sexist message and where organized religion is seen as but one element of a lived life, a life that is not seen as diminished by deep associations with people of other religions. In other words these schools' views are part of the pluralist consensus. Yet they operate in a relatively homogeneous climate where some basic assumptions and institutional practices operate unchallenged and where some of these have a direct or indirect influence on how students come to view other religions.

Students are quite naturally taught to be partial to their own religion, and as I have suggested earlier, partiality toward a particular conception of the good and a willingness to reproduce it across generations are conditions of pluralism. They create the plurality that pluralism in the concrete requires. Yet in addition to partiality, pluralism requires a reasonable level of respect for other traditions. In this chapter I look at religious partiality and some of the different ways in which it is expressed in religious schools, and I ask, given the religious homogeneity of faith-based schools, how can those that are committed to both religion and to pluralism advance the one without disadvantaging the other?

The Confusion between Plurality and Pluralism

Political and educational plurality take different forms, and some of these must be distinguished from normative, democratic pluralism. In normative pluralism multiple communities, existing side by side and whose members have equal status regardless of their communal affiliation, are recognized as a desirable social state and promoted both politically and educationally. Mere plurality may exist where one group maintains political, legal, and economic dominance while providing limited rights to other cultural or religious groups. Here rights and obligations are assigned to groups, not to individuals, and groups are expected to police the behavior of their members and are similarly held accountable for them. This describes the status of religious groups under the Ottoman Empire, for example. Another form of plurality assigns a group identity to each person at birth, sets a status hierarchy between groups, restricts interaction between members of different groups, and prohibits mobility from one group to another. Laws prohibiting intermarriage are signs of this kind of plurality.

Education within a plurality is authorized and conducted by and for the group, and the group itself is the object of loyalty. While students must learn the rules of the larger political society, they do so with the expectation that they will obey them rather than with the expectation that they will engage in deliberations to evaluate or change them. And because of this limited expectation, they are not expected to develop loyalty to anything but their own primary group. Here there is a mutual indifference. Members of primary groups are indifferent to the quality of the larger society except insofar as it affects them, and the larger society is indifferent to the quality and internal practices of primary groups except as they might interrupt the status hierarchy.

In contrast democratic pluralism depends upon internalizing a number of values that extend beyond the immediate group, values that are designed to produce excess loyalty, which can be used to promote the ideals of the larger society, some of which entail the values and practices that sustain the plurality in its democratic form.

In contrast to mere plurality, democratic pluralism is anchored in the individual, not the group, and therefore the boundaries across groups are expected to be reasonably porous.[2] Education is expected to promote the capacity to interact within and across different group formations and, if one chooses, to provide the skills required to exit one formation and enter another. This means that the internal quality of the group is of concern to those outside of it. Opportunities for interaction between members of different groups are a desirable norm for pluralism, and pluralism has an interest in education that enables students to engage with those whose background and beliefs are considerably different than their own. One of these qualities is what Rawls calls "the burden of judgment." This involves a basic assumption about the reasonableness of those with whom we radically disagree. It also entails a willingness to assess our own and other's claims not just in terms of our own well-being but also in terms of the well-being of the larger democratic institutions.[3]

These qualities are furthered by an overall sense that all value systems, including our own, have their limitations, and we must select only a part of "the full range of moral and political values" available.[4] Because equality and stability are conditions for the smooth and just working of democratic pluralism, there must be public acknowledgment of these norms, and thus the commitment of members of different groups to them needs to be transparent. Stability requires not only that I hold these norms but that you hold them as well, and it also requires different levels of knowledge, or transparency. I need to know that you know that I hold them. Transparency is a condition of stability in democratically pluralist societies because there is no single and dominant ethnic or religious group to enforce the rules and because the rules must be a feature of the internal disposition of citizens. This means trust that everyone understands and accepts the basic rules of the plurality itself and the reasons for them is a basic ingredient in pluralism. Transparency is, thus, a condition of stability in democratic pluralism in a way that it is not in other forms of pluralism. Isolation or extreme chauvinism can be a problem for democratic pluralism because it introduces static and distortion in the way in which members of one group perceive the commitment of members of another group to the basic foundation of democratic pluralism, and hence endangers political stability by narrowing one's sense of justice and fairness.

Political stability in a fair and just society is both a condition and a goal of democratic education. As a condition, democratic education requires a reasonably predictable political order where the benefits of education are realistically available to all, where the laws of the society are known and administered fairly, and where each citizen has representation in determining them. As a condition of democracy, education is required to establish the intersubjective understandings, attitudes, and responses needed to sustain the loyalty a democratic system requires. Thus, in contrast to education under mere plurality, education in pluralism extends loyalty beyond the local group and presents ideas of justice and fairness as proper expectations for all members of the society, including those whose beliefs and values are shaped by religious traditions that are considerably different from one's own. One concern about faith-based schools has been that their religiously homogeneous population reduces the value of other groups and places limits on the application of this extended loyalty.

Stability and transparency traditionally have served as justifications for public education. Stability requires that public norms constrain group-centered tendencies and aim at enlarging sympathies beyond the members of one's immediate group.[5] Hence many reformers felt that public schools could reshape group loyalties to coincide with those of a larger national community. It was also felt that as children of one group came into contact with those of another, both hearing the same message, transparency would be established. While formal racial segregation and informal income segregation have hindered efforts to bring children from different groups together as much as reformers might like, have these norms still influence the expectations for public schools, and, while hardly successful, they are considerations in evaluating the success or failure of public education. One of the concerns about religious schools is that they need not be measured against these standards and that they can allow isolation and chauvinism at the expense of pluralism. There is a fear that we can have plurality without pluralism.

To some extent this fear has been mitigated by the ecumenical turn among a number of religions, Catholicism being the most prominent. In the past, children in Catholic schools were expected to memorize large passages from the Baltimore Catechism where Jews were described as Christ killers, Mohammed as a murdering thief, and Protestants as heretics whose only future is eternal damnation.[6] The picture today is quite different, and a spirit of ecumenicalism has been infused in the most recent catechism and in most of the schools themselves. Yet even in the most ecumenical classroom, the homogeneous population can leave certain assumptions and practices unchallenged. In this chapter I look at some of these assumptions, how they are expressed in school practice, and the way in which they can be addressed.

The Prayer on the Anniversary of the World Trade Center Attack

I was at Saint Dillon High School in Mr. P's class on the one-month anniversary of 9/11. At the beginning of every class, P asks a student in his moral theology class to come to the front of the classroom to lead the class in prayer. The student, who has been selected the day before, then reads a section from the Bible, explains why he or she selected the passage, and concludes by leading the class in prayer. On this day a boy reads a section from the Gospel that spoke of the Jews betraying Jesus, and then he followed the reading by explaining that "one month ago some non-Christians took their religion to the extreme and bombed the World Trade Center, killing thousands of Americans." And then he told the class how "we Christians turned around and provided food to their children."

My Response

As he was reading from the original passage, as a Jew I felt uneasy for the first and only time in this class. I thought the idea of Jews as Christ killers had been put to bed by the Second Vatican Council in the early 1960s. However, this uneasy feeling was sublimated as I listened to his explanation and the way in which he had interpreted the conflict as one between forgiving Christians and extremist non-Christians (by which he meant Muslims).

The week passed, and I wondered whether P noticed this episode. I thought that if he had, he might have found it difficult to confront, given that it had occurred during the prayer session, a time that was largely given over to the students. It was still early in the year, and our relationship was still being developed. Nevertheless, when I did bring up the issue, it became clear that my presence in the classroom broke its homogeneity and made a difference in the way P remembered the episode and possibly his subsequent teaching as well.

A Jew in the Classroom

At our next meeting I approached the issue indirectly, asking P whether he viewed the moment of prayer as strictly a religious moment or whether he also saw it as pedagogical,[7] thinking that if it was the former, there would be few venues in which he could intervene, but if the latter, there would be possibilities for intervention.

I do not take notes while a student is reading from the Bible or while a class is praying (I bow my head in respect, but do not say the prayer). I do take notes immediately after, though. In this case this put me at a disadvantage because my ill ease about the comment regarding "non-Christian" extremists bombing the United States replaced my uneasiness about the passage about Jews from the Gospel of John. Thus, even though at the moment I felt uneasy about the reference to Jews, by the time the explanation ended I had subsumed the passage about Jews under that broader heading, *non-Christians*, and then allowed the entire category of non-Christian to be occupied by Islam.

As the days passed before my next meeting with Mr. P, I forgot about the Bible reading and focused instead on the student's commentary and on its implications for Muslims. I was reminded of my original unease only when I returned the next week and spoke about the incident to P, who, as it turns out, had remembered the topic of the Bible reading vividly but had forgotten the commentary that followed. When we probed our partial but complementary memories, it was clear that P's recall was prompted by his concern for me and that my Jewishness had made a difference in what he recalled. I began with the question of whether he saw the moment of prayer as a religious or a pedagogical moment. He responds as folllows:

P: I'd say it's both. I see it more as a religious moment. . . . Now it's interesting that you've mentioned. Last week I was very cognizant of the fact that the kid chose a prayer from John's Gospel when you were in here. And John's Gospel, okay, is the latest of the Gospels. It's written at the time when there had been a split, pretty clear split from Judaism. And so in John's gospel, there's a certain anti-Jewishness in there. . . .

I: Did you comment?

P: I didn't. I was thinking while the kid did it, and I was like, "Should I say something?" But I always try and let them, because they need to, it's like kids need to, you know, "They're going to have their falls before they can walk" kind of thing.

I: That's their moment.

P: Right.

I: Last week I was wondering how you responded, because in his explanation to the prayer, you know, he talked about the World Trade Center. He did it in the context of religion and Christianity and non-Christianity. I wondered, did you have any thoughts on that?

P: Could you refresh me? If you remember what he said, because I don't at this point.

I: Well, basically he said, because it was the anniversary, a month ago some non-Christians took their religion to the extreme and . . .

P: Oh, okay.

I: And of course I, I mean, I'm not Muslim, but you know, I sat there as a non-Christian and had a response. I was wondering whether you picked that up in the same way I did or . . .

P: I remember very clearly being apprehensive because of the reading, and because it being from John.

There are pieces in the Gospel of John where he refers to the Jews being responsible for Christ's death. I'm not sure that I remember hearing what you just said the first time, because I was thinking "Oh, should I say something, you know. I feel bad for Walter."

Mr. P's Response

The episode was more than simply a moment in our relationship, but after the talk Mr. P began to take steps to introduce his students to the views of other religions. He invited a teacher from a Hebrew day school in to teach a class on Judaism to his students, he encouraged his students to attend a visitors' day sponsored by members of a mosque in a nearby town, and he began to view some of the long-standing features of the school in a new and more critical way. In other words, my *Jewish* presence and the opportunity to discuss the incident may have provided the opportunity for P to consider additional ways in which to incorporate other religious perspectives into his teaching.

As time went by, he began to discuss with me other features of Church doctrine that he thought problematic. For example, he criticized as excessively chauvinistic, the doctrine of the anonymous Christian.[8] He said that it belittled the religious beliefs of non-Christians. The doctrine of the anonymous Christian holds that some non-Christians can be saved because unbeknown to either themselves or others, they were really Christians in the eyes of God. To P, this was patronizing because in order for a non-Christian to be saved, it required that they must be mistaken about their own religious identity.

Some weeks after the prayer incident, Mr. P offered to show me something in the small school. One wall of the chapel was taken up with four beautiful, full-length, stained-glass windows depicting four saints. Mr. P told me that a renowned craftsman had constructed them in the early

1950s and that they depicted events in the lives of saints who were important to the founding order of the school.

Mr. P had been in this space many times before, but as we walked past the first window he paused, as if he were seeing it for the first time. The saint resting on his sword was standing in a victorious position, with each one of his feet planted on a different book. The spine of the first book said "schism," indicating the saint was important because he has been victorious in a certain schismatic dispute in the Church. The spine of the second book, however, was blacked out, and no words were written on it. Mr. P. looked at me and said, with some puzzlement, that he had not noticed before this moment that the spine had been blacked out with paint. He told me that the last time he looked, it had said "Jew." Thus, whereas the word *Jew* had once stood alongside the word *schism* as an object of conquest, now, with the simple and very deliberate stroke of a brush, Dillon, founded in the 1920s, joined the ecumenical spirit; and Mr. P, now noticing the change for the first time, clearly saw it as a moment of progress.

Whereas it is quite unlikely that my presence in the classroom contributed to Mr. P's underlying openness to different points of view, to his genuine decency, or to his acceptance of people of different faiths, it did seem to influence his sensitivity to an outsider's view. It was after the prayer that he discussed his problem with the anonymous Christian doctrine, for example, and directed me to the stained-glass window and the role that it played in the informal curriculum. That he responded to the reading from John about the Jews killing Jesus but not to the implicit slander of Islam suggested to me that my presence as a Jew actually did make a difference in his perception of the messages passed on through the informal curriculum. And given his genuine openness to other perspectives, at times he seemed to doubt whether he should teach a religion course because of his reservations about some of the Church doctrine. Yet from the standpoint of pluralism, this openness, even if accompanied by doubt, and perhaps *because* accompanied by doubt, is an asset that needs to be promoted.

Shaping Commitment: Institutional Habits and the Example of Moses Hebrew Day School

As I use the term, *institutional habits* are systemic patterns of dispositions, expectations, and standards that are used to construct shared meanings and practices. They normally remain unquestioned and form part of the social world that we take as "natural." In their very naturalism, they express and shape shared emotions, attitudes, and perspectives. Their expressions are so common that, like a pair of eyeglass frames that we have incorporated into our activity of seeing, they no longer have the status of an object that is out there to be seen.

Moses Day School, for example, takes it for granted that their students should come to feel a close identity with the Israeli state and its Jewish population. This aim provides the context for much of the pedagogical work that takes place in the school. The Israeli flag flies along with the American one. Corridors are named after streets in Jerusalem, and members of the Jewish Defense Force help children prepare a mural to celebrate Jewish Independence Day. The institutional habits serve to establish and to reinforce the children's identity as Jews and as inexorably tied, first to the experience of the Holocaust and then, as the rabbi tells me, to the redemption of Jews by the founding of Israel.

The identification with Israel is visible in the speakers who are invited to the school and the way in which topics are addressed. Moses Day School does not have an explicit political agenda regarding Israel and its proper relation to the Palestinian population, but the teachers who I met are generally progressive, hoping that the two people could live in peace, and in at least one class students were taught how Jews flourished under Islamic rule in Spain. I never heard the Palestinians demonized or denounced in this school in any way or saw any evidence that their culture or the Islamic religion was belittled or disrespected. Nevertheless, Moses Day School shapes the boundaries of intelligence and imagination in ways that both connect students to the state of Israel and take that connection for granted as the way they ought to be. Below is an example.

Celebration of Israeli Independence Day

Moses Day School is celebrating Israeli Independence Day and has invited an American Jew to talk to the students. He is involved with Magen David Adom, the Israeli equivalent of the Red Cross. The speaker informs the students that his organization is neutral with regard to politics, it has no connection to the Israeli political system, and it seeks none.

Much of his message is consistent with the requirement of democratic pluralism to widen identifications and sympathies beyond one's own group. He tells students the following: "We are all human beings." "[His] group sends people to disasters all over the world." "A Jewish life is not worth any more than any other life. A life is a life, and they are all equally precious." "Palestinians are human beings, and real person-to-person cooperation does occur between Israelis and Palestinians." He illustrates this theme by telling them of the "good news" and the "bad news."

The bad news is that one of their ambulances was set upon by Palestinian protesters. A shot was fired and hit an oxygen tank in the ambulance. There was an explosion. The good news is that no one in the ambulance was hurt because a Palestinian ambulance was nearby and came to the rescue of the Jews in the ambulance. The other bad news is that when he tried to get the United States media to report on this incident of cooperation, none of them were interested, neither the media in New York nor in Chicago or Los Angeles. Continuing with the bad news, he tells the students that while the Red Cross recognizes its Arab equivalent, the Red Crescent, it does not recognize his organization (a fact that seems to me as well as to others inconsistent with the very universalism on which the Red Cross was founded), and this observation sets the stage for the subtext of his talk, Israel's isolation and unfair treatment by the rest of the world.

He tells the children of the generosity of Norway, which, after hearing that his organization lost forty-nine ambulances since the latest violence began, donated ten ambulances to Israel. The "bad" news, he tells them, was that nine of those ambulances were to be directed toward the Palestinians while his organization received only one. The good news is that the Norwegians sent the ten ambulances through Israel because it understood that if it sent them through the Palestinians, Israel would not get even their one.

Critical silences shape the presentation, providing a subtext of unfairness and isolation. He does not mention that the American Red Cross supports Israel and withholds dues from the national organization in protest to the fact that it refuses to recognize Mogen David Adom, a fact that might mitigate the subtext of the isolation of Israel. Nor does he address the fact that Israel, together with Egypt, have received more aid from the United States than any other country and that in this context, nine ambulances are more significant for the Palestinians since the Israelis can easily provide them for themselves. And he does not account for the number of ambulances—state, army, hospital, voluntary organizations, and so on—available to each side. The subtext functions to strengthen the alignment of the children's identity with that of Israel as a Jewish state and as the victim of international isolation and exclusion. The talk was given three times: first to sixth graders, then to seventh graders, and finally to eighth graders. The younger students talked more and fidgeted as the lecture progressed, and it seemed hard to hold their attention. The older students were quiet and more attentive than usual.

This identity work pervades both the formal and the informal curriculums and perhaps shows itself most clearly when things don't work and the old tried and true is brought out as a fitting substitute. Following the talk about the ambulances and after a break for lunch, an assembly was held where children were to be shown a film about Sephardic Jews, their culture, and their history. Unfortunately, there was a snag and the staff had not realized that the film was in Spanish with very unclear subtitles. The hundred or so students present began to fidget as the teachers scurried around for a substitute. They finally came up with a film moderated by Dan Rather, valorizing the Israeli military victory in the Six-Day War. Once the film was rolling, the students were quiet again. In this moment, the institutional habit comes into play to reconstruct the normal assembly and to literally repair the breakdown.

Analysis: Religious Partiality, Democratic Pluralism, and Conditions of Stability

To review: democracy in a religiously pluralistic society is aided by making the commitment to pluralism transparent to everyone regardless of his or her religious beliefs. A commitment to pluralism is consistent with confidence in the truth of one's own faith as long as it allows equal confidence to members of opposing faiths. It is also important that these commitments be transparent. Transparency involves three levels of knowing:

1. You need to know that regardless of my religious belief and the strength with which I hold it, I also hold a commitment to pluralism, or to your right to worship (or not to worship), to express your beliefs, and to the maintenance of the conditions that will enable you to do so.
2. I need to know that regardless of your religious belief and the strength with which you hold it, you hold a similar commitment to pluralism and thus to my right to worship (or not to worship) as I see fit, and so on.
3. We both need to know that the other knows this.

The ideal of public school education has been that children can develop other strands of relationships—sports, academic interests, clubs, and so on—that can minimize the conflicts that can arise over religious differences. As these additional levels of contact thicken, the requisite assumptions hopefully take hold in an implicit way, often without need of articulation. If these additional layers cannot be developed implicitly as a result of informal interaction, then they need explicit development.

This is not to say that public schools have always been successful in providing the needed transparency. Indeed, the unwillingness to acknowledge the legitimacy of other religions was one of the major charges that Catholic schools had to address in the 1800s, and in turn Catholic educators believed that public schools were a thin disguise for Protestant education.[9] The failure was one of both commitment and transparency, and it contributed greatly to the riots that occurred around the issue of religious education in the 1800s[10] and the attempt to reject Catholic schools as illegal in the early part of the twentieth century.[11] While these battles may be largely behind us, the complexities of the new age of globalization and the increasing appeal of private and religious schools mean that the lessons of pluralism need to take place in a different kind of environment. It means that what might have been learned informally through friendship and interaction in the classroom and on the playing field needs to be made explicit as part of a religiously separate education if, as Callen suggests, separate religious schools are to serve a common good.[12] I now turn to these possibilities.

Promoting Democratic Pluralism in the Context of Religious Schools

One advantage of successful transparency through the public schools was that children got to know each other as individuals. One disadvantage is that they got to know each other as individuals. In other words, they were not encouraged to know each other in terms of their deeper commitments and attachments. If this happened, it was as a result of informal friend-ships. While religious schools have not generally been known to encourage this kind of contact, they have an advantage that could be exploited and that could go a long way in dispelling simplistic stereotypes. Four examples from schools in my study can illustrate the point.

1. Liberation High, a Catholic school in the inner city, employed a Jewish rabbi part-time on its counseling staff.
2. After the events of September 11, 2001, Mr. P at Dillon High School encouraged his students to accept an open invitation to visit a mosque and learn more about Islam.
3. Mr. P invited a teacher from a Jewish day school to talk about her religion to his class.
4. A teacher in the Jewish day school discussed how Jews flourished under Muslim rulers in Spain
5. A picture of Martin Luther King, Jr., a Protestant, hangs on the wall of both the Jewish day school and an inner-city Catholic high school.
6. A unit on the Holocaust, critical of the Church's position, is taught to students in the Catholic high school.

Stereotypes are also challenged in some Catholic schools by academically sound courses in world religions. Some of the texts are models of critical self-reflection. For example, one text voices criticism of the treatment of Jews in the Gospels (e.g., "The Gospels seem to overemphasize the involve-ment of the Jews in the arrest and trial [of Jesus]").[13] It is critical of the historical Church, acknowledging the corrupt practices of some of the popes.[14] This book, which is used in some upper grade schools and high schools, also alerts students to the unique problems involved in studying one religion from the standpoint of another, and encourages them to try to explore other religions from their own perspective.[15] As one example, it notes, "For Judaism the Tanakh is in no sense the 'Old Testament.' Nothing new has ever superceded it, and it remains the vital center of Jewish understanding."[16] In terms of the question of tolerance toward Jews, this Catholic text gives a considerably higher score to Muslims than to Christians. "Entire Jewish populations were massacred . . . by wandering bands of Christian penitents. Meanwhile the Spanish Inquisition also targeted Jews, putting many to death. . . . But we must not lose sight of the haven of relative peace and prosperity in which some Jews lived in Moslem Spain."[17] And the book ends with a Muslim prayer calling for unity and understanding.[18]

There is no formal diocese requirement mandating world religion, and courses in world religion are a contested domain in many Catholic high schools, with more tradition-minded Catholics lobbying for courses in Church history or apologetics as substitutes. Nevertheless, Catholic students in some schools learn more about other faiths in the formal curriculum than do children in most public schools, although public school students in general have more opportunity to interact with students of different religions.

Transparency as a Condition of Stability

Democratic stability requires, among other things, that

1. People, regardless of their group, understand the rules of interaction and engagement. This is a minimal condition for stability and applies to nondemocratic as well as to democratic forms of education.
2. They accept these rules as applying both to themselves and to others. This is a condition of fairness. This requirement is critical for supporting ideals such as equal opportunity.
3. Long-term and systematic inequalities are addressed through education and other means.
4. Students are willing to abide by these rules and to accept them as fair and to support their enforcement.
5. Students learn that others are willing to abide by them and that they too accept them as fair and are willing to support their enforcement.
6. They learn that others know that they are willing to abide by them, and they know that this knowledge is mutual.
7. They are represented in the process of making and changing the rules.

Knowing the rules of interaction and engagement is, by definition, a cognitive matter. It is something that people can be told. However, it is not merely cognitive. It is a condition of social trust, of trust in the goodwill of people you do not know and may never meet.

The knowledge that others are willing to abide by these rules is a condition of their mutual acceptance and is a condition of commitment and loyalty to the larger institutional and cultural practices that guarantee enforcement of the rules. It makes little sense to participate in a game in which you believe that the other side will break the rules whenever it is to its advantage to do so. The belief that others also have faith in your willingness to abide by the rules is a condition of stability across different identity groups such as religions. If one party believes that the other will break the rules, then, in the absence of the threat of force, it will try to get the advantage of breaking them first and will try to gather the commitment of others to support these efforts. Too much force, however, is itself a problem for prosperous stability, breeding feelings of resentment and habits of inertia and passivity. This is one reason why deliberation is critical to democracies. It allows perspectives to be shared and taken into account as partisans on different sides of an issue hammer out decisions.

For example, as I mentioned earlier, one of the traditional arguments for public education is that by including students from many different backgrounds, it provides the conditions to address and correct inequality and the attitudes of superiority and inferiority that extreme inequality breeds. It is an empirical question just how well public schools do this, and there are many who argue that they have failed to live up to expectations,[19] but to the extent that they do not include students of different backgrounds, they are vulnerable to criticism. The presence of both boys and girls from different economic, ethnic, and religious backgrounds can be an important element in developing an active standpoint of equality and in weaving a thick web of relationships among different kinds of children.

If these are not present because of racial, economic, or religious isolation, the web is thinner and the standpoint of equality more difficult to develop. In the absence of certain kinds of children, teachers may do their best to weave a thicker web by providing students with more information about the group that is not present. A unit on the labor movement or on civil rights in a wealthy, all-white suburb would be examples of this. While this may well produce greater understanding in some academic sense, it need not produce the competence required to interact with the other from the standpoint of social equality. A unit on feminism taught in an all-male setting, for example, could help a student to develop some understanding of the history of the movement without developing the skills required to address women as political, intellectual, and moral equals.

In this same sense, religious homogeneity in even the more progressive faith-based schools has a special challenge, as institutional habits of thought and action are channeled in fairly standardized and normalized forms according to the frame of reference of a given religious group. When others are present, it becomes possible for students to incorporate another perspective and hence to raise habit and routine to the status of objects for evaluation. This can happen in modest ways, as when the minister at Saint Martin, recognizing my position as a university professor, began his discussion of creationism with the humorous aside that he "hoped he did not wind up as a case study in an abnormal psychology text." Or, it can provide an occasion for serious reflection and reevaluation, as occurred in the prayer episode at Dillon where the perspective of the other is incorporated into Mr. P's reconsideration of his responsibility to encourage his students to learn about and engage members of different religious communities.

Conclusion: The Requirements of Religious Pluralism

Now that it is constitutional to appropriate public funds to pay for tuition at religious schools, their popularity will most likely increase, and as it does funds may be withdrawn from public schools, thereby reducing their quality and increasing the pressure for parents, religious or otherwise, to send their children to faith-based schools. While there is some question how far the Constitution will allow states to regulate religious schools,[20] there is a need to examine the requirements of democratic pluralism under conditions of increased religious schooling where

1. Students from different religious background do not share the same classrooms;
2. Textbooks are as likely to be chosen for their appeal to a given religion as for their accuracy;
3. Teachers are not necessarily educated under conditions in which democracy holds the highest priority;
4. Public scrutiny of schools has been reduced or eliminated;
5. Global forces bring people from unfamiliar religious background into political and economic contact with one another in the larger society; and
6. Global communication makes it possible to mobilize discontent on the basis of religious identities.

A condition of pluralism is its transparency and the understanding that my freedom to think and worship as I see fit is dependent on your freedom to think and worship as you see fit and that both of us understand that this is the condition of pluralism. To the extent that a stable pluralism is valued, it is important that students are taught this as the basic condition of their own religious freedom and that it be incorporated into their own identity. One of the premises of public education was that early contact between children of different religions made this lesson easier to learn and that religiously isolated education made it harder. The idea that institutions develop habits that serve to unconsciously reinforce the norms of one specific religious community as the norm for all gives some credibility to this premise. The prayer about 9/11 and the scurry to replace the film in the Hebrew day school are examples of this tendency and the way it is played out, even in schools that embrace democratic pluralism. The lessons may still be taught in some abstract way, but the absence of the religious other means that if pluralism is to be reinforced by concrete examples, teachers will need to consciously engage students in hearing the voice of the religious other even as they engage their own religious commitments. Without this voice, the saint's foot would forever remain on the spine of the Jew and films shown to Jewish children will replay Israel's victory in the Six-Day War whenever other plans break down.

PART III

The Reconstruction of Religious Education: A Pragmatic Framework

CHAPTER **8**

The Challenge of Religious Education for Pluralism

Liberal democracies have an interest in religious education, but they also face a major dilemma when it comes to the regulation of religious schools. If they insist that religious schools teach the values of liberal pluralism, they risk injecting the state into the affairs of religion and interfering with the parents' right to educate a child as they think appropriate.[1] However, if they fail to intervene in religious schools, they may find schools promoting illiberal attitudes toward other groups, toward socially and politically weaker members of their own group (e.g., women and homosexuals), or toward democracy.

In this and the next chapter, I explore the character of the public's interest in religious schools and suggest a way it can be expressed without compromising pluralism. I believe that the public should have an influence over the education of those who teach religion courses in denominational schools that children attend full-time, ensuring that these teachers are aware of the developmental needs of students and the educational requirements of pluralism.[2] Regulating aspects of the education of religion teachers is a compromise between direct oversight of the schools and the present system, where satisfaction of the public interest must remain a matter of chance.

The Tension between Liberalism and Pluralism

Religious education actually reveals a tension in the concept of liberal pluralism as a social ideal. Liberalism requires that children acquire the

171

skills needed to develop their own conception of the good life. This means, among other things, that children in liberal societies are not *destined* to live the life of their parents. They may, if they wish, choose different occupations from their parents, marry a spouse from a different background, live in different communities, root for different teams, vote for different political parties, and adopt different religions. Rational choice requires that children develop the knowledge and reasoning skills necessary to understanding the possibilities available to them and that they grasp the likely consequences of selecting one or another possibility.

Contemporary liberalism has promoted public schools as the major institution for assuring the development of the knowledge and skills required to make intelligent choices. Not all schools meet this standard, but to the extent that they do not, they are subject to fair criticism. However, many public schools are reluctant to provide students with information on different religions, and some established practices such as vocational counseling would arguably be unconstitutional if extended to religious counseling. Imagine the uproar if publics schools had neutral religious counselors who would work with students to match them to the religion that would best suit their spiritual needs, talents, and interests independently of their parents' religious preferences. When it comes to religious counseling and education, public schools have a hands-off policy, leaving parents as the sole guide to a religious education.

Among the reasons for this is the idea of religious respect embedded in conceptions of normative pluralism. Normative pluralism is that component of philosophical liberalism that requires the encouragement of many conceptions of the good as a condition for rational choice. Religious variety provides a plurality of conceptions of the good along with the historical and collective conditions required to sustain them. The need to sustain multiple conceptions of the good is one reason why public schools are required to respect religious differences. Respect is generally expressed here in a negative way, namely, by avoiding the topic.[3] And when it is treated, critical discussion is largely neglected.[4]

The practical result is that at least in this area, parents are provided an official monopoly over the formative experience of their children. Parents not only can determine what and how children choose to worship but also can legitimately expect schools not to challenge religious preferences even when children develop these preferences uncritically and hold them dogmatically.[5] Thus the way in which religious respect is interpreted has meant that children often grow into a religious tradition without the critical distance that is helpful in directing choice in other areas, whether those areas be vocational, political, personal, or recreational.

If parents view the public school's version of negative respect as inadequate, they retain the right to send their children to the religious school of their choosing. This choice may serve to decrease the chance that their children will have an opportunity to become impartially informed about the advantages of other religions, about the problems inherent in their own religion, and about the reasons some people choose a life of faith and others do not. Of course, children do not, as adults, always follow their parents' religious preferences, but when they do not, it is more often by accident than by deliberation. In many cases of conversion, judgment is based less on critical reflection and careful reason than on companionship, convenience, or comfort. Indeed, some scholars mistakenly assume that the rejection of the parents' religious preference is, by itself, a sign of an informed decision.

The problem of uncritical commitment is paralleled by the problem of uncritical rejection where many nominal believers reject a faith-mandated practice because they find it inconvenient or harsh, without understanding the reason the faith advances the practice. Many Roman Catholics do not follow the Church's teachings on divorce, homosexuality, or birth control. Many Jews and Muslims eat pork, and many "fundamentalists" do not accept a literal interpretation of the Sixth Commandment when it comes to capital punishment or war. While rejection often arises from accident rather than reasoned consideration as liberalism would prefer, a hands-off policy is consistent with pluralism's concern to enable and respect difference across religious and nonreligious communities. Yet when it comes education and religion, the respect that pluralism requires may hobble the critical thinking that liberalism demands.

In this chapter I address the problem of pluralism, which I define in terms of the question "What is the preferred meaning of respect in a religiously pluralist society, and how can it be promoted in the context of a deep belief in the primacy of one religion?" In the next chapter I address the problem of liberalism, which I define in terms of the question "How can an education into a faith tradition be maintained while reflective critical thinking about one's own religious tradition is promoted?"

While the problem of pluralism is directed toward the religions of others, the problem of liberalism is directed toward one's own religion. Its question is directed inward: how can one's own religious doctrine be taught so as to allow the widest possible scope for critical reflection within a faith tradition?

Commitment and Respect

A central feature of exclusivist religious schools is the encouragement of belief in the doctrine of a single religion. Children in these religious schools are expected to learn the doctrines of "their" religion in a way that will insure belief in them. Not only do they learn what the doctrine says but also, ideally (from the standpoint of the school), they come to believe that it is true. Doctrines advanced as absolute and universally true by one religion will, at some point, diverge from the doctrines of other religions also advanced as absolute and universally true. Jesus is the son of God. Jesus is not the son of God. Faith alone will open the gates to heaven. Faith alone is not sufficient without good works. The Koran is or is not the most complete word of God. Wives should or should not be submissive to their husbands.

Philosophers of education have pointed out the problem of indoctrination that resides in such an educational state of affairs.[6] If it is true that Jesus is divine, then any claim to the contrary is, given rules of ordinary binary logic, false. And if Jesus is the son of God, then any claim that he is not is false. It may be possible to complicate the rules of ordinary logic, as I will attempt to do, but that is the place we need to begin. Under the rules of such logic, if one doctrine is true, then a contradictory claim is false. And, if one religion teaches children that Jesus is God's son and another rejects this claim, then one of them is teaching something as true that in fact is not, and this is one important component of indoctrination.

Universalism

Fearing the effects of religious indoctrination, the pragmatist John Dewey offered an alternative to traditional religious education that he thought would preserve the spirit of religion without falling prey to dogma and indoctrination. In his book, *A Common Faith*, he advanced an argument against *religion*, which he understood in terms of the promotion of irrational dogma, and he argued for a kind of spirituality, which he called the "religious."

Dewey wanted to separate the religious from anything to do with dogma about the supernatural and to ground religious experience in the world of nature. The "religious," for him, refers to the quality of an experience rather than to an institution and its doctrine. The religious emancipates the wholeness of experience from religions and their prejudices. Dewey explained that "the adjective 'religious' denotes nothing in the way of a specifiable entity, either institutional or as a system of beliefs."[7]

He held that the religious quality in experience refers to a kind of wholeness, a complete sense of adjustment, and a sense of security and stability,[8] not to the cause of the experience in some supernatural being.[9] He saw the wholeness of the religious attitude as arising from the ability of human beings to cooperate with nature to make a world that is more dependable and more secure. "The essentially unreligious attitude is that which attributes human achievement and purpose to man in isolation from the world of physical nature and his fellows. Our successes are dependent upon the cooperation of nature."[10]

In a critique and rejection of dogma and the idea of absolute truth, Dewey remarked "that some fixed doctrinal apparatus is necessary for *a* religion. But faith in the possibility of continued and rigorous inquiry does not limit access to truth to any channel or scheme of things."[11] To many people affiliated with traditional dogmatic religions, this understandably seems to suggest a rejection of religion itself.

Problem with Universalism

Whatever the correct interpretation of Dewey, he is not particularly helpful to religious educators who are committed to advancing the beliefs and practices of one particular faith. From their point of view, he fails to understand that the spiritual source of religious spirituality lies precisely in those experiences that are beyond our control and where nature does not always seem to be cooperative. Certainly it lies, as I mentioned in the first chapter, in awe and gratitude for our own being, and here Dewey is correct. A religious response acknowledges the cooperative features of the universe. However, it is also a response to the knowledge that each of us and our loved ones will also pass out of existence. In other words, it is to be found as much in grief as in joy, as much in death as in birth—in those features of experience where "nature" seems unfriendly and uncooperative. To the religious educator these inchoate feelings need to be shaped if they are to be acknowledged and communicated.

Much of religion is involved in trying to help us communally shape experiences that otherwise overwhelm us. It does this by engaging individuals in a collective construction, in a staging and retelling of stories that give shape to the awe and the terror of existence. The stories literally shape emotions and thereby enable them to be communicated within and across generations. They enable us to share the joys of birth, to mark emergence into adulthood, and to provide comfort to the bereaved, allowing them to go on when going on might be the last thing that they think they can do.

When principles of right living are drawn from these stories, when these principles are extended to cover new conditions, and when priests are selected to communally mark the events, thereby giving a communal shape to emotions, we have a religion. When the principles of right living are systematized to address tensions and contradictions, when theologians are identified and educated to calibrate different principles and their applications, and when protective regulations are established to discourage competing stories from being taken seriously, we have dogma. Dogma commands belief about a state of affairs even in the absence of independent, public evidence that such a state of affairs is or was the case—that is, without the kind of evidence that would be convincing to those people not already committed to the belief system.

Now, when Dewey suggests that a spiritual attitude without dogma is the preferred state of religious education, he is proposing a constraint on the stories that pluralism can allow, and this constraint is in tension with the basic idea of normative pluralism: that different conceptions of the good, including nonscientific ones, be allowed to coexist within the same society.

Indeed, to some, Dewey seems to be advancing a new religion, one in which science and science alone has the last word. Fundamentalists and others[12] use this interpretation to advance the idea of providing equal time to creationism as to evolutionary theory. This is the basis of the largely erroneous charge that, by teaching the theory of evolution, public schools are teaching a religious doctrine—secular humanism—and that they thus should give equal weight to creationism. The U.S. Supreme Court has rightly found this charge wanting.[13] As long as a teacher does not lead her students to infer from the theory of evolution anything about the existence or nonexistence of God, there should be no conflict between religion and the teaching of evolution.

However, to privilege evolution in a science class should not be taken to imply that only stories that conform to science should be accepted as religious. To make this leap is to deny one of the critical principles of normative pluralism—that there be many conceptions of the good available. Rather, pluralism as a standpoint prefers a generous reading of different religious narratives, a reading that will allow religious differences to flourish even in cases where one religious group has more members or is potentially more powerful.

In providing this reading it is important to take into account Dewey's legitimate concern that individuals maintain a capacity for intelligent choice between different conceptions of the good. Dewey feared that because many religions rest on a dogmatic foundation, such choice is discouraged, and that much of religious "education" amounted to indoctrination. The problem for him was that dogma resisted empirical tests. Yet the problem with Dewey from the standpoint of the religious educators is that he cuts out the foundation of their faith and its capacity to communally shape human emotion.

The Workings of Dogma

Yet Dewey has a real concern. Take the statement "Jesus is both fully human and fully divine" as an example. Those of us on the outside can give this statement various meanings that make logical sense, but those inside the tradition will reject many of these commonsense meanings.

An outsider might translate the statement as analogous to saying, "This box contains all apples, and this box also contains all fruit," thus allowing no contradiction because all apples are fruits. However, if humanity implies mortality and divinity implies immortality, then this interpretation works only by changing the meaning of the basic terms and must be rejected by those on the inside. In some way the translation must hold on to the ordinary sense of *human* and *divine* as contrary terms. To be human in ordinary language means to not be divine, and to be divine in ordinary terms means to not be human.

From the inside the translation is inadequate because it is incompatible with the larger belief system that holds that *human* and *divine* are not congruent terms and that the miracle of Jesus is to be found in the simple fact that he transcended the boundary between them. The interpretation is thus inadequate because it does not allow that Jesus is special and that there is an unexplainable mystery to it all.

Others might try to make sense of the statement by interpreting it metaphorically—Jesus suffered like a human, but acted like a god. Yet this interpretation falls short. "If we meant to say Jesus was *like* a human or like a God, we would have said so." What is taken as a metaphor to those outside is taken as truth and as mystery to those inside.[14] Jesus did not just act like a God. He is God! *And he is also human.* From the inside the statement is bedrock. From the standpoint of the believer if you don't believe it and accept its mystery, you are not a Christian.

Yet this insider's truth is the outsider's dogma (in the negative sense of the term). From the point of view of someone who has gone halfway and posed a perfectly sensible but metaphorical meaning that has been rejected, this stubborn insistence on nonmetaphorical literalness is dogmatic. To the believer, however, to accept the meaning as metaphorical is to belong to a different religion. To the insider it might seems as if Dewey and similar critics are appealing not just to the spirit of scientific inquiry but also to the spirit of Unitarianism where, with enough ingenuity, we can all live together under one big tent. Yet is the spirit of the Unitarian also that of the monolithic imperialist, where we will all live together but under my set of rules? Science over all!

Can this impasse be resolved? Can we allow for a plurality of religious interpretations, some of which contradict others, without allowing that some of these are necessarily indoctrinatory in the derogatory sense of the term? I am not sure whether we can, but I want to attempt an interpretation of religious dogma that might allow for an opening for faith-based *education* that is not an oxymoron—where both faith and *education* about belief and nonbelief are real possibilities, and where it is possible to allow that other conceptions of the good are sensible even while holding firm to the ideals and practices of one's own religion. Whether this interpretation needs to be taught to children in religious schools is to me an open question. I offer it, however, because, if taught to religious educators in an interreligious setting, it likely would serve to advance the interest of pluralism.

I want to begin, then, by returning to the theme developed in Chapter 1 and exploring again the genesis of religious dogma—the sense of awe, powerlessness, dependency, and terror that arises out of the understanding of the contingency of our own existence.

The Genesis of Dogma

An important source of religion is the need to give meaning to our coming into and passing out of being, and to mark the joy, suffering, terror, awe, and wonder that human existence entails. It arises from the childlike need to understand the incomprehensible. A parent dies, and a child is comforted by a story. The story cannot be told as one among many stories: "Yes, we believe that your mother is watching over you in heaven, but others believe that her spirit has entered into a different state of being and will be expressed in another earthly form—a whale, or a newborn child." The problem is that where one story is sufficient, two or more unconnected stories may be too many. Moreover, the effectiveness of the story depends on it being ready at hand and on having it told by many people, even those who have not yet experienced the death of a loved one, with an aura of authority; and it may also depend on the solidarity that it reinforces, through comforting words, closeness, and touch with an entire community. When a Jewish person dies and the family sits shivah, the tradition whereby friends are not supposed to greet the family with a traditional "Hello" or "Goodbye," whatever else its reasons, is also a way of saying, "We understand, we care, we are one with you and your loss."

Thus religion provides meaning for the most powerful events of our lives, but it does so where there is an abundance of possible meanings. We die, and a story is told. The story is one among many. Our death is just a fact. "He died." But it is a fact that demands a meaning. The story may be "He went to heaven," or it may be its opposite: "He did not go anywhere, but he would want us to continue his work (or to remember his goodness, etc)." The various stories arise from the demand for excess meaning—for meaning above and beyond the simple observable "fact" that he is gone and will, as far as we know, never return. The stories that are told entail the construction of difference, and such constructions are markers of a tradition. "*They* believe that people go to heaven, but *we* believe that their spirit is carried on in our memory," or "They believe that the spirit lives on in memory, but we believe that it is manifested in other life forms, in a cow or a rabbit."

I call the meaning *excess* because it goes beyond the information available and therefore beyond what we can expect everyone to agree to and for which the evidence is unshakable—"He died, there is the body that was once him." Yet even here language fails us. Is it "the body that was once him"? Or is it the "body that was once part of him," assuming that he might have had a mind or a soul that was separable from the body? I also call it *excess* because it is one story among many possible ones.

However, while the story is drawn from excess meaning, it is not excessive. We need words to reshape experience that is overwhelmed by its object, experiences such as awe, joy, and grief. We participate in one of these stories, and the shape that it gives to our experience allows it to be shared with and communicated to others. That we participate in a story and that we do not simply create it on the spur of the moment mean that it will be preserved so that it can be told (*staged* might be more accurate). The institution of religion serves to preserve these stories and the structure required to sustain participation over many generations. Of course, the term *story* is really too thin to fully appreciate the religious experience. The story is not just told. It is also enacted in rituals that bring people together and that provide renewal and continuity for each individual as part of a larger community.

Dewey would have acknowledged the need to share, communicate, and preserve experience, but his treatment of faith downplays the role that *religions* play in this process because he wished for a commonality across religious differences. Yet commonality needs to come as a result of recognizing differences and in recognition of the fact that a common faith is not always the most sustaining.

Nevertheless, if dogma is taught in such a way as to constrain thinking, or to interfere with the autonomy of those within the group or the freedom of those outside of it, it can likely lead to intellectual and spiritual bondage. A dogmatic presentation, without reasonable opportunity as one matures to encounter different approaches, narrows people by denying them the opportunity to contextualize one's own beliefs into a larger set of possibilities

Yet the quality of understanding that is developed through a particular tradition, especially for children, should not be minimized. To shape overpowering emotions effectively, a story may demand a monopoly on truth, at least for some—it is presented as *the* truth. It is not just a candidate for truth, not one among many possible truths. If it is presented as one story among other, equally valid stories, it risks losing some of its power to shape emotions and provide them with a communal foundation.

The above presents a serious educational problem for pluralism and also for religious educators, a problem that is the opposite of Dewey's pragmatic "universalism." Namely, how can democracy sanction religious education, and how can religious educators develop respect for different religions when, among the stories told by different religions as absolutely and indisputably true, some will be in contradiction with others, and at least traditional logic tells us all except one member of a contradicting pair will be false?

The problem suggests that if we are really concerned with truth, then—at least in principle, even if not in content—Saint Martin's[15] pedagogical approach is the most defensible: inoculate students against "false" doctrine. Yet, in the absence of mitigating factors, such as a broad-based, nonsectarian, public education, if this approach were generalized to every religious school, the result could well be the destruction of normative pluralism itself, or the balkanization of educational life. Plurality could remain, depending in part on the balance of power and what those in charge would allow, but pluralism, or the idea that there is much value to be gained by supporting the conditions for a wide range of communal expressions, is weakened if it is not acknowledged. Yet what is this value, and how can those who stand on the inside of one faith community and are committed to advancing the primacy of its teachings express it?

Thinking about Truth

To respond to this question, I want to return to the distinction made in an earlier chapter between propositional and pragmatic rationality[16] and to expand here on a certain feature of the pragmatic as an enactment not just of rationality, which speaks to the process of coming to hold a belief, but to the truth of an idea, which is a quality of the beliefs one holds. When the eighth graders were teaching the second graders how to pray, they were in effect bonding them to a certain religious community, a community whose continuing existence will depend upon these students engaging, along with others throughout the Catholic world, in acts of prayer. This act entailed certain beliefs about God, Jesus, and so on. Thus, affirming the truth of these beliefs in a collective and intergenerational setting; that is, in this enactment, Catholicism is reconstituted as a subject. Taking some license with the term, I want to call these moments *enacted truths* and to distinguish them from *propositional truth*, or the claims that we mark as true when evidence and reasoning support them over other claims. To see this distinction, consider that there are different ways in which truth is conceived. One way, mentioned above, is a proposition that conforms to some real state of affairs. This is the point of the worn philosophical example "The cat is on the mat." The proposition is true only if there is a mat and only if there is a cat on it. Yet there are other senses in which we use the word *true*. Truth may be an enactment, as when we say of a book or a play that it "gets at truth." In this sense it may get at something that eludes propositional truth—the sense of truth as a touching or even a making.

The pragmatist William James captures some of this idea of truth in his essay "The Will to Believe."[17] Although James has sometimes been criticized wrongly for holding that truth can be whatever we want it to be, his pragmatic notion of truth allows that where the evidence is uncertain, affirming a truth may create conditions required to bring it about. Thus, if I believe that you are basically honest and act as if you are, and if you do the same with me, then this may lead to an open and honest relationship. The belief that you are honest thus can make the proposition "You are honest" a true proposition. It is truth as making. James's notion is by no means without difficulty, and what he alluded to as truth might be thought of in more traditional terms as a hypothesis—albeit a hypothesis that adds its own weight to its likely truth. As James puts the point:

> The knower is not simply a mirror floating with no foot-hold anywhere, and passively reflecting an order that he comes upon and finds simply existing. The knower is an actor and co-efficient of the truth . . . [and] action. . . transforms the world—helps to make the truth they declare.[18]

An *enacted truth*, as I am appropriating the term, differs from James in that it is neither hypothetical nor propositional. It is a creation or a re-creation. It is what it represents, and in that sense it creates the subject and the standard for evaluating propositional claims such as "She is a good Catholic." It differs from James in that it is the result of a collective, not simply an individual, endeavor. Mutual engagement creates the truth of the belief. It is not simply a hypothesis that may or may not refer to a real state of affairs. In an enacted truth, we are transformed as dancers who, believing in each other's talent, flow together as dance. If I believe and if you believe as well that the eucharist brings us together as part of the same divine spirit, then as dancers are transformed into dance, we are transformed into that spiritual union called Christianity. We now constitute a spiritual *we*.

Viewing religious truth in this way does not exhaust all the meanings of truth or reject other conceptions. It simply provides religious educators with a vantage point from which they can teach how different religions may dwell together without requiring students to accept a logic that holds that if their religion is true, then those whose propositions seem to contradict it must be false. It is pluralism's way of understanding how religions work to construct a way of being that is what it claims to represent.

While this is the desired view of truth from the standpoint of pluralism, it is also consistent with the way in which some theologians now understand religious truth, and hence the idea of an enacted truth is not necessarily one that religious educators need to see as imposed from an exclusively secular standpoint. Consider, for example, the words of the liberal Catholic theologian Antoine Vergote:

> Christian faith in God the Father is not the theoretical affirmation of a truth pronounced by a religious man. It is the active acceptance of a proffered relationship. 'I believe' is a *performative* expression. In it I implicate myself, and commit myself to a lived relationship which transforms my existence in the same way as and more basically than the man and woman who, when they marry, establish a relationship and commit themselves to live in accordance with the terms of that establishment.[19]

Transubstantiation may be more than an enacted truth in the mind of a believer. For the pragmatic pluralist, though, it is *at least* an enacted truth and possibly more. *We* come together as Jesus did to partake in his spirit and to make visible the Church, which is a continuation of the works that he performed. While this interpretation may not be sufficient to capture the meaning that the eucharist holds for Catholics or for Catholic theologians like Vergote, the sense of truth that it does provide is a sufficient foundation for pluralism. McGrath speaks to the divide between insider and outsider when he writes,

> Doctrine arises within the community of faith, as it seeks to make sense and give order and structure to its experience. . . . Doctrine is thus an 'insider' phenomenon, reflecting the specific perspective of the community of faith. Outside this context, it seems barren and lifeless. . . . The source of pressure within the community to generate doctrinal formulations is its wish and perceived need to give substance and expression to its corporate experience of God in Christ. The impulse which animates the genesis of doctrine is thus prior to any specific doctrinal formulation as

such—yet, paradoxically, requires some such doctrinal formulation if it is to be transmitted from one generation to another.[20]

To participate in the eucharist is, from the Church's point of view, to acknowledge one another as created by God and as members of Christ. However, in establishing the community as part of Jesus Christ, the act makes us the *us* that we are. By enacting, there is now a *we* that is acting.

An outsider can know that this is how the thing is *seen* to work from the inside, but further than this he may not be able to go. When Pope Paul VI in 1965 affirmed again that the bread and wine are the real presence of Christ, the mystery that he affirms also stands as a wall separating Catholics from non-Catholics? While the specific claims may, to the outsider, appear barren and lifeless, as McGrath suggest, all that the outsider needs to know for pluralism's sake is that from the inside it gives substance and expression to the communal life of the believers. It stands as a form of the good for many people, and pluralism is required to nurture multiple conceptions of the good.

It is not clear that people in constructing an enacted truth actually think of what they are saying as a propositional truth, unless they are challenged to do so. And hence for educators to acknowledge the enacted quality of religious truth may not be all that far from the way many experience their faith. Even if a religious utterance is taken as a propositional truth, it is not always clear that it has the same literal meaning for all believers. When Jews pray, "Blessed art thou O Lord Our God King of the Universe," are they picturing God sitting on a throne with a crown *on* his head like we might picture the cat *on* the mat? It is hard to tell without asking, and we would probably get different answers from different Jews. Indeed, the enactment may depend on that very vagueness.

Nevertheless the most important word in the prayer is *our*. The prayer is uttered, and in uttering it the community is enacted—re-created. In saying *our God*, we create a *we*. The community is formed around these rituals, but the rituals alone are not sufficient. When the Jew asks his relative on Yom Kippur, "Did *you* fast today?" he is repairing a potential rift in the community. To have not fasted without sufficient reason is to distance one's self from the community. Hence, as ties to a religious community loosen, fewer Jews notice whether one fasted or not, and fewer Catholics ask, "Were you sick last Sunday? We noticed you missed the mass."

Tensions between Enacted and Propositional Truth

There is, nevertheless, a potential tension between the enacted truth function of religious utterances and their role as propositional truth claims.

The more an enacted truth resembles a testable propositional truth, the more problems it may create for people to adopt the faith. Is there, for example, a DNA test for the eucharist service, or is the "literal" turning of the host into flesh and blood not literality as we understand it in normal, everyday, or scientific discourse? As the believer might respond, "Whoever said that God had DNA tracers, anyway?"

Pluralism cannot override ordinary logic, but it can allow that ordinary logic is not the only test of enacted truths. To allow that in communion I partake of the flesh and blood of Jesus is taken as a condition of belonging to this community. *Allow* here need not mean overt agreement such as "when I '*allow*' I '*agree*' that this is real flesh and blood." It may just mean that I don't raise questions about propositional truth, but as a believer I participate in the act. *Communion* here is literal in the sense that it is the "literal creation of *this* community." It may be that I join in without thinking about the meaning in all of its possible operational senses. Nevertheless, pluralism's view is compatible with a thin understanding of the sacraments, even in the Church's eye, as a sacrament of initiation.[21]

From within each religion, of course, the sacraments (or their equivalent) have a fuller and richer role to play. They bring people into the community, shape their relations to one another, and, through ceremonies marking birth (for example, baptism and circumcision) and death, provide for its renewal. Part of a religious education involves engaging students in these occasions and hence teaching them to live within the meaning given to these events. Yet part of a religious education in a pluralistic society requires that teachers understand the potential openness entailed within their own belief system and that they leave a window available for students to appreciate the value that other religions hold for their believers. Thus the larger society has an important stake in the way full-time religious teachers, as advocates of both religion and of pluralism, are educated into the doctrines of their own tradition.

Dogma as a Place in a System of Belief: The Education of the Religious Educator

The beliefs that comprise doctrine and stamp a collective identity do not all have the same status. Some are more easily discarded than others. For Saint Paul, for example, it was easier to give up the dietary rules than it was to give up a belief that the Gospel was meant to be heard by all people, not only Jews. The example suggests that beliefs are not the only practices that stamp an identity. Diet, circumcision, common holidays, rituals, and so on are all parts of the fabric of a religious identity providing collective markers depicting who belongs and who does not. Dogma says what these markers are about, what holds these practices together, and how they are related. While the term *dogma* is identified only with some religions, such as Catholicism, its function as a distinguishing feature of a given religion is essential to all religions.

Dogma is a part of a belief system and, as such, serves as a stamp for a collective identity. *Dogma* is the word we use to indicate the core of a belief system. When we speak of dogma, we have two things in mind. The first is content. To say that Muslims believe that Mohammed was the last prophet and that the Koran is the most complete prophetic vision is to identify the content of dogma. Content varies from religion to religion. The second feature of dogma is that it indicates the place of a belief in a system of beliefs. It is those ideas that believers are most reluctant to change because when such ideas are viewed as truth claims, so many of other beliefs rest on them. Taken together, the proclamation of these beliefs along with the practices and rituals that express and represent them constitute a particular religious community.

Dogma is held much in the same way as our beliefs in logical or mathematical truths in science. Because so much depends on them, they are the slowest to change.[22] New logical and math systems do develop, but with considerable resistance and usually not by overturning the old but by finding new niches for it. Beliefs that occupy the place of dogma actually do change over the long run, but they change very slowly, often keeping their basic form but allowing for different interpretations. To affirm a belief in dogma is centrally important because it affirms you and me as a *we* and so identifies all of the others who take on "our" collective identity.

The view that religious doctrine functions as other than just a propositional truth claim is again consistent with some theological thinking. The theologian George Lindbeck, for example, advances a regulatory theory of religion, stressing the similarities between religion and language.[23] "The function of church doctrines that become most prominent in this perspective is their use, not as expressive symbols or truth claims, but as communally authoritative rules of discourse, attitudes and action."[24] Departing from more familiar ideas of the relationship between religion and rules, Lindbeck, in an attempt to establish an anthropological and linguistic foundation for ecumenical understanding, defines religion as "comprehensive interpretive schemes . . . which structure human experience and understanding of self and world . . . shap[ing] the entirety of life and thought."[25] And he then suggests that this is "the only job that doctrines do in their role as church teachings,"[26] although they may do other things besides teaching, such as evoking emotional responses.

Lindbeck's view allows seemingly contradictory doctrine to exist side by side without conflict in the same way that one country requires its drivers to stay on the left-hand side of the road while another requires its to stay on the right-hand side. Lindbeck is not arguing that this is the only function of religion, but that this is the only function of religious *doctrine*. In other words, as he puts it, *doctrines* function to "regulate truth claims by excluding some and permitting others."[27]

This interpretation does not minimize the importance of religious doctrine, but it does allow that its importance and validity are not necessarily confined to its singular agreement with a preexisting reality and that, whatever its relation to an external reality such as the will of God or the biblical text, it provides the framework for the thoughts and feelings that many people have and for the acts they perform. Turning the other cheek is not a natural response, but it does become possible to exchange good for harm under a certain system of regulatory rules where it is recognized as a communal exemplar. Thus to become religious is to interiorize, through its art, music, and rituals, "a set of skills by practice and training. One learns how to feel, act, and think in conformity with a religious tradition that is, in its inner structure, far richer and more subtle than can be explicitly articulated."[28] To take Lindbeck's point seriously would give teachers a way to acknowledge what is implicit in religious conceptions such as charity and forgiveness. That doctrine always points beyond itself to something that is neither instinctual nor expressible in mere words, but that can only come into being by a collective human enactment.

Doctrine as Marker

While the regulatory function of doctrine is part of identity formation, equally important is the public proclamation of belief. Public proclamation makes the commitment to a particular religious community visible. Unlike simple spirituality, religion requires proclamation. The religious community itself is constituted only through a series of mutually audible affirmations and shared rituals. Here enactment entails constitution.

Religious teachers need to understand how doctrinal proclamation works in the formation of the community of believers. The enactment of the community requires, in addition to the profession of sameness of belief, markers that will distinguish this community of believers from other religious communities. Thus the beliefs of a particular religious community will both overlap with some of the beliefs of other communities and depart from each of them in different ways. It is the differences that mark off one community from others. And it is the totality of different kinds of differences and similarities across the boundaries with other religions that enables this religion to secure a separate identity—to take its place in a religious "geography." Thus, in contrast to the example of driving on one side of the road or the other, an example intended to suggest the historically arbitrary character of belief, faith communities require difference. It would be equivalent to the requirement that we drive on the left *if* they drive on the right and vice versa as the prerequisite for there being any automobiles at all.

Summary: Dogma versus Dogmatic

The interaction between the microlevel religious belief and its incorporation into a larger understanding of democratic pluralism requires that a distinction be made between the noun *dogma* and the adjective *dogmatic*. *Dogma* refers to the place a particular belief has in a belief system of a community, while *dogmatic* refers to the way in which the belief is communicated. Dogma may be held reflectively, such as when a person says something like "If I did not believe X, I would be a different person" or "X is the foundation of all of my most important beliefs; if I do not hold on to X, I could not continue." Here the person shows an awareness that X is more than just a truth claim but holds an important place in her life and in defining who she is and where she belongs. It may also be held not only reflectively but also self-consciously: "My identity requires that I believe X to be the case" or "If I did not believe in X, I would be a different person." Dogmatic claims are of the form "X is the case, and you should acknowledge X" or "If you do not believe X, you will go to hell" (which is different from "I believe you will go to hell"). The distinction between propositional and enacted truth and between dogma and dogmatic allows for a pluralistic understanding of respect that remains open to the worth, if not the full propositional truth, of other religions, and in this sense the requirement of pluralism is satisfied.

In religiously pluralist societies, doubt and conflicts in faith are common, and students are likely at some time to question the dogmas of their faith, comparing them to other religious and nonreligious systems. Students who are taught to see their religious education as a question of not just what to believe but also where to belong may have a better basis on which to evaluate their doubt and to make a wiser decision when a conflict of faith comes along. If this is the case, then religious teachers who understand how religions works within a pluralistic context will in the long run have an important theoretical instrument with which to address doubt.

CHAPTER 9

The Challenge of Religious Education for Liberalism

The Constitutional Minimalist and the Argument for Parental Rights

In recent years some legal and political scholars, whom I refer to here as *legal minimalists*, have advanced the idea of public support for religious schools on legal and constitutional grounds. Legal minimalists hold that the right to determine one's child's education is part of a more basic and fundamental right such as freedom of expression or freedom of religion, and they thus believe that religious schools should be required to meet very few externally imposed standards. To intrude the state into the educational choice of the parent is akin to introducing a noise machine into a poetry reading—it overwhelms the event.

Yet, as we will see, a careful exploration of these arguments suggests that the public interest in religious education is considerably greater than the legal minimalists acknowledge, and that the requirements of liberalism for the education of autonomous citizens is a substantial limit to the authority of parents to educate their children. While my argument has legal ramifications, I make it on educational grounds. It is intended as a philosophy, not a politics, of religious education.

The Legal Argument

William Galston writes, "The ability of parents to raise their children in a manner consistent with their deepest commitments is an essential element of expressive liberty."[1] Galston believes, "One of the most disturbing features of illiberal political regimes is the wedge their governments

189

typically seek to drive between parents and children, and the effort they make to replace a multiplicity of family traditions with a unitary, state-administered culture."[2] While Galston places some limits on parental authority, such as teaching children to be servile, he believes that these days the larger danger comes from the state and the media.[3] Thus for Galston increasing the parental rights over children's education protects democracy and inhibits tyranny.

Stephen Gilles, a legal scholar, views the right of parents to control their children's education as an extension of their right to free speech and thus as part of a concept of minority rights. He believes that parental speech should be subject to a high degree of court protection via the First Amendment's Free Speech Clause, and that such speech includes the direct speech of parents and their indirect speech through a chosen educational agent. He also holds that selective funding for compulsory *public* education burdens that speech, and thus believes that public funds should be used to support parents who wish to send their children to religious schools.[4] He places the burden on the state to show that a parent's comprehensive view of the good is unreasonable and proposes a thin theory of what is "reasonable." Any comprehensive view that acknowledges the importance of human development, embraces *civic* toleration and respect for law, and acquiesces in basic constitutional standards is, for him, reasonable.[5] He views compulsory *public* education as an intrusion by the state on the parents' right to communicate their views to their children, and argues that selective funding of public, secular schools is coercive.

Gilles's argument is only incidentally about religious schools, and the implications are not nearly as one-sided as he makes them sound. For example, he implicitly allows that children have an interest in their own education, an interest that goes beyond that of their parents, when stating that a condition for exercising this right is that husbands and wives remain "parents in good standing," which seems to suggest they meet certain basic standards of care and competence. Gilles also acknowledges a state interest in education when he requires that children be taught respect for the law. These softer interests not withstanding, Gilles holds that parental speech and the speech of their children's designated teachers should be categorized as being entitled to the same high-level protection against content- or viewpoint-based state action that political and religious speech receive. Again, because he appeals to *parents*, and not just *religious* parents, his argument could be persuasive to many who believe that their educational choice is overly restricted by exclusive state support of public schools.

Despite the softer implications of his argument, Gilles nevertheless gives the impression that the state has no legitimate role in providing incentives for parents to send children to public schools, that parents are unfairly burdened, and that their right to free speech is improperly interfered with whenever a state supports secular public education but not religious education.[6] However, this impression is misleading, as we will see shortly by examining closely the constraints he proposes—an education must be consistent with what we know about human development, and it cannot teach *civic in*tolerance or disrespect for law or our basic constitutional standards. While these may seem quite minimal on the surface, their implications for the expression of public interest in parental choice is actually a bit more robust than Gilles suggests.

Clearly Gilles has a point. In a legal context, parents may hold any belief they want—anti-Semitic, antiblack, or antigay—and in certain settings (say, their home or at a political rally), it would be an interference with their right to free speech if they were silenced. However, the regulation of speech changes depending on the social and institutional context. You may yell "Fire!" any time you please as long as you do not do so in a crowded theatre or other locations where it will constitute threat of a stampede. The same is true of hate speech. It is permissible except in contexts where it is delivered as an immediate threat. I may be able to burn a cross on my lawn but not on yours (and possibly not even on mine if the context serves to intimidate or provoke you). These rules are obviously flexible, and lawyers can debate their elasticity, but context matters, and some things that are permissible to say in one context are not permissible in another. Education, whether carried on in a home school or in a private, religious, or public school, changes the character of permissible speech. Children are vulnerable to the ideas and opinions of the adults around them, which impacts their own-well being and the well-being of others.

Human Development and Self-Esteem

The more robust implications of Gilles's proposals can be seen best by asking for the basis of the exclusive parental control that he advocates. One likely reason for allowing parents an exclusive say in their children's education has to do with the importance of self-esteem and the fact that children's self-esteem is often tied to the esteem with which their parents are held. Assault on the self-esteem of children can be crippling. It can lead them to give up on a task because they feel themselves inadequate; it can lead to unreasonable caution and fear of risk and novelty. Because children's self-esteem is tied to the esteem with which their parents are held, it is important for schools to respect parents and their beliefs.

Because self-esteem has to do with one's assessment of self-worth, an assault can discourage students from working hard in school on tasks that they find difficult. If a child does not believe that she has any mechanical ability, she will look on every momentary failure not as a challenge to be worked on by scrutinizing the situation more closely, but as confirmation of her mechanical inadequacy. As a result she may shy away from mechanical tasks, hence contributing to her mechanical inadequacy. At the more global level, assaults on the fabric of a child's identity, her skin color, her religion, or her sexual identity or orientation may take even deeper tolls. As an adult she may be able to avoid a mechanical task by hiring a mechanic, but she cannot, without doing serious damage to herself, deny those things that constitute her social identity. And, because the self-esteem of children is so dependent on that given to their parents, teachers must be extremely cautious in the way they address those features of a child's life, language, skills, and beliefs that are tied closely to the esteem with which the child's parents are held.

Yet the self-esteem of the child is not tied inexorably to that of the parent, and parents can be a source of low self-esteem if, say, they belittle a child's efforts or reject a child's basic sense of herself, as for example when a youngster becomes aware of homosexual or bisexual desires and a parent belittles him because of it. In these cases, the way in which schools treat these students should not depend on how the parents think they should be treated. Teachers need to exercise independent judgment, and they need to do so precisely for the reason Gilles suggests: to fail to do so violates basic considerations of self-esteem and hence threatens to stunt human development. Further, in an educational context there are other students to consider as well. Any hate speech is appropriately controlled and limited to the extent that it contributes to an environment that threatens the self-esteem of other students. Thus, a concern for human development allows for a significant degree of constraint over parent choice.

Even the idea of free speech, which Gilles appeals to as a major justification for his strong view of parental rights, is complicated when asserted in an educational context. There is some speech that in an abstract legal context is and should be free, but that in an educational context should be curtailed to the extent that it is likely to harm the development of others. Consider, for example, the situation described by Barbara Applebaum in one of her graduate teacher education classes where one of the white, Christian, heterosexual students, a prospective administrator, said that she would have no difficulty with homosexual students because she "has learned to 'love the sinner but hate the sin.'"[7] When Applebaum challenged her, the student defended herself on the grounds of freedom of speech.

This situation strains Gilles's position. Would he agree with the graduate student and affirm her right to free speech as long as parents chose the schools in which this person was the administrator? Or, would he agree with Applebaum on the grounds that educators who treat their gay students as sinners are likely inhibiting their development and contributing to an educationally hostile environment? As we have seen in Chapter 3, it is one thing to talk openly about "the Church's" position on an issue, but it is quite another to do so in a way that diminishes the self-esteem of students.

Applebaum points out that there is a distinction between speech that, in its utterance, harms, and speech that is uncomfortable to hear, and she fears that hating "the sin" does real harm to young, vulnerable students. It is an assault on their self-esteem. To make the distinction between harmful and uncomfortable speech clear, Applebaum, an Orthodox Jew, wonders why her graduate student has never mentioned her (Applebaum's) sin—failing to accept Jesus as her savior. She speculates that anti-Semitism is much more difficult to express today than antihomosexuality.

Applebaum's point is that homophobic speech harms because it is uttered in the context of and contributes to a climate in which gay people can be denied jobs and housing and where gay students are subject to psychological and physical harm, and to self-abuse and suicide. This context makes homosexuals an oppressed group in today's world, and in the context of oppression, such speech is not just uncomfortable—it is dangerous. However, for the purposes of this argument, the question of what is and what is not harmful or what stunts human development is secondary to the point that the importance of human development legitimately constrains parental choice. If we truly take the ideal of human development seriously, the education of private and religious schools' teachers would, at the very least, require study in the area of child development.

Gilles's other constraints also entail more robust implications than he initially would seem to allow. Take, for example, the importance of *civic* toleration, respect for law, and acquiescing with our basic constitutional standards. *Teaching* civic tolerance is a complex topic, but Gilles seems to have in mind a negative conception of tolerance where I let you live and you let me live. However, the pedagogical limits of this negative conception can be seen as soon as one asks, "Why should I let you live as you wish to do? Is it because there is something about *you* that requires my respect [a strong reason for tolerance], or do I let you live as simply part of the bargain whereby you let me live [a weak form of tolerance]? If it is the latter, and if you are a member of a weak minority, I need not feel obliged to keep my end of the bargain if expediency allows me to break it. Yet this weak idea of tolerance—be tolerant only if you cannot get away with being intolerant—requires that children be taught that hypocrisy, which is a character trait that is parasitical on true virtue, is itself the highest virtue.

Yet if it is strong tolerance that is required, then we need to see just what we teach when we teach respect for others. Here it is useful to begin with the observation that there are always too many people with too many different lifestyles to teach a specific lesson of respect for them all. We can have a day to remember Martin Luther King, Jr., as a symbol of the struggle of black people or a unit on the Holocaust to recall the destruction of European Jews, but we are unable to teach students about each and every group or idea that they are likely to encounter. Moreover, even those groups that do serve as the objects of instruction change, and the practices that students are taught to associate with a particular group may, over time, become less characteristic of that group. To teach ideas of tolerance, students will need to learn some general lessons that they can apply to people who they may never hear about in school but whose practices need to be tolerated even under conditions of unequal power. How is this kind of tolerance to be taught?

First, we frequently tolerate people and practices that we essentially disapprove of. To say "I tolerate her because I love her" is a contradiction unless it is shorthand for, say, "I tolerate her messiness because I love her." Here it is really not *her* that I tolerate but a certain habit that she has, a habit that I do not like. The person I love may have habits I tolerate, but it is not the habits that I love; it is the person.

In many cases we may even have a visceral reaction to that which we come to tolerate. We may feel disgust or revulsion. Even though there are times when feelings of disgust or revulsion are appropriate emotional responses—say, when we come upon a piece of rancid food—toleration calls on us to *not* act on those feelings in certain kinds of instances. So when we teach toleration of this kind, we are teaching students to transcend their initial response and check the more impulsive reaction that provoked it. This is similar, say, to what a parent does when encouraging a child to overcome her repulsion to the way lobsters look and take a taste.

This need not mean that one must deny the initial feeling; it simply means that one must learn to respond to it in a new way. Imagine, for example, a new medical student who faints upon first seeing a body cut. The initial response is quite physical: blood rushes away from the brain, and the student falls to the ground. While fainting is an extreme reaction, general revulsion at seeing a person cut is an appropriate, indeed empathetic response in most situations, but the medical student needs to reshape the response in *this* kind of situation and get down to work. In the case of tolerance, something like this is going on as well.

Imagine a southern white who, during an earlier period of our history, might have viewed with disgust a black man kissing a white woman. Disgust involves a physical reaction—the body recoils, the throat constricts, the nostrils tighten as if to protect the body from a rank odor, and the body itself shivers as if it escaped a close call with polluted matter. These physical states are mentally linked to a larger picture of racial impurity and even potential national impotence. They shape and are in turn shaped by a special vocabulary consisting of words like *colored, mulatto, miscegenation,* and so on. And this vocabulary leads, in turn, to a certain conception of order where people and their status are arranged according to the color of their skin, which leads in turn to a certain understanding of obligation—to protect white women—and then to a propensity to action, including violence.

To teach minimal tolerance in this case would then be to teach this person ways to interrupt this chain so that the initial physical state did not lead to the final act of violence. The act can be short-circuited by reshaping the feelings, by rechanneling them into a different emotion (say, pity), by denying them, by redirecting the action (say, into sports), or by reflecting back on their source (say, in features of one's own socialization).

It is possible that changing the final action may even work in reverse and have an effect on the emotion and possibly even on the physical state, as philosophers like William James have suggested, but tolerance need not go this deep. It is sufficient to short-circuit the action. In the example above the desired learning is straightforward—interrupt the chain from physical state to emotion to act. Even privately hitting a punching bag instead of a person in this case is an act of civic tolerance—minimal, but still the act has been interrupted. Here tolerance is static and passive—do not harm people. If they do not intend to hurt me, leave them alone. I do not have to watch the kiss. If I don't like it, I can turn away.

Yet in many instances the issue is not simply to tolerate an existing practice, but also to be able to engage in the possibility of new practices in a reasonable and fair-minded way, even if the initial state of revulsion remains. True, we tolerate practices we do not like just because we believe that people who practice them have a right to do what they want. For educators, however, the problem is not only to short-circuit the chain from feeling state to action, but also to refine the process of reflection so that students learn when it is appropriate to short-circuit this chain and then do so by themselves. This involves a reflective engagement with one's own responses so that the feeling state can be raised to consciousness and evaluated.

Unless students learn to do this, tolerance must always be dependent on an outsider to provide the short-circuiting when needed, and we never transfer the process from one object to another. It would be akin to a person having the ability to multiply, but only on those combinations of numbers that he has practiced on. Thus, the reformed anti-Semite remains the unreformed racist and the reformed racist remains the unreformed sexist. But even this would be too generous, since each one of these breaks down into finer categories. The person who learns not to discriminate in housing would have to be taught anew not to discriminate in employment and education. Teaching tolerance is a complicated affair and requires constant intervention both in the formal and the informal curriculums. And it requires teachers who are able to read the atmosphere of a school and to take action when it is likely to produce intolerance. When Mr. P from Dillon decided to teach a unit on discrimination against homosexuals, he was taking charge of a situation in which homosexuals are a likely target of intolerance and abuse.

Yet even taking into account all of the educational considerations that need to be addressed when deliberating about the character of a good education, the issues raised by both Galston and Gilles remain. Parents do have special rights over their children's education, and there is reason to be concerned when states deny without strong reasons the right of parents to pass on their own faith to their children through religious schools. This, however, is a different question than whether other tax-paying citizens are to be obliged to support the exercise of this right with public funds. Different societies may choose to respond in different ways to the question of public support, but regardless of the way in which religious schools are supported, the public has an obligation to safeguard the right of children to self-esteem and intellectual development.

The Nature of the Public Interest in Critical Reflection

People in a democracy have many different interests that are expressed through many different associations, with each serving as part of the environment in which the interests of the others will be advanced or frustrated. In this environment it is inevitable that some of these interests will evolve and take on new shapes. It is also inevitable that priorities change as some interests are more realizable than others, that coalitions of interests will form, and that individuals and groups will seek out strategic allies at those points where interests merge. Moral education involves, among other things, the development of the disposition needed to call up these interests and to identify them as part of a field of other interests. Critical thinking is simply the mechanism that we use to recognize conflicts, to define problems, and to engage in evaluating the stakes involved in advancing some interests over others, in projecting alternative courses of action, and in reconstructing interests when conditions make it advisable.

Critical reflection is a public interest as well as an individual interest precisely because we all stand in different places and are shaped by different experiences, and because our individual interests will be worked out successfully to the extent that they anticipate the demands that the interests of others impose on our own actions. The public interest arises from the fact that every individual and every group are subject to conflicting interests, and that every individual and group have a meta interest in developing the skills required to address these conflicts when necessary. In principle, then, there need be no inconsistency between the substantive commitments to a particular conception of the good, advanced through a religious education, and the development of students who are capable of reflective critical inquiry. The latter is simply one of the instruments available for students to function within a world in which difference is inevitable.

Granted, some religious educators believe that there is a risk in teaching their students to be reflective critical thinkers, fearing that they will hold up the teachings of their own faith to critical analysis or that they will come to hold the teachings of their faith in more complex ways. This fear leads to the kind of education as inoculation that we saw at Saint Martin with regard to the teaching of evolution. However, this risk is entailed in the fact of living in a complex, interdependent society and cannot be avoided for long by shielding students from complexity.

Critical reflection need not work against a religious commitment. As we saw in Chapter 4, with Mr. S and the Nicene Creed, there are strong pragmatic as well as religious reasons to favor one's own religious community. Critical thinking thus does not require that teachers present all traditions in a neutral way and encourage students to reflect on the merits of their own from outside of the tradition. It only requires teachers who are aware of the interpretive opportunities within their own tradition, and who use this awareness, to help students grow within their own faith tradition, while, as argued in the last chapter, learning to respect the ideas and beliefs of others.

In previous chapters I provided examples of many religious teachers who worked hard to advance a single, unique conception of the good while still providing their students with the skills required for critical thinking. Granted, there are times when, because of age or the level of intellectual or emotional maturity, it is not wise to push critical religious inquiry all the way down, but this is a local judgment that can be made by competent religious educators.

Yet the fact that this judgment may best be made on the local level does not reduce the public's interest in promoting the capacity of all children, including those in religious schools, to engage in a critical reflective inquiry regarding competing claims to religious truths. The development of this capacity will require religious teachers who are comfortable with transmitting both the beliefs and rituals of their own religion and with contextualizing that religion within the context of the multiple beliefs and practices of the larger community. In the last chapter I suggested that educators needed to understand religious doctrine both as a statement of beliefs and as a marker that sets one religion off from others, hence stabilizing its identity. In the sections that follow, I show how the interest that liberalism has in critical reflective thinking can be served by providing religious teachers with an understanding of the interpretive opportunities that their own and other religious doctrines provide.

A Rule-Based Reading of the Claim to Universal Truth

Religious doctrine can be thought of as a fabric of beliefs and interpretations about spiritual and moral truths existing across time and including mechanisms for changing and refining its articulations of truth. Thought of in this way, doctrine transcends any single belief, and even when the claim is made that the doctrine is fixed and absolute, there is often considerable room for flexibility. An analogy would be to say that the truth of the U.S. Constitution is fixed and universal, while granting there are vast differences between the way the Constitution was understood in, say, 1850 and the way it is understood now. It is universal and fixed if we allow that our idea of the Constitution includes its formula for self-correction and for the development of new interpretations. Interestingly, popes and other members of the Catholic hierarchy may use the word *irreformable* to describe infallibly tinted doctrines.[8] The link between religious dogma and the U.S. Constitution is captured by Supreme Court Justice Robert Jackson's interpretation of the Court's authority: "We are not final because we are infallible, but we are infallible only because we are final."[9]

From a religious standpoint this interpretation of doctrine should leave open the possibility for religious reconciliation, because each group is potentially more complex and varied than commonly thought and because at the end of the day, it could be argued that all religions are on the way to the same truth, however distant and contradictory their beliefs may be at the present moment. Moreover, it allows for religious chauvinism, since one religion may claim that it has the lead in this common journey, as Muslims do when they see Mohammed as the last and most complete prophet, and as Christians do when they hold that they follow the example of the son and spirit of God.

From the standpoint of pluralism, this is good. It allows different communities of the good to be sustained while providing some reason for dialogue across group boundaries. From the standpoint of the believer within all and any groups, it is also good because it allows for mistaken interpretations to be corrected and for development between and across religious groups. Hence it is possible to sustain commitment, even amidst disagreement and disapproval.

Understanding the importance of this overriding commitment is likely one reason some people on very different sides of issues of doctrinal truth want to remain within the same religious community at all costs. They see themselves as important to its future unfolding. Thus Muslims do not abandon their faith when terrorists hijack it and turn it into a weapon, although many other people might wonder why peace-loving Muslims remain committed to Islam. Nor do many Catholics leave the Church when they discover that there is a sexual abuse scandal involving priests and cover-ups by bishops, even though many non-Catholics are con-founded by the continuing commitment of *indignant* believers. And many Jews, angered by the use of the Bible to justify the Israeli government's response to the plight of the Palestinians, do not quit their religion because of its appropriation by some of its spiritual spokespeople. Believers remain, both because they may well continue to love their religion[10] and because many feel that it is at these moments when it needs them the most. The motive may not be that much different from the reason a parent continues to love a child even after the child has committed a serious crime. It is at such a time when love is most called for.

The Function of Religious Doctrine

Religious dogma presents an obstacle to the development of the skills of critical inquiry if, in its emphasis on the promulgation of "eternal truth," it affirms that all-important questions have been answered and thus concludes that inquiry is unnecessary.[11] Yet religious dogma has changed over time, and inquiry can be aided by understanding the nature of this change and the way in which it compares to changes in other areas such as science.

Changes in religious beliefs are different than changes in science as nor-mally conceived. In science, differences of opinion will often set off a series of hypotheses and experiments, which, while not always conclusive, hold out a reasonable possibility of closure for people who hold different hypotheses. Religious differences are addressed largely in terms of arguments that are internal to the competing faiths, and rarely is there a definitive challenge that will be acceptable to all sides. Yet this is a simple fact of life and does not deny the possibility of religious inquiry, even in matters where dogma holds a claim on truth.

Certainly religious inquiry will never settle certain critical questions. A Unitarian will never win a wager with a Catholic about the truth of the eucharist based on the evidence of DNA. While Catholicism does hold that there is a literal transformation of the flesh and blood, Catholics are unlikely to be convinced that any DNA test will demonstrate the truth or falsity of that belief.[12] Apology, not experimentation, is the usual device for defending the faith. Apology works by trying to locate points of agreement, often referencing a sacred authority or text. This is then treated as a point of consensus from which logical inferences and conclusions may be drawn about right belief and correct action. While the flow from text to dogma may be presented as seamless, changes over time do occur in the way dogma is interpreted. Religion teachers need to be aware of these interpretive moments if their students are to develop an appreciation of inquiry. Below is an example of such an interpretive moment.

Changes in Dogma: The Example of Usury

Consider the change that has occurred in the teaching of the Catholic Church against usury. Originally the Church prohibited usury (in the original context, lending money for interest). The biblical reason for this prohibition is to be found in a number of passages. For example:

> If you lend money to any of my people, even to the poor with thee, thou shalt not be to him as a creditor; neither shalt thou lay upon him interest. (Exodus 22:24)

> Thou shalt not lend upon interest to thy brother: interest of money, interest of victuals, interest of anything that is lent upon interest. Unto a foreigner thou mayest lend upon interest; but unto thy brother thou shalt not lend upon interest; that the Lord thy God may bless thee in all that thou puttest thy hand into, in the land whither thou goest in to possess it. (Deuteronomy 23:20–21)[13]

Originally these passages were taken to mean simply that money should not be lent for interest. I do not know the exact reason for the original prohibition, but let's imagine a possible historical reason. Assume that once the prohibition served to enhance harmony in tightly knit communities where members were living close to the edge with no yearly surplus of food and where mutuality—knowing your neighbor, serving his needs, and trusting that he would serve yours—could mean the difference between life and death. In this kind of world, a system that allowed one person to hold another hostage to high interest rates would threaten the bonds that mutual aid required, blurring the line between debtor and friend. At those rare moments when someone needs extra funds that the community could not provide, the party must go outside to receive it. By going outside of the community, harmony is maintained within. The role of moneylender is then assigned to those who are beyond the mutual tie of the community. Historically, for Christians it was assigned to Jews. Thus, when the Church disallowed usury in the usual sense, it would have been, given this speculative history, preserving trust and mutuality within a community of believers.

Now imagine that the material foundation for this prohibition changed as opportunities for wealth arose in far and distant lands. There is now less need to maintain mutuality. As greater opportunities for profitable investments grow beyond the confines of the local or the national community, there are possibilities of living beyond the limits of mere sustainability, which less adventurous members of the community might want to profit from. To exploit these possibilities, greater capital is needed and the non-adventurous members of the community can begin to share in the gain by lending money to the adventuresome ones, but now with a prospect of large returns. If there were a surplus to be spent, it would seem unreasonable not to allow people within the faith to do so, while expecting a reasonable return.

Yet, from both a doctrinal and a political point of view, it seems arbitrary to just throw the concerns about usury to the wind or to say that times have changed and therefore divine doctrine has changed. To do so could cast suspicion on the authority of the whole tradition. It makes considerably more sense to provide the doctrine with a different interpretation. Yet in providing this interpretation, as the Catholic theologian Jacques Maritain acknowledges, the inerrancy of the Church must be preserved.

As Maritain notes, "The teaching of the Church concerning the doctrine of morals [must be] as infallible as her teaching concerning the doctrine of faith."[14] Having set the limits of the interpretation, he now gives new meaning to the injunction against usury. *Usury* now refers not to the lending of money for interest but to the way in which an act contributes to or subtracts from human good. In modern times, usury applies to the increase of misery created by undiluted capitalism. He writes, "If men had understood the whole bearing of the condemnation of usury by the Church, there would not have been any capitalist regime or any society of consumption."[15] Thus, while religious truths may be fixed, this does not exclude highly significant changes in the way they are interpreted and applied over time.

In providing a modern interpretation to the prohibitions against usury, Maritain also provides a demonstration of the flexibility of dogma. He has saved biblical infallibility by providing an interpretation of the meaning of usury as any systematic practice that contributes to human misery on a large scale. Lending money for interest may fit, but then again it may not. The quality of the interpretation suggests that at least some units of dogma may allow significant room for accommodation and development.

Dogma, according to the Catholic Church and other dogmatic religions, flows from Scripture. One need not be Catholic to accept this as accurate, and one need not be a non-Catholic to allow that *its* dogma need not be the only possible interpretation implied by a specific biblical passage. Intervening between the text and its application are implicit rules of interpretation. Reflection involves, in part, making these rules transparent, and doing so allows educators to leave a role for contingency in the construction of religious identities and for alternative interpretations to be viewed as credible, even if not preferred.

The study of this transparency by prospective religion teachers, or what I call the study of the logic of dogma, involves two different phases. The first entails understanding the interpretive rules for generating dogma from text—the logic of origin. The second, the logic of structure, involves understanding the way in which specific elements of dogma are constructed to give shape to one religious community and to differentiate it from others.

The Logic of Origins and the Evolution of Interpretation

By the *logic of origins*, I mean an investigation that makes the rules for generating dogma from text transparent. One may study this logic while taking a position internal to a faith community, or one may study it without any commitment to that community whatsoever. In either case to study the logic of dogma opens up possibilities for new or more nuanced interpretations such as exemplified in this book by Father J and his understanding of the Church's doctrine on procreation and homosexuality. The Catholic theologian Maritain can be used again to help demonstrate the movement from scripture to dogma. Here are two examples where he anchors dogma to Scripture. He begins with Scripture:

Husbands, love your wives, as Christ loved the church. He gave himself up for her to make her holy, purifying her in the bath of water by the power of the word, to present to himself a glorious church, holy and immaculate, without stain or wrinkle or anything of that sort" (Ephesians 5:25–27).[16]

Maritain comments, "The Church is *the Bride* of Christ. And she is *without stain or wrinkle or anything of that sort but holy and immaculate* ('indefectibly holy,' the second Council of the Vatican will say)."[17] Here are some of the rules Maritain employs to bind Scripture to Catholic dogma:

1. Read the parts of the analogy as follows A. Husbands love as Christ loved but also as B. Christ marries as husband marries. Thus C. Husband takes bride = Christ takes bride. D. Bride of husband is woman. Bride of Christ is Church, Church = woman.
   Thus: Transposing "husbands, love your wives, as Christ loved the church" to *Christ married the Church* and then to *Church is the bride of Christ.*
2. Allow that the point of the message is a statement about the relationship of Christ to the Church and only secondarily about the treatment of wives by their husbands.
3. Christ gives Bride = Church (his purity). Read, *church* as the historical Catholic Church.
4. Allow that the Church remains pure even after Christ's crucifixion.

This latter direction rests on other directions that Maritain does not recite. These have to do with how to take what Jesus meant when he told Peter, "You are Peter, and on this rock I will build my Church, and the gates of hell will not prevail against it" (Matthew 16:18). To understand that the statement should be read to include not just Peter but his successors as well, and that these successors are the subsequent popes, Maritain then goes on to make the inerrancy of the Church more explicit: "I am writing to you about these matters so that if I should be delayed you will know what kind of conduct befits a member of God's household, *the church of the living God, the pillar and bulwark of truth*" (I Timothy 3:14–15).[18]

Maritain remarks on the meaning of the "Inerrancy of the Church. She is *the pillar and bulwark of truth*."[19]

Thus the doctrine of the inerrancy of the Church becomes anchored in Scripture as one moves from the "church of the living God, the pillar and bulwark of truth," to the "Inerrancy of the Church." The implicit rules for reading the passage are as follows:

A. Interpret pillar of truth as entailing knowing rather than inquiring. In other words, the integrity of the Church is to be found in the truth of its established doctrine, not in the open-minded, methodical testing of competing truth claims.
B. Interpret "pillar of truth" as an achievement that must be protected, rather than just an aspiration. The Church has the truth, and this truth serves to hold up the entire superstructure upon which ethical, moral, and religious claims are established.
C. Read *church* (lowercase *c*) as *Church* (uppercase *C*).
D. And, implicitly, read *inerrancy of the Church* as the *inerrancy of the pope*.

In the cases described above, dogma develops out of the New Testament, but it is not a direct route from what is written in that text to where dogma directs belief. A set of other directives and rules intervene that direct the reading in one way, rather than in others. The fact that a reading is circumscribed in a certain way does not close off all issues, however. Consider the following:

"You, however, are 'a chosen race, a royal priesthood, a holy nation, a people he claims for his own to proclaim the glorious works' of the One who called you from darkness into his marvelous light. Once you were no people, but *now you are God's people*" (I Peter 2:9–10).[20] And Maritain comments, "The Church is the People of God, a name which has been brought to full light by the second Council of the Vatican."

Here "a people" becomes "The Church is the People of God."[21] The rule here is as follows:

1. Take the passage starting with "'a people he claims for his own to proclaim the glorious works' of the One who called you from darkness into his marvelous light. Once you were no people, but *now you are God's people*," and read it in the following way:

    1A. "a people" becomes *the People*.
    1B. "the People" becomes *the Church*.

2. Do not read "a people" as one of God's people.
3. Read "priesthood" (lowercase) as *Church* (uppercase).

The rules that allow Scripture to be recast as dogma provide opportunities for new interpretations to develop and for new understandings to be articulated across generations. Although the idea of dogma is advanced as fixed and absolute, there are important changes as the doctrine is passed down to students of different generations. New beliefs are added, and old ones downgraded. Beliefs that were once seen as heretical are incorporated into the official doctrine. Even the words of the Bible change through different translations and interpretations as different scholars, theologians, and educators from different generations and different cultures take from it what the times require.

The Logic of Structure

Branches of the same religion, for example Lutheranism and Catholicism as forms of Christianity, share certain core beliefs—Jesus is the son of God—while other beliefs serve to differentiate them from one another, say, whether good works are sufficient for salvation. Differentiating beliefs may be *symmetrical* or *asymmetrical*, where the terms indicate the placement of the belief in the system. Symmetrical beliefs are contradictory assertions within two different belief systems in which each assertion occupies a core position in its respective system. If one religion requires the belief that good works will not provide the key to heaven, and the other requires the belief that it does, the beliefs, while contradictory, are symmetrical.

Asymmetrical, or nonsymmetrical, beliefs occupy different places in separate belief systems. If one religion holds a belief that good works will not get you into heaven, while the other holds that good works may well be sufficient but members are free to decide the question for themselves, the beliefs are asymmetrical. They do not have equal weight in the two religious systems. The more orthodox a religion, the more beliefs will tend to occupy the core. Outside of the core are beliefs that individual members are allowed to differ about but that are still religiously relevant. "Could God forgive Hitler?" is a question that was asked in more than one of the schools I observed, and the students were allowed to debate the answer. Their religious identity, however, does not depend on how they answer the question.

There are also claims that are held by the official body of the religion but which congregates may debate without sanction. These include previously settled core truths that have sunk in status and are now objects of official debate, such as the question in some churches of the ordination of women. There are also discarded beliefs, beliefs previously accepted as official but that now have been abandoned by the faith and reside in the dustbin of previous beliefs. Perhaps the most notorious of these is the view that the Church held that the earth was the center of the universe. Conversely, there are beliefs that rise into the official teachings of the church as dogma that did not previously occupy that position. In Catholicism, the infallibility of the pope, officially established in the 1800s, became a central dogma of the Church. Another, the doctrine of worker rights articulated by Leo XIII in 1891,[22] does not have the standing of a dogma such as the doctrine of infallibility and the immaculate conception of Mary, but it has the standing of official teaching and is able to borrow the aura of dogma.

We can label these additional belief locations in the following way:

1. Shared dogma is any set of core beliefs common to two or more religions or distinct denominations. They are core beliefs for three reasons. First, public rejection of them disqualifies one from membership. Second, public acceptance is strongly expected for undisputed membership. And third, these beliefs are protected more thoroughly than others from the effects of criticism and are therefore the least likely to be changed.

2. Differentiating dogma is any set of beliefs that distinguishes one religion, sect, or denomination from another and that one is required to accept to be recognized as a member of that religion, sect, or denomination rather than the other. To believe that Christ is divine is a qualifying belief for Christians and a disqualifying one for Muslims. Differentiating dogma may also be described as a symmetrical pair, or two contradictory beliefs, each of which occupies the place of core dogma in an opposing religious system.

3. A nonsymmetrical pair is two contradictory beliefs, only one of which occupies the place of core dogma in one of two religious systems.

4. An optional belief is a religiously relevant belief that occupies a nondogmatic place in a religious system.

5. A fallen belief is one that has fallen from the status of dogma and is now subject to official debate.

6. A discarded belief is a belief that once occupied positions 1–3 but has now been rejected.

Religious education involves many things that do not have to do directly with beliefs. It has to do with celebrations, passages, prayer, devotion, developing a sense of the sacred, and so on. However, insofar as it does concern belief, there are four important lessons that are suggested by this typology that relate to students' understanding of their religion in the context of others. The first is learning the content of the beliefs of their own religion. The second is learning where to place the belief in this system, to know whether it is core or optional. The third involves learning how to negotiate the place of the belief among believers where there is internal disagreement. The fourth involves mapping these beliefs in relation to those of other religions.

It is important for religious educators at various levels to have an idea of the nature of each one of these stages and not to teach the first two so as to obstruct the critical engagement called on by the last two. Reflection is compatible with religious education at the higher level, if the earlier stages do not teach dogma dogmatically and if students are taught to respect the role other belief systems and religions play in people's lives. When this occurs, then pluralism exists in the service of liberalism, and liberalism works to strengthen pluralism.

It is important not to leave the impression that only the Catholic Church is tied to a dogmatic foundation. What distinguished the Church from many other religions in this regard it that there is reasonably clear institutional structure for pronouncing and maintaining dogma. Yet even a religion like Judaism that is seen to emphasize "practice" rather than "belief" may be seen to reserve a space for dogma. Right practices can be traced back to belief statements. Consider the following:

"We light the candles because we are told to keep the Sabbath."

"Where were you told?"

"In the Bible." (Statement of legitimate source of practice—I believe that we should do what the Bible tells us to.)

"Why follow the Bible?"

"It is the word of God." (Belief about the source of the Bible.)

Even though the topic is about practice—lighting candles—the justifications are belief statements that appeal to a core of dogma.

Different religions may be marked off from each other in different ways, depending on the way in which dogma is understood. Sometimes religions differ because one must affirm as true and the other must deny as false a particular item of belief; however, because there is no single way to prove or to disprove the belief, both affirmation and denial are dogma. They are not just dogma, however, because they are believed or not believed. Nor are they dogma just because they cannot be proved to be true or false, although both are elements of dogma. They are dogma because in addition to these two elements, they must be professed as a condition of belonging to a certain religion. Catholics must profess, as Mr. P put it, that Jesus is both one hundred percent human and one hundred percent divine, and Jews and Muslims must advance the belief that Jesus was not divine.

An interesting example is the group that calls itself Jews for Jesus. Unless read as a noun phrase (*Jews-for-Jesus*), the term, for those Jews who are *not* for Jesus, stands as an oxymoron and an assault on their belief system—a kind of fifth column. If it is read as a noun phrase, it allows that these people are not real "Jews." *Real* Jews, by definition, do not believe that Jesus was the Messiah. These people are *Jews-for-Jesus* and a Christian group. They are not, nor could anyone ever be, a *Jew* for Jesus. If a Jew comes to believe in Jesus, then, in the view of many tradition-minded Jews, he has left one religion for another. The label is troubling to Jews in the same way as a restaurant once called Snacks Fifth Avenue was troubling to the Saks Fifth Avenue department store. It was a trademark infringement. Yet, there is no crystal ball to say that Jews-for-Jesus might not take over Reform, Conservative, and Orthodox synagogues and become Jews for Jesus—or just plain Jews, with the remnant relabeled *Jews-not-for-Jesus*. After all, Snacks did not, but it still might have won the lawsuit and taken over Saks Fifth Avenue. The point is that religion is a process whereby change occurs as beliefs move from one place to another. Any belief can, given enough time, change position, and what was once viewed as core may at a later date have fallen to a different place.

There may be a question as to whether some beliefs are so important that to change them is to abandon the religion altogether. I don't have a definitive answer to this question. However, it is useful to think of a belief system as a cluster of individual beliefs that evolve over time in terms of their status within the system as a whole. Change can occur in either an evolutionary or a revolutionary way. Evolutionary changes appeal to the authority within the system itself and connect new beliefs to old ones in ways that respect the existing authority structure. Revolutionary change appeals to the basic principles of the system as a way to overthrow the existing authority structure and construct a new one. The first, then, stresses continuity of authority and reform within, and the second stresses discontinuity and revolution. While it may be seen as unlikely, one could conceivably reconstruct a religion over time, slowly, perhaps almost imperceptibly, and wind up with a radically different set of core beliefs. If all of the microchanges were reasonable in terms of a more slowly evolving core, there would be no reason to call the resulting beliefs by a different name than the original. Even fairly swift and major changes, such as those resulting from Vatican II, may maintain the recognizable identity of the community of believers. Pre-Vatican II Catholics are different from post-Vatican II ones, but few anymore question that they are still Catholics.

Thus, the core should not be understood as an essential component of an identity, the content of which must remain the same forever. Rather, it is the place where beliefs that *are taken* as central to a religious identity at a certain point in time reside and about which there is internal certainty and a great reluctance to change. Dogma occupies a central position in a belief system; it is held unquestionably, and changes at a much slower pace than beliefs that occupy the periphery; but given enough time, any belief may come to occupy a different position.

Positional change may be very subtle, often entailing a change in the instructions for reading a passage rather than an obvious change in position. "Yes, my child, we still believe that we do literally partake of the blood and the flesh of Jesus, but no, a DNA test is really not necessary because the process is a mystery. It is the blood and the flesh transformed." Here the reading says, "Yes, we still accept the literal meaning of this, but we do not accept what others often count as the 'literal' meaning." Religious stability depends upon these beliefs not changing so rapidly that members become hopelessly confused about their collective identity or become unable to distinguish themselves from members of other religious systems. Nevertheless, they do change in ways that it is important for religious educators to understand if they are to enable their students to be reflective about their own commitments.

Doctrine as Presented: The Study of the History of Religious Pedagogy

To study the logic of doctrine in both its origin and its structure provides religious educators with a kind of map that enables them to engage with the interpretive opportunities their religion provides. Father J did not tell his students that he believed the Church's doctrine on homosexuality was a doctrine about adding life to the world, but by pushing this interpretive moment, he could justify his appropriation of a story about homosexuality to illustrate the love of Jesus. And similarly, Maritain maintained the credibility of the dogma regarding usury by understanding the interpretive possibilities the text allowed.

Although a clearer understanding of the logic of dogma provides a wider berth for religious educators to encourage reflective critical engagement, the *pedagogical* unit of analysis for the religious educator is not doctrine as such, but doctrine-as-presented. It is that shape and interpretation that is given to doctrine at particular points in time and not some abstract, timeless ideal. Doctrine-as-presented is the religious ideals as articulated in official doctrine at a given point in time, in textbooks and catechisms, in the activities of clergy, and by teachers in churches and classrooms.

The idea of "pure" doctrine to which religious officials may allude serves as a constraining force and provides, among other things, the rules for adding new truths, rejecting inadequate claims, and eliminating old, worn-out ones. It provides a template whereby truths within a faith are generated and evaluated. In contrast, doctrine-as-presented is what different generations of students experience in classrooms. The study of it is the study of how meanings and interpretations are developed at different times and how they are communicated to students. It would then be the object of study for courses on the history of religious pedagogy, and would provide teachers with a historical perspective on their own practice. A large part of this study would be drawn from teacher and student diaries and official reports, but it would also include a study of the changes in religious texts.

Two Catechisms, 1894 versus 1994: An Example

A catechism is a teaching document that contains many of the most important doctrines of the Church. Today Catholic school publishers use the catechism as a guide and then submit their textbooks for approval by an official Church body. If approved, the text is granted an imprimatur and officially legitimated by an affirmation that it is without error. Some schools may use other texts as supplementary material, but the imprimatur provides the text with a special status. In the past catechisms were used directly by teachers to question students who were expected to memorize the answers and to recite them while standing erect.

The most famous of these, the Baltimore Catechism mentioned in Chapter 3, was published in 1894 and was largely addressed to American European immigrant children. It has served as the subject matter for novels and plays (often farces) about the rigidity of Catholic education. The preface to the Baltimore Catechism notes it was written with Sunday school students in mind but is appropriate for the majority of Catholics, including adults, who are *"children as far as their religious knowledge goes."*[23]

The Baltimore Catechism is divided into thirty-seven lessons. Each lesson is further subdivided into a series of questions and answers and an accompanying explanation. Children were expected to memorize the answers to specific questions that the teacher would ask. For example: the teacher would ask, "Why did Christ live so long on earth?" and the child is expected to respond, "Christ lived so long on earth to show us the way to heaven by his teaching and example."[24] They were not required to memorize the explanations, however. Rather, the teacher used these if she wished to elaborate on the questions and answers.

While the Q and A session has been satirized by Catholics and non-Catholics alike, because of its stiff and programmed quality, the anxiety and guilt that it is reported to have produced, the low level of sophistication required by student and teacher, and the heavy reliance on rote memory, the catechism provides a snapshot of Catholic schools prior to the reforms that began with the Second Vatican Conference in the early 1960s. It also provides a benchmark with which to compare Catholic education subsequent to these reforms and the latest catechism, published in 1994. The 1994 Catechism, a larger and more sophisticated book, unlike the Baltimore Catechism, is used more as a teacher guide than a text to be committed to memory. Even though some liberal Catholics are critical of the 1994 Catechism for its conservative bent, it is a significantly more progressive and ecumenical document than the Baltimore version, and together they illustrate different points in the evolution of the Church doctrine as presented to children.

The basic theme of the Baltimore Catechism is salvation and damnation. The saved go to heaven, and the damned to hell. Purgatory is an intermediate stage, a kind of communal bathhouse, where we are washed clean of our sins in preparation for the final judgment. Limbo, a place once reserved for nonsinners who were never baptized, is reduced in importance even in the Baltimore Catechism. It is mentioned, but, unlike the discussions of heaven, hell, and purgatory, there is some uncertainty about its reality. About limbo it says, "It does not exist now, or, if it does, is only for little children who have never committed actual sin and who have died without baptism."[25] The wording "*It does not exist now, or if it does,*" contrasts with descriptions of heaven, hell, and purgatory, which are presented as real places to which we are all are assigned after death.

Whether we ultimately make it to heaven or are damned in hell depends on a number of factors. These include the kinds of sins we commit (venial or mortal), whether we have confessed in the proper way to the right person, and whether we have received absolution from a priest. Every saved person, except for saints, must spend some time in purgatory. Saints go directly to heaven. Baltimore is not clear about whether those destined to go to hell must also spend time in purgatory, where the efforts at purification ultimately must fail, or whether, as the saints go directly to heaven, they will go directly to their eternal destiny in hell. Nor is it clear from the Baltimore just what steps are taken in purgatory to cleanse the sinner, but the final hoped-for result is an exalted place in heaven.

In the new catechism, published first in 1994,[26] psychology has made its way into Catholic theology. Hell has been shorn of its physical discomforts and is a place of psychological disquietude. Purgatory has been significantly reduced in stature, and a person's psychological state weighs heavily in the judgment attached to particular sinful acts. Moreover, in line with a move toward pluralism, other religions have a more elevated, although not fully equal, place alongside of Catholicism. The 1994 Catechism has added an entire new theme—social justice. Jews are no longer Christ killers, and the founder of Islam is no longer the murderer and thief that Baltimore depicted. Both religions are to be respected for the truths they present and the values they represent. In other words, the changes are deep and significant, even if they do not go as far as many liberal Catholics would wish.

The Education of the Religious Educator

The subjects I have suggested are intended to be only suggestive and are proposed as complements to the faith-based study that religious instructors presently receive. However, because this part of the study is intended to express the interest that the larger public has in religious education, it must be planned and executed outside of the authority of any single religious denomination and needs to include secular as well as denominational voices. The fact that a significant number of students are educated in religious schools, usually in one faith tradition, speaks to the need for some regulation. The fact that many of these schools do a good job with their students does not minimize the difficulties that arise when parents are given a monopoly on the experiences and education of their children.[27] That some of these schools distort other religious as well as nonreligious traditions and that students may not be introduced to alternative points of view on vital personal, political, and even scientific issues speak to the need for the public interest to be expressed. Given the hands-off policy that has largely governed religious education in the United States, there is no simple way to effect this change, but it must be done with respect for different religious traditions as well as for the pluralism that enables them all. At this point in time, the most acceptable approach may be to insert the public interest into the education of the religious educator.

In studying the logic of origins, educators can begin to understand how their own doctrine is shaped through the interpretive moments that scripture allows, and how other interpretive possibilities are bypassed, rejected, or abandoned. In studying the logical structure of dogma, they can understand both the beliefs of other faiths in relation to their own and how their own religion is constructed through points of similarity and difference that mark their tradition off from others. In studying doctrine-as-presented to children in different time periods, the religious teacher has an opportunity to place the doctrines of a single religion in a larger historical context and to understand the evolution of belief as presented to children. The idea of these studies is not to challenge doctrine as such but to allow dogma to be taught nondogmatically and as sharing some space with other systems of belief and with other religions.

Granted, to think that all religious educators would welcome this addition is somewhat ideal. However, those who already have a working commitment to pluralism might welcome the opportunity to deepen their contribution to it, and if they do, the resources need to be provided for them to do so.

There is, of course, the question raised by Galston and Gilles about the rights of parents to educate their children even in exclusivist religious traditions. Perhaps the most that can be said at this point is that this is a political question, not an educational one. In other words it is not a question that requires a lot of deep thinking about what the best form of education or religious education is for a child. It is rather a question of what a political system can or should allow parents with regard to the education of their children, and whether it is wise, all things considered, to place the burden of proof on the parent or the state for determining a child's schooling—and then, given a fairly wide berth to the parent, whether the state should set certain requirements for the teachers and schools the parents do select. These questions will take us in quite a different direction—from a philosophy of religious education to a politics of religious education. And the response to the latter will need to differ from country to country depending upon historical traditions and local conditions.

Nevertheless, this much can be said: in all cases, one important consideration must be whether the school simply opposes liberal democracy for its own members or whether it teaches students to be actively antidemocratic by promoting racist, anti-Semitic, and authoritarian ideals for the society at large. The latter is simply not justifiable as an exclusive form of schooling, and most likely both Galston and Gilles would agree. With the former it depends perhaps on the character of the exclusivist position that is promoted and whether it provides the information and skills that its students will need to eventually choose for themselves. Here Galston's antisubservience standard is not a bad one to adopt.

However, for the majority of schools, which would include most of those in this study, where there is a genuine appreciation of the pluralist environment that enables them to flourish, and for teachers in these and many other religious schools, an opportunity to deepen their understanding of their own faith as they also contribute to the flourishing of liberal pluralist ideals would likely be welcome.

Postscript: Religious Education in the Context of Public School

In recent years some educators and political leaders have turned to religious schools as a possible corrective to the problems that they see in public education, and this was one of the reasons I undertook this study. I wanted to understand the benefits that religious schools provide as well as some of their limitations. I was then, and remain, committed to the importance of a strong public school system where students from different religious backgrounds are encouraged to learn to work and play together. In addressing the education of the religious educator, it should not be forgotten that we have in many public schools the kind of interreligious contact that pluralism requires.

In the rush to privatize public education and to provide public funds to support private, and religious schools, the important role that a secular public school system serves needs to be remembered. Indeed, where religious schools have advantages—in matters of discipline, for example—some of the advantage can be attributed to the fact that they can reject or expel troubled students much more readily than public schools.

After completing this study and viewing many dedicated and impressive religious schools' teachers, I have also come to appreciate the role that they play in our democracy. However, I believe, perhaps even more strongly than I did when I started this research, that religious schools serve democracy best where there is a strong and viable public school system that serves to provide the religious contact and diversity that is lacking in most religious schools. Religious schools can teach their students to cherish their own specific conception of the good, but they must be able to count on the public schools to reproduce the understandings and dispositions needed to secure the political climate where all deeply held religious ideals can be expressed.

Public schools, when working as they should, can provide the trust and understanding that can allow single-tradition religious schools to flourish at the educational margins. True, Catholic schools may be at least as culturally diverse, and perhaps even more economically diverse, than many public schools, but many other religious schools are not, and certainly even in Catholic schools religious diversity—of both teachers and students—does not stand up to the religious diversity found in most public schools. In addition, some parents send their children to religious schools to escape the racial and economic diversity that otherwise would be found in public schools. It is thus a mistake to think that public schools should closely mirror religious ones or, more importantly, that government should take away critical resources from public schools to support private ones that remain free from public scrutiny and controls. Indeed, liberal societies can best enable religious instruction to flourish when religious schools can depend on public schools to assure a climate in which openness and diversity are cherished.

Notes

Introduction

1. Meira Levinson, *The Demands of Liberal Education* (Oxford: Oxford UP, 1999), 157–58.
2. Anthony S. Bryk, Valerie E. Lee, and Peter B. Holland, *Catholic Schools and the Common Good* (Cambridge: Harvard UP, 1993), 59–63. Recent studies complicate these findings suggesting that public schools do better than Catholic and other private schools when certain critical variables related to social class are controlled for Sarah Theule Lubienski and Christopher Lubienski, "A New Look at Public and Private Schools: Student Background and Mathematics Achievement", May 2005, pp 696–699.
3. *Pierce v. Society of Sisters*, 268 U.S. 510 (1925) Docket no. 583
4. *Zelman, Superintendent of Public Instruction of Ohio, et al. v. Simmons-Harris et al.* US Supreme Court, 536 U.S. 639 (2002) 00–175.
5. Stephen Macedo, *Diversity and Distrust: Civic Education in a Multicultural Democracy* (Cambridge: Harvard UP, 2000), 231–53.
6. Warren Nord, *Religion and American Education: Rethinking a National Dilemma* (Chapel Hill: U of North Carolina P, 1995), 138–59; Nel Noddings, *Educating for Intelligent Belief of Unbelief* (New York: Teachers College, 1993); and Robert J. Nash, *Faith, Hype and Clarity* (New York: Teachers College, 1999).
7. Stanley Fish, "One University, under God?" *Chronicle of Higher Education*, 7 Jan. 2005: C4.
8. Research suggests that prejudice among students in Catholic schools toward non-Catholics has been decreasing starting in the 1960s; Andrew M. Greeley and Peter H. Rossi, *The Education of Catholic Americans* (Chicago: Aldine, 1966), 132–33. This research also suggests that Catholic school students have higher tolerance scores than do public schools students (although public schools students' scores are higher than those of students in non-Catholic religious schools). David E. Campbell, "Making Democratic Education Work," in *Charters, Vouchers, and Public Education*, ed. Paul E. Peterson and David E. Campbell (Washington, DC: Brookings, 2000), 21. Moreover, in recent years many Catholics schools have become especially assertive in addressing racism and anti-Semitism. Gerald Grace, *Catholic Schools: Mission, Markets and Morality* (London: Routledge, 2002), 134; and Tomas C. Hunt, "Catholic Schools Today: Redirection and Redefinition," *Living Light* 17.3: 203–10. And, as mentioned earlier, ethnic and racial minority students in Catholic schools score higher on standardized tests than similar students in public schools. Andrew M. Greeley, *Catholic High Schools and Minority Students* (New Brunswick: Transaction, 2002), xiii; Anthony S. Bryk, Valerie E. Lee, and Peter B. Holland, *Catholic Schools and the Common Good* (Cambridge: Harvard UP, 1993), 59–63.
9. There is John Rawls's idea of the "veil of ignorance," behind which you have to decide how to run things without knowing your place in the system. Or, there is the functionalist

standpoint that allows people to ask, for example, whether the functions once served by restricting marriage to union between a man and a woman—child rearing, economic efficiency, moral education, a loving and caring relationship, property control, and so on—might now be separated and each served in other ways as well. There is the utilitarian standpoint that, in recent years, has added the interest of animals to the moral concerns of humans—hence going beyond even species interests, let alone individual ones. And there is the critical standpoint where unequal power relationships are exposed for silencing certain moral standpoints.

10. See Patricia White, "What Should We Teach Children about Forgiveness?" *Journal of Philosophy of Education* 36.1 (2002): 57–67, for a critical analysis of the role of forgiveness in education.

11. William Galston, *Liberal Pluralism: The Implications of Value Pluralism for Political Practice and Theory* (Cambridge: Cambridge UP), 2002.

12. Eamonn Callan, *Creating Citizens: Political Education and Liberal Democracy* (Oxford: Clarendon, 1997), 178–82; and Levinson, *The Demands of Liberal Education*, 72–73.

13. Joel Feinberg, *Freedom and Fulfillment: Philosophical Essays* (Princeton: Princeton UP, 1992).

14. Stephen Gilles, "On Educating Children: A Parentalist Manifesto," *University of Chicago Law Review* (Summer 1996): 937–1034.

15. Harry Brighouse, *School Choice and Social Justice* (Oxford: Oxford UP, 2000).

16. Eric Bredo, private correspondence, 9 Jul. 2004.

17. Walter Feinberg, "Religious Education in Liberal Democratic Societies," in *Citizenship and Education in Liberal-Democratic Societies: Teaching for Cosmopolitan Values and Collective Identities*, ed. K. McDonough and W. Feinberg (Oxford. Oxford UP, 2003), 385–413.

18. This is not to suggest that public schools do not turn out students who are also scientifically misinformed. The issue is whether standardized tests are adequate to address teaching that is intentionally biased against evolution.

19. Some evangelical Christians have begun to understand this issue and a few have begun to argue that creationist science is harmful to the evangelical cause because it has "undermined the ability to look at the world." See Mark A. Noll, *The Scandal of the Evangelical Mind* (Grand Rapids: Eerdmans, 1994), 196.

20. Numbers alone merit the attention provided here to Catholic schools. They educate more students than any other private or religious system. The Chicago Diocese for example, operates the tenth largest school system in the nation, public or private, and provides a practical reason for extra attention.

Chapter 1

1. Special thanks to my colleague Robert McKim for his comments on this chapter.

2. Wayne Jackson, "Religion and Morality: The Connection," *ChristianCourier.Com: Investigating Biblical Apologetics, Religious Doctrine and Ethical Issues*, <http://www.christiancourier.com/penpoints/religionMorality.htm>.

3. One of the problems with the command theory in its unqualified form is that it would require that were God to order us to cause human suffering for no other reason than it would please him, we would be obliged to see it as a moral good. For an interesting attempt to correct this problem, see Robert Merrihew Adams, *The Virtues of Faith and Other Essays on Philosophical Theology* (Oxford: Oxford UP), 1987), 97–122.

4. It is still possible to argue, as Robert Adams does, that morality is ontologically conditioned on the will of a loving deity and consists in following that will. See Adams, 139–42. As I will argue shortly, I believe that Adams is correct in his characterization of religious morality but that secular morality takes a different turn.

5. There is one important objection to this point that needs to be noted. Because many secular theories take the benefit or harm intentionally done to another person as the critical factor in moral behavior, there is some question whether secular morality can condemn as immoral the harm we might intentionally do to ourselves. For the religious person, because the concern is whether we act in accordance with or against God's will, we can act immorally even if the only harm we do is to ourselves. This is one reason many religions oppose

suicide. There are two possible responses here that should be noted. First, some secular theorists do take into account the way an act reverberates back on the actor as an element in shaping character. Hence it is believed that harming ourselves is a problem because of the long-run effects it has on the quality of future acts. This argument does not cover suicide, but it remains a matter of conjecture whether the pain that might lead a person to commit suicide is less harmful than the suicide itself. Because of the complexity of these theories, I do not take them up here except to note that some religions do appeal to them to restrict harmful self-regarding acts as against God's will and hence as immoral. Yet even here it seems that the wrongness of the act is a result not of the direct harm it does to the actor but rather because of the harm it does to God. Hence it is questionable whether religious morality is completely successful in addressing the immorality of self-harm. In any event, secular theories may be able to address harmful acts to the self but would likely appeal to more prudential reasons such as the long-term effects on health, well-being, or character to make the case. Similarly, it would not necessarily be inconsistent for a religious person to believe that God willed the suffering to end, even if suicide was the only means for doing so.

6. John Stuart Mill, *Utilitarianism, On Liberty, Essay on Betham*, ed. Mary Warnock (New York: Meridian, 1962), 265.

7. Heinz W. Cassirer, *Grace and Law: St. Paul and the Hebrew Prophets* (Grand Rapids: Eerdmans, 1988), 168.

8. Antoine Vergote, "God Our Father," in *Moral Formation and Christianity*, ed. Franz Bockle and Jacques-Marie Pohier (New York: Seabury, 1978), 8–9.

9. Ibid., 9.

10. Ibid., 10–11.

11. See Patricia White, "What Should We Teach Children about Forgiveness?" *Journal of Philosophy of Education* 36.1 (2002): 57–67.

12. Ibid., 62.

13. These distinctions are not absolute. Witness, for example, the popularity of the character development movement in public schools.

14. Eamonn Callan, *Creating Citizens: Political Education and Liberal Democracy* (Oxford: Clarendon, 1997), 56.

Chapter 2

1. Thomas P. Rohlen, *Japan's High Schools* (Berkeley: U of California P, 1983).

2. Michael Walzer, *Interpretation and Social Criticism* (Cambridge: Harvard UP, 1987), 31–32.

3. These are two black leather boxes that contain sections of the Pentateuch and that are strapped to the arms and forehead by adult men during Morning Prayer. Geoffrey Wigoder, ed., *Encyclopedic Dictionary of Judaica* (New York: Keter, 1974), 589.

4. My appreciation to Deborah Feinberg for this information.

5. When they recognize ambiguities and tensions in the text, they believe it will be resolved by examining other sections of the text. However, it is thought that clarification and resolution are gained not by looking outside of the Bible toward scientific or modern interpretive theory but by exploring other passages in the Bible.

6. I am indebted to Sarah M. McGough and the additional work she did at Saint Martin for my Religious Educational Policy seminar for some of this material.

7. Appreciation to McGough for this observation.

8. LCMS, "Chosen People of God," <http://www.lcms.org/cic/chosen.htm>.

9. Office of the President, "What about Jehovah's Witnesses?" *What Lutherans Believe*, <http://www.lcm.org/president/aboutcms/whatabout/jw.asp>.

10. Office of the President, "What about Mormons?" *What Lutherans Believe*, <http://www.lcm.org/president/aboutcms/whatabout/mormonism.asp>.

11. Fauzia Rahman, "Muslim Alternatives to Public Education and Issues of Citizenship," seminar paper, Urbana: University of Illinois 14 Dec. 2004.

12. "Meaning a sin, unlawful" (Rahman's explanatory note). It should be added that many of the students in this school are immigrants, and a number of parents, usually those who are economically mobile according to this student, are seeking more modern Islamic alternatives.

Chapter 3

1. Reverend Thomas L. Kinkead, *An Explanation of the Baltimore Catechism of Christian Doctrine* (New York: Benzinger, 1891/1921), 126.
2. Ibid., 131–32.
3. Among these changes is the change from ·a largely clerical teaching staff to mostly lay teachers.
4. These categories are meant as convenient constructs, not as labels that exhaust an individual's or school's identity.
5. In point of fact, dogma almost never rises to the level of infallibility, and recent Church interpretations of the doctrine continue to restrict its scope. In *Mysterium Ecclesiae*, a Vatican document issued in 1973, "doctrinal definitions are affected by the limited context of human knowledge in the situation in which they are framed." Quoted in Richard P. McBrien, *Catholicism: Completely Revised and Updated* (San Francisco: Harper, 1994), 765.
6. The names of all schools and individuals have been changed.
7. Many Catholic high schools have a division of labor between the president, usually a priest, who works on external relations and development issues, and a principal, who works on internal issues of discipline, curriculum, staffing, admissions, and so on.
8. Pope Paul VI, *Humanae Vitae*, Encyclical Letter, 25 Jul. 1968

Chapter 4

1. Martha C. Nussbaum, *Cultivating Humanity: A Classical Defense of Reform in Liberal Education* (Cambridge: Harvard UP, 1997), 28–29.
2. Charles S. Peirce, "The Fixation of Belief," *Popular Science Monthly* 12 (November 1877): 1–15.
3. This term was used by John Dewey to express a conception of pragmatic truth.
4. Charles Peirce called this process "abduction." See Jürgen Habermas, *Knowledge and Human Interest*, trans. Jeremy J. Shapiro (Boston: Beacon, 1968), 114.
5. Amy Gutmann, *Democratic Education* (Princeton: Princeton UP, 1987).
6. Richard M. Hare, "Adolescents into Adults," in *Aims in Education: The Philosophical Approach*, ed. H. B. Hollins (Manchester, UK: Manchester UP, 1964), 47–70; John Wilson, "Education and Indoctrination," in Hollins, 24–46; Anthony Flew, "What Is Indoctrination?" *Studies in Philosophy and Education* 4 (1966): 273–83; and Ivan Snook, "Indoctrination and the Teaching of Religion" (Ph.D. diss., University of Illinois at Urbana, 1968).
7. Alan Peshkin, *God's Choice: The Total World of a Fundamentalist Christian School* (Chicago: U of Chicago P, 1986); and James G. Dwyer, *Religious Schools v. Children's Rights* (Ithaca: Cornell UP, 2001).
8. Alasdair C. MacIntyre, *After Virtue: A Study in Moral Theory*, 2nd ed. (Notre Dame: U of Notre Dame P, 1984).
9. Ibid.
10. Shelly Burtt, "Comprehensive Educations and the Liberal Understanding of Autonomy" in *Citizenship and Education in Liberal-Democratic Societies: Teaching for Cosmopolitan Values and Collective Identities*, ed. K. McDonough and W. Feinberg (Oxford: Oxford UP, 2003), 179–207.
11. The classic works on this are A. J. Ayer, *Language, Truth, and Logic* (New York: Dover, 1952); and Karl Popper, *The Logic of Scientific Discovery* (New York: Basic, 1959).
12. The point here is not that these may be the activity of religiously sponsored schools. Historically this would be wrong, since until a U.S. Supreme Court decision in the early 1960s, children in most public schools prayed. The point is that this feature of education, whether performed in private or public schools, is a religious feature.
13. While there is a similar ceremony for girls, the readings are often shorter.
14. This is almost by definition the case. A school that had a religious affiliation but did not give a high priority to prayer might best be called a *religiously sponsored school* rather than a *religious school.*
15. There is a sense in which my self identity is tied to my extended identity and that had, say, I been adopted at birth by a Mexican family, in some sense I would be a different person than the one I am.

16. Paul Willis, *Learning to Labor: How Working Class Kids Get Working Class Jobs* (Westmead, UK: Saxon, 1977). Willis certainly valorized resistance, but he was well aware of its limitations when it was both blocked by and served to block alternative visions.

Chapter 5

1. The two were the Islamic Day School, prior to the attacks of 9/11, and a school operated by Opus Dei, a lay order with a strong traditional bent. Both schools were in wealthy suburbs.
2. National Conference of Catholic Bishops, *To Teach as Jesus Did* (Washington DC: National Conference of Catholic Bishops, 1972). Quoted in Edwin J. McDermott, S.J., *Distinctive Qualities of the Catholic School* (Washington, DC: National Catholic Education Association, 1997), 1.
3. These were topics that students in our interviews mentioned as especially salient in their retreat experience.
4. At this writing, a small crack seems to have appeared in this teaching. The Catholic Church in Spain says it supports the use of condoms to prevent the spread of AIDS. It is not clear at this time whether Rome will alter its position or whether the American bishops will follow Spain's lead. "Church Policy Shifts on Condoms." *FindLaw Resources.* <http://news.findlaw.com/ap_stories/i/1102-19-2005/20050119033>.
5. Vatican Congregation for Catholic Education, "Educational Guidance in Human Love: Outlines for Sex Education" (Vatican: Vatican Congregation for Catholic Education, 1983), arts. 101–3.
6. I address this logic in the next chapter.
7. Mark W. Roche, "Voting Our Conscience, Not Our Religion," *New York Times,* 11 Oct. 2004, A29.
8. See Michael J. S. Maher, Jr., *Being Gay and Lesbian in a Catholic High School: Beyond the Uniform* (New York: Harrington Park, 2001); and Cris Mayo, *Disputing the Subject of Sex: Sexuality and Public School Controversy* (Boulder: Rowman & Littlefield, 2004).
9. Sister Mary Ellen Gevelinger, O.P., and Laurel Zimmerman, "How Catholic Schools Are Creating a Safe Climate for Gay and Lesbian Students," *Educational Leadership* 55 (October 1997): 66–68.
10. Gerald D. Coleman, "The Teacher and the Gay and Lesbian Student," *Momentum* 28 (April/May 1997): 46–48.
11. Chris Collins, M.P.P., et al., *Abstinence Only vs. Comprehensive Sex Education: What Are the Arguments/What Is the Evidence?* policy monograph (San Francisco: AIDS Policy and Research Center, U of California, San Francisco, 2002), ii.
12. Research suggests that education and strategies that promote abstinence but withhold information about contraception in general and condoms in particular can actually place young people at risk of pregnancy and STDs. For example, a study of teenagers who pledged to abstain from sex until marriage and subsequently broke their pledge were one-third less likely to use contraceptives than those who had not pledged virginity in the first place. Alan Guttmacher Institute, *Sex Education: Needs, Programs and Policies* (Washington, DC: Alan Guttmacher Institute, 2005), 35.
13. Mayo, 2004.
14. People for the American Way report that there are about six hundred such groups in the country; People for the American Way, "ReligiousTolerance.org," <http://www.religioustolerance.org/hom_psgr1.htm>.
15. *BOE of Westside Community Schools v. Mergens,* 496 U.S. 226 (1990), docket no. 88-1597.
16. Thomas Kuhn, *The Structure of Scientific Revolutions* (Chicago: U of Chicago P, 1962); and Imre Lakatos and Alan Musgrave, *Criticism and the Growth of Knowledge* (Cambridge: Cambridge UP, 1970).
17. Daniel A. Dombrowsi and Robert Deltete, *A Brief Liberal, Catholic Defense of Abortion* (Urbana: U of Illinois P, 2000), 33.
18. Ibid.
19. John T. McGreevy, *Catholicism and American Freedom: A History* (New York: Norton, 2003), 244.

20. Andrew M. Greeley, William C. McGready, and Kathleen McCourt, *Catholic Schools in a Declining Church* (Kansas City: Sheed & Ward, 1976), 28–40.
21. Ibid., 33.
22. Dombrowski and Deltete, 2000; and Richard P. McBrien, *Catholicism: Completely Revised and Updated* (San Francisco: Harper, 1994), 982–92.

Chapter 6

1. Jean-Jacques Rousseau, *Emile: or, on Education*, trans. Allan Bloom (New York: Basic, 1979).
2. Charles Taylor, *The Ethics of Authenticity* (Cambridge: Harvard UP, 1992), 29.
3. Charles Taylor provides a fine examination of this standpoint in Charles Taylor, *Sources of the Self* (Cambridge: Harvard UP, 1989), 368–92.
4. See John Rawls, *A Theory of Justice* (Cambridge: Harvard UP, 1974).
5. The acknowledgment of the potentially bad effects of sublimation was recognized by both Augustine and Aquinas in their permissive attitude toward prostitution: Aquinas "notes that the state should allow fornication and prostitution to exist for the sake of the common good. Relying on the well-known passage from Augustine's De ordine, Aquinas advocates tolerance of prostitution by noting: 'Accordingly in human government also, those who are in authority rightly tolerate certain evils, lest certain goods be lost, or certain evils be incurred: thus Augustine says [De ordine 2.4]: If you do away with harlots, the world will be convulsed with lust.'" Vincent M. Dever, "Aquinas on the Practice of Prostitution," *Essays in Medieval Studies: Proceedings of the Illinois Medieval Association* 13 (1996): 39.
6. To have exhibited growth in the way I am describing brackets a question like "Just how sophisticated does a casuist need to be before growth is recognized?" The quick answer is that some minimal recognition of potential conflict in justification is required, but a Saint Thomas is not expected. The focus is not on development within a level—say, Sally knows more rules than Jed. The comparison point is acknowledgment of complexity and the capacity to work it through.
7. These students were presently attending a non-Catholic, public university. All of the students had gone to Catholic high schools, and all, with the exception of the last, were living in the Catholic dorm, one that was independent of the university and run by the local diocese, which supported a full-time priest. The dormitory also included a chapel, Catholic library, and dining room. The students we interviewed selected the dormitory for a variety of reasons, but all mentioned that it was important for them to be able to maintain a Catholic influence in their lives, and we took this as a sign of the strength of their commitment. I draw on these interviews to suggest some of the factors that are involved in critical reflection and growth toward autonomy as they might occur within a religious tradition, as well as some of the factors that might serve to limit such growth.
8. Richard P. McBrien, *Catholicism: Completely Revised and Updated* (San Francisco: Harper, 1994), 1007–13.
9. Judith Jarvis Thomson, "A Defense of Abortion," *Philosophy & Public Affairs* 1.1 (Fall 1971): 47.
10. McBrien, 1994, 1009.
11. Dever, 1996, 39.
12. McBrien, 1994, 1010–11.
13. In 1968 a commission appointed by Pope Paul VI reported its findings on birth control to him. Before the commission was established, the Catholic Church strictly forbad any form of birth control except abstinence based on calculations relating to the wife's menstrual cycle. The commission came back with a surprise, recommending that the Church's long-standing position on contraception be liberalized to at least allow what it calls *artificial* contraceptive devices. The recommendation was ultimately rejected, to the regret of many of the faithful, and surveys indicate that more than eighty percent of Catholics of childbearing age do not follow the teachings on contraception. Yet there are many devout Catholics who still believe that the Church's views on birth control are the correct ones, and they are even more adamant in their support of the Church's strong prohibitions against abortion. The Church's reasons for its stand on these two issues are, even though related, somewhat difference.

14. Joseph Cardinal Bernardin et al., *Consistent Ethic of Life* (Kansas City: Sheed & Ward, 1988).
15. McBrien, 1994, 983.
16. Andrew M. Greeley, William C. McGready, and Kathleen McCourt, *Catholic Schools in a Declining Church* (Kansas City: Sheed & Ward, 1976), 35–39.
17. It is not clear that practical considerations were left out of the decision, since one persuasive argument was that if the Church changes its opinion on birth control, it would reduce its legitimacy in the eyes of many believers.
18. *Catechism of the Catholic Church*, 2nd ed. (1994), 547–48, nos. 2270-72.
19. McBrien, 1994, 1009–10.
20. Greeley, 1976, 35.
21. "In situations of rape or incest, the Catholic church does firmly uphold a woman's right to prevent conception from happening. A number of considerations must be taken into account, but chief among them would be this: If it is known that she is not already pregnant, a woman who has been raped or a victim of incest may seek immediate medical assistance—within a day—to prevent ovulation or kill the sperm, thus preventing conception from occurring." In Julia Ahlers, Barbara Allaire, and Carl Koch, *Growing in Christian Morality* (Winona, MN: Saint Mary's Press, 1996), 250 (nihil obstat, Rev. William M. Becker, STD Censor Librorum, 18 May 1995; and imprimatur, Most Rev. John G. Vlazny, DD, Bishop of Winona, 18 May 1995).
22. Not all choice need be autonomous. For example, if one is drunk, incapacitated, under threat, or manipulated to believe that things are other than they are, one may choose but not do so as an autonomous agent.
23. Heinz W. Cassirer, *Grace and Law: St. Paul, Kant, and the Hebrew Prophets* (Grand Rapids: Eerdmans, 1988).
24. John Dewey, *Human Nature and Conduct* (Carbondale: Southern Illinois UP, 1922/1988); and Albert R. Jonsen and Stephen Toulmin, *The Abuse of Casuistry: A History of Moral Reasoning* (Berkeley: U of California P, 1988).
25. Catharine A. MacKinnon, *Sexual Harassment of Working Women: A Case of Sex Discrimination* (New Haven: Yale UP, 1978).
26. Steve Maas conducted some of these interviews.
27. The position of the Greek Orthodox Church on abortion in cases of the disease is somewhat more ambiguous than we presented it at the time of these interviews. Officially the Orthodox Church still disapproves of abortion, but "[t]he church requires only premarital screening and genetic counseling for its certificates, but that counseling includes information on prenatal testing and abortions. However, in addition to mandatory genetic testing, the Church approves of information given to couples who test positive and this information includes material on abortion." Lila Guterman, "Choosing Eugenics: How Far Will Nations Go to Eliminate a Genetic Disease?" *Chronicle of Higher Education, Section: Research & Publishing* 49.34: A22, <http://www.racesci.org/in_media/choosing_eugenics.htm>.
28. McBrien, 1994, 966–67.
29. This was the only interview conducted through e-mail and not face to face.
30. The way I framed the interview may have handicapped this consideration.
31. Jeff McMahan, *Ethics of Killing: Problems at the Margins of Life* (New York: Oxford UP, 2002).
32. Dombrowsi and Deltete, 2000.

Chapter 7

1. Fauzia Rahman, "Muslim Alternatives to Public Education and Issues of Citizenship," seminar paper, 14 Dec. 2004.
2. Even when the social group becomes the object of moral consideration, as discussed in the last chapter, it is understood in terms that encompass the well-being of individuals and not as existing independent of those individuals. It is through individual participation that groups are constituted (see Chapter 8). Will Kymlicka makes this point in Will Kymlicka, *Multicultural Citizenship: A Liberal Theory of Minority Rights* (Oxford: Clarendon, 1995).
3. John Rawls, *Political Liberalism* (New York: Columbia University Press, 1993) 55–56.

4. Ibid., 57.
5. Ibid., 71.
6. Reverend Thomas L. Kinkead, *An Explanation of the Baltimore Catechism of Christian Doctrine* (New York: Benzinger, 1891/1921).
7. Asking the question in this way was the suggestion of my assistant at the time, Rashid Robinson.
8. The doctrine of the anonymous Christian is a way theologians have found to allow that non-Christians may enter heaven. Only God knows the true identity of the anonymous Christian. It remains hidden both to other Christians and to the person himself.
9. Kinkead, 1891/1921, 32–52.
10. Ibid.
11. This attempt was finally put to rest by the U.S. Supreme Court in *Pierce v. Society of Sisters*, 268 U.S. 510 (1925), docket no. 583.
12. Eamonn Callan, *Creating Citizens: Political Education and Liberal Democracy* (Oxford: Clarendon, 1997), 182.
13. Jeffrey Broad, *World Religions: A Voyage of Discovery* (Winona, MN: Saint Mary's Press, 1997), 219 (nihil obstat, Rev. William M. Becker, STD; and imprimatur, Most Rev. John G. Blarney, DD).
14. Ibid., 231 (brackets added for clarification).
15. Ibid., 18.
16. Ibid., 193.
17. Ibid., 200
18. Ibid., 255.
19. S. Bowles and H. Gintis, *Schooling in Capitalist America: Educational Reform and Contradictions of Economic Life* (New York: Basic Books, 1976).

Chapter 8

1. This is the stance taken by William A. Galston in *Liberal Pluralism: The Implications of Value Pluralism for Political Theory and Practice* (Cambridge: Cambridge UP, 2002), 25.
2. Some may find this attempt futile, arguing that the most that can be expected is a passive and nonviolent acceptance of other religious, one where I begrudgingly realize that allowing you to practice your religion is one of the conditions for me to practice mine. The problem with this view is the potential instability that arises when one or another faith community dominates. Nevertheless, it may well be the case that at the extremes, this may well be all that we can expect. However, what we might allow at the extremes should not be confused with what we should count as educationally sound.
3. Warren Nord, *Religion and American Education: Rethinking a National Dilemma* (Chapel Hill: U of North Carolina P, 1995), 138–60.
4. For an insightful statement of how this might be overcome, see Nel Noddings, *Educating for Intelligent Belief or Unbelief* (New York: Teachers College, 1993).
5. James Dwyer, *Religious Schools v. Children's Rights* (Ithaca: Cornell UP, 1998).
6. Ivan Snook, "Indoctrination and the Teaching of Religion" (Ph.D. diss., University of Illinois at Urbana, 1968).
7. John Dewey, *A Common Faith* (New Haven: Yale UP, 1934/1962), 9.
8. Ibid., 14.
9. Ibid.
10. Ibid., 25.
11. Ibid., 26.
12. Nord, 1995.
13. *Edwards, Governor of Louisiana, et al., v. Aguillard et al.*, Supreme Court of the United States, 482 U.S. 578, argued December 10, 1986, decided, June 19, 1987.
14. My appreciation to Jill Wightman and Rashid Robinson for a discussion in which the suggestion about mystery arose. And also to Eric Bredo for reinforcing the point later.
15. See Chapter 2.
16. See Chapter 4.

17. William James, "The Will to Believe," in *Essays in Pragmatism*, ed. A. Castell (New York: Hafner, 1957), 88–110.

18. William James, "Remarks on Spencer's Definition of Mind as Correspondence," as quoted by Louis Menand, *The Metaphysical Club: A Story of Ideas in America* (New York: Farrar, Straus and Giroux, 2001), 357 (brackets mine).

19. Antoine Vergote, "God Our Father," in *Moral Formation and Christianity*, ed. Franz Bockle and Jacques-Marie Pohier (New York: Seabury, 1978), 5.

20. Alister E. McGrath, *The Genesis of Doctrine: A Study in the Foundations of Doctrinal Criticism* (Oxford: Blackwell, 1990), 12.

21. *Catechism of the Catholic Church* (St. Paul, MN: Wanderer, 1994), 311.

22. W. V. O. Quine, *From a Logical Point of View* (Cambridge: Harvard UP, 1953).

23. George A. Lindbeck, *The Nature of Doctrine: Religion and Theology in a Post Liberal Age* (Philadelphia: Westminster Press, 1984), 18.

24. Ibid., 18.

25. Ibid., 32–33.

26. Ibid., 19.

27. Ibid., 19

28. Ibid., 35.

Chapter 9

1. William A. Galston, *Liberal Pluralism: The Implications of Value Pluralism for Political Theory and Practice* (Cambridge: Cambridge UP, 2002), 102.

2. Ibid., 103.

3. Ibid., 106–8.

4. Stephen G. Gilles, "On Educating Children: A Parentalist Manifesto," *University of Chicago Law Review* (Summer 1996): 937–1034.

5. Ibid., 3.

6. I have addressed both of these questions elsewhere. See Walter Feinberg, "On Public Support for Religious Schools," *Teachers College Record* 102.4 (August 2000): 841–56; Walter Feinberg, "Choice, Autonomy, Need-Definition and Educational Reform," *Studies in Philosophy and Education* 20.5 (2001): 402–9; and Walter Feinberg, "Religious Education in Liberal Democratic Societies: The Question of Accountability and Autonomy," in *Citizenship in Liberal-Democratic Societies: Teaching for Cosmopolitan Values and Collective Identities*, ed. K. McDonough and W. Feinberg (Oxford: Oxford UP, 2003).

7. Barbara Applebaum, "Social Justice, Democratic Education and the Silencing of Words That Wound," *Journal of Moral Education* 32.2 (2003): 151.

8. See, for example, the Vatican II document *Lumen Gentium*, para. 25. My appreciation to Jason Odeshoo for this reference. And this infallibility, with which the Divine Redeemer willed his Church to be endowed in defining doctrine of faith and morals, extends as far as the deposit of Revelation extends, which must be religiously guarded and faithfully expounded. And this is the infallibility which the Roman pontiff, the head of the college of bishops, enjoys in virtue of his office, when, as the supreme shepherd and teacher of all the faithful, who confirms his brethren in their faith, by a definitive act he proclaims a doctrine of faith or morals. And therefore his definitions, of themselves, and not from the consent of the Church are justly styled *irreformable*, since they are pronounced with the assistance of the Holy Spirit, promised to him in blessed Peter, and therefore they need no approval of others, nor do they allow an appeal to any other judgment. Dogmatic Constitution on the Church, *Lumen Gentium*, Solemnly Promulgated by Holiness Pope Paul VI, 21 Nov. 1964, <http://www.cin.org/v2church.html>.

9. In *Brown v. Alley*, 344 U.S. 443, 540 (1953). Appreciation to Odeshoo for this and the above reference.

10. Garry Wills, *Why I Am a Catholic* (Boston: Houghton Mifflin, 2002).

11. This was Dewey's most important concern about religious dogma.

12. I am putting aside obvious scientific problems with the example like the way in which digestion alters the character of food, and how this would affect any DNA.

13. Appreciation to Nathan Raybeck for locating these passages.

14. Jacques Maritain, *On the Church of Christ* (Notre Dame: U of Notre Dame P, 1975), 29 (brackets mine).
15. Ibid., 30.
16. Ibid., 9.
17. Ibid.
18. Ibid., 4.
19. Ibid., 4.
20. Ibid., 4.
21. Ibid., 4.
22. Pope Leo XIII, *Rerum Novarum*, May 1891.
23. Reverend Thomas L. Kinkead, *An Explanation of the Baltimore Catechism of Christian Doctrine* (New York: Benzinger, 1891/1921), 4 (emphasis mine).
24. Ibid., 91.
25. Ibid., 98.
26. *The Catechism of the Catholic Church* (St. Paul, MN: Wanderer, 1994).
27. David Blacker, "Fanaticism and Education," *American Journal of Education* 106 (1998): 241–71.

Works Cited

Adams, Robert Merrihew. *The Virtues of Faith and Other Essays on Philosophical Theology.* Oxford: Oxford UP, 1987.

Ahlers, Julia, Barbara Allaire, and Carl Koch. *Growing in Christian Morality.* Winona, MN: Saint Mary's, 1996. Nihil obstat, Rev. William M. Becker, STD Censor Librorum, 18 May 1995; and imprimatur, Most Rev. John G. Vlazny, DD, Bishop of Winona, 18 May 1995.

Alan Guttmacher Institute. *Sex Education: Needs, Programs and Policies.* Washington, DC: Alan Guttmacher Institute, 2005.

Applebaum, Barbara. "Social Justice, Democratic Education and the Silencing of Words That Wound." *Journal of Moral Education* 32.2 (2003): 151.

Ayer, A. J. *Language, Truth, and Logic.* New York: Dover, 1952.

Blacker, David. "Fanaticism and Education." *American Journal of Education* 106 (1998): 241–71.

BOE of Westside Community Schools v. Mergens, 496 U.S. 226 (1990), docket no. 88–1597.

Bowles, S., and H. Gintis. *Schooling in Capitalist America: Educational Reform and Contradictions of Economic Life.* New York: Basic, 1976.

Brighouse, Harry. *School Choice and Social Justice.* Oxford: Oxford UP, 2000.

Broad, Jeffrey. *World Religions: A Voyage of Discovery.* Winona, MN: Saint Mary's, 1997. Nihil obstat, Rev. William M. Becker, STD; and imprimatur, Most Rev. John G. Blarney, DD.

Brown v. Alley, 344 U.S. 443, 540 (1953).

Bryk, Anthony S., Valerie E. Lee, and Peter B. Holland. *Catholic Schools and the Common Good.* Cambridge: Harvard UP, 1993.

Burtt, Shelly. "Comprehensive Educations and the Liberal Understanding of Autonomy." *Citizenship and Education in Liberal-Democratic Societies: Teaching for Cosmopolitan Values and Collective Identities.* Edited by K. McDonough and W. Feinberg. Oxford: Oxford UP, 2003. 179–207.

Callan, Eamonn. *Creating Citizens: Political Education and Liberal Democracy.* Oxford: Clarendon, 1997.

Campbell, David E. "Making Democratic Education Work" *Charters, Vouchers, and Public Education.* Edited by Paul E. Peterson and David E. Campbell. Washington, DC: Brookings, 2000. 21.

Cassirer, Heinz W. *Grace, and Law: St. Paul and the Hebrew Prophets.* Grand Rapids: Eerdmans, 1988.

Catechism of the Catholic Church. St. Paul: Wanderer, 1994.

Catechism of the Catholic Church. 2nd ed. New York: Catholic Book, 1994.

"Church Policy Shifts on Condoms." *FindLaw Resources.* <http://news.findlaw.com/ap_stories/i/1102-19-2005/20050119033>.

Coleman, Gerald D. "The Teacher and the Gay and Lesbian Student." *Momentum* 28 (April/May 1997): 46–48.

Collins, Chris, M. P. P., et al. *Abstinence Only vs. Comprehensive Sex Education: What Are the Arguments/What Is the Evidence?* Policy monograph. San Francisco: AIDS Policy and Research Center, U of California, San Francisco, 2002.

Dever, Vincent M. "Aquinas on the Practice of Prostitution." *Essays in Medieval Studies: Proceedings of the Illinois Medieval Association* 13 (1996): 39.

Dewey, John. *A Common Faith*. New Haven: Yale UP, 1934/1962.

Dewey, John. *Human Nature and Conduct*. Carbondale: Southern Illinois UP, 1922/1988.

Dogmatic Constitution on the Church. *Lumen Gentium*. Solemnly promulgated by Holiness Pope Paul VI. 21 Nov. 1964. <http://www.cin.org/v2church.html>.

Dombrowsi, Daniel A., and Robert Deltete. *A Brief Liberal, Catholic Defense of Abortion*. Urbana: U of Illinois P, 2000.

Dwyer, James G. *Religious Schools v. Children's Rights*. Ithaca: Cornell UP, 2001.

Edwards, Governor of Louisiana, et al. v. Aguillard et al., Supreme Court of the United States, 482 U.S. 578, argued December 10, 1986; decided June 19, 1987.

Feinberg, Joel. *Freedom and Fulfillment: Philosophical Essays*. Princeton: Princeton UP, 1992.

Feinberg, Walter. "Choice, Autonomy, Need-Definition and Educational Reform." *Studies in Philosophy and Education* 20.5 (2001): 402–9.

Feinberg, Walter. "On Public Support for Religious Schools." *Teachers College Record* 102.4 (August 2000): 841–56.

Feinberg, Walter. "Religious Education in Liberal Democratic Societies: The Question of Accountability and Autonomy." *Citizenship and Education in Liberal-Democratic Societies: Teaching for Cosmopolitan Values and Collective Identities*. Edited by K. McDonough and W. Feinberg. Oxford: Oxford UP, 2003. 385–413.

Fish, Stanley. "One University, under God?" *Chronicle of Higher Education* 7 Jan. 2005: C4.

Flew, Anthony. "What Is Indoctrination?" *Studies in Philosophy and Education* 4 (1966): 273–83.

Galston, William. *Liberal Pluralism: The Implications of Value Pluralism for Political Practice and Theory*. Cambridge: Cambridge UP, 2002.

Gevelinger, Sister Mary Ellen, O. P., and Laurel Zimmerman. "How Catholic Schools Are Creating a Safe Climate for Gay and Lesbian Students." *Educational Leadership* 55 (October 1997): 66–68.

Gilles, Stephen. "On Educating Children: A Parentalist Manifesto." *University of Chicago Law Review* (Summer 1996): 937–1034.

Grace, Gerald. *Catholic Schools: Mission, Markets and Morality*. London: Routledge, 2002.

Greeley, Andrew M. *Catholic High Schools and Minority Students*. New Brunswick, NJ: Transaction, 2002.

Greeley, Andrew M., William C. McGready, and Kathleen McCourt. *Catholic Schools in a Declining Church*. Kansas City: Sheed & Ward, 1976.

Greeley, Andrew M., and Peter H. Rossi. *The Education of Catholic Americans*. Chicago: Aldine, 1966.

Guterman, Lila. "Choosing Eugenics: How Far Will Nations Go to Eliminate a Genetic Disease?" *Chronicle of Higher Education, Section: Research & Publishing* 49.34: A22. <http://www.racesci.org/in_media/choosing_eugenics.htm>.

Gutmann, Amy. *Democratic Education*. Princeton: Princeton UP, 1987.

Habermas, Jürgen. *Knowledge and Human Interest*. Trans. Jeremy J. Shapiro. Boston: Beacon, 1968.

Hardy, Thomas. *The Mayor of Casterbridge*. New York: Penguin, 1886/1997.

Hare, Richard M. "Adolescents into Adults." *Aims in Education: The Philosophical Approach*. Edited by H. B. Hollins. Manchester, UK: Manchester UP, 1964. 47–70.

Hunt, Tomas C. "Catholic Schools Today: Redirection and Redefinition." *Living Light* 17.3: 203–10.

Jackson, Wayne. "Religion and Morality: The Connection." *ChristianCourier.Com: Investigating Biblical Apologetics, Religious Doctrine and Ethical Issues*. <http://www.christiancourier.com/penpoints/religionMorality.htm>.

James, William. "The Will to Believe." *Essays in Pragmatism*. Edited by A. Castell. New York: Hafner, 1957. 88–110.

Jonsen, Albert R., and Stephen Toulmin. *The Abuse of Casuistry: A History of Moral Reasoning*. Berkeley: U of California P, 1988.

Joseph Cardinal Bernardin et al. *Consistent Ethic of Life*. Kansas City: Sheed & Ward, 1988.

Kinkead, Reverend Thomas L. *An Explanation of the Baltimore Catechism of Christian Doctrine.* New York: Benzinger, 1891/1921.

Kuhn, Thomas. *The Structure of Scientific Revolutions.* Chicago: U of Chicago P, 1962.

Kymlicka, Will. *Multicultural Citizenship: A Liberal Theory of Minority Rights.* Oxford: Clarendon, 1995.

Lakatos, Imre, and Alan Musgrave. *Criticism and the Growth of Knowledge.* Cambridge: Cambridge UP, 1970.

Lutheran Church Missouri Synod. see http://www.lcms.org/pages/internal.asp.htm>.

Levinson, Meira. *The Demands of Liberal Education.* Oxford: Oxford UP, 1999.

Lindbeck, George A. *The Nature of Doctrine: Religion and Theology in a Post Liberal Age.* Philadelphia: Westminster, 1984.

Macedo, Stephen. *Diversity and Distrust: Civic Education in a Multicultural Democracy.* Cambridge: Harvard UP, 2000.

MacIntyre, Alasdair C. *After Virtue: A Study in Moral Theory.* 2nd ed. Notre Dame: U of Notre Dame P, 1984.

MacKinnon, Catharine A. *Sexual Harassment of Working Women: A Case of Sex Discrimination.* New Haven: Yale UP, 1978.

Maher, Michael J. S., Jr. *Being Gay and Lesbian in a Catholic High School: Beyond the Uniform.* New York: Harrington, 2001.

Maritain, Jacques. *On the Church of Christ.* Notre Dame: U of Notre Dame P, 1975.

Mayo, Cris. *Disputing the Subject of Sex: Sexuality and Public School Controversy.* Boulder: Rowman & Littlefield, 2004.

McBrien, Richard P. *Catholicism: Completely Revised and Updated.* San Francisco: Harper, 1994.

McDermott, Edwin J., S. J. *Distinctive Qualities of the Catholic School.* Washington, DC: National Catholic Education Association, 1997.

McGrath, Alister E. *The Genesis of Doctrine: A Study in the Foundations of Doctrinal Criticism.* Oxford: Blackwell, 1990.

McGreevy, John T. *Catholicism and American Freedom: A History.* New York: Norton, 2003.

McMahan, Jeff. *Ethics of Killing: Problems at the Margins of Life.* New York: Oxford UP, 2002.

Menand, Louis. *The Metaphysical Club: A Story of Ideas in America.* New York: Farrar, 2001.

Mill, John Stuart. *Utilitarianism, On Liberty, Essay on Bentham.* Edited by Mary Warnock. New York: Meridian, 1962.

Nash, Robert J. *Faith, Hype and Clarity.* New York: Teachers College, 1999.

National Conference of Catholic Bishops, *To Teach as Jesus Did.* Washington DC: National Conference of Catholic Bishops, 1972.

Noddings, Nel. *Educating for Intelligent Belief of Unbelief.* New York: Teachers College, 1993.

Noll, Mark A. *The Scandal of the Evangelical Mind.* Grand Rapids: Eerdmans, 1994.

Nord, Warren. *Religion and American Education: Rethinking a National Dilemma.* Chapel Hill: U of North Carolina P, 1995.

Nussbaum, Martha C. *Cultivating Humanity: A Classical Defense of Reform in Liberal Education.* Cambridge: Harvard UP, 1997.

Office of the President. "What about Jehovah's Witnesses?" *What Lutherans Believe.* Now defunct. <http://www.lcms.org/president/aboutcms/whatabout/jw.asp>.

Office of the President. "What about Mormons?" *What Lutherans Believe.* <I>http://www.lcms.org/president/aboutcms/whatabout/mormonism.asp<D>.

Peirce, Charles S. "The Fixation of Belief." *Popular Science Monthly* 12 (November 1877): 1–15.

People for the American Way. "ReligiousTolerance.org." <http://www.religioustolerance.org/hom_psgr1.htm>.

Peshkin, Alan. *God's Choice: The Total World of a Fundamentalist Christian School.* Chicago: U of Chicago P, 1986.

Pierce v. Society of Sisters 268 U.S. 510 (1925) Docket Number: 583

Pope Leo XIII. *Rerum Novarum.* May 1891.

Pope Paul VI. *Humanae Vitae.* Encyclical letter. 25 Jul. 1968.

Popper, Karl. *The Logic of Scientific Discovery.* New York: Basic, 1959.

Quine, W. V. O. *From a Logical Point of View.* Cambridge: Harvard UP, 1953.

Rahman, Fauzia. "Muslim Alternatives to Public Education and Issues of Citizenship." Seminar paper, 14 Dec. 2004.

Rawls, John. *Political Liberalism.* New York: Columbia UP, 1993.

Rawls, John. *A Theory of Justice*. Cambridge: Harvard UP, 1974.

Roche, Mark W. "Voting Our Conscience, Not Our Religion." *New York Times*, 11 Oct. 2004: A29.

Rohlen, Thomas P. *Japan's High Schools*. Berkeley: U of California P, 1983.

Rousseau, Jean-Jacques. *Emile: or, on Education*. Trans. Allan Bloom. New York: Basic, 1979.

Snook, Ivan. "Indoctrination and the Teaching of Religion." Ph.D. diss., U of Illinois at Urbana, 1968.

Tait, Katharine. *My Father Bertrand Russell*. New York: Harcourt, 1975.

Taylor, Charles. *The Ethics of Authenticity*. Cambridge: Harvard UP, 1992.

Taylor, Charles. *Sources of the Self*. Cambridge: Harvard UP, 1989.

Thomson, Judith Jarvis. "A Defense of Abortion." *Philosophy & Public Affairs* 1.1 (Fall 1971): 47.

Vatican Congregation for Catholic Education. *Educational Guidance in Human Love: Outlines for Sex Education*. Vatican: Vatican Congregation for Catholic Education, 1983.

Vergote, Antoine. "God Our Father." *Moral Formation and Christianity*. Edited by Franz Bockle and Jacques-Marie Pohier. New York: Seabury, 1978. 8–9.

Walzer, Michael. *Interpretation and Social Criticism*. Cambridge: Harvard UP, 1987.

White, Patricia. "What Should We Teach Children about Forgiveness?" *Journal of Philosophy of Education* 36.1 (2002): 57–67.

Wigoder, Geoffrey, ed. *Encyclopedic Dictionary of Judaica*. New York: Keter, 1974.

Willis, Paul. *Learning to Labor: How Working Class Kids Get Working Class Jobs*. Westmead, UK: Saxon, 1977.

Wills, Garry *Why I Am a Catholic*. Boston: Houghton, 2002.

Wilson, John "Education and Indoctrination." *Aims in Education: The Philosophical Approach*. Edited by H. B. Hollins. Manchester, UK: Manchester UP, 1964. 24–46.

Zelman, Superintendent of Public Instruction of Ohio, et al. v. Simmons-Harris et al, US Supreme Court, 536 U.S. 639 (2002) 00-175.

Index